Freedom's Promise

PROMISES
A ROMANCE

Freedom's Promise

SUZANNE D. HELLMAN

Chariot Victor Publishing
A Division of Cook Communications

Chariot Victor Publishing,
a division of Cook Communications, Colorado Springs, Colorado 80918
Cook Communications, Paris, Ontario
Kingsway Communications, Eastbourne, England

FREEDOM'S PROMISE
© 1998 by Suzanne D. Hellman.
Printed in the United States of America.

Editor: L.B. Norton
Design: Bill Gray
Cover Illustration: Matthew Archambault

1 2 3 4 5 6 7 8 9 10 Printing/Year 02 01 00 99 98

Library of Congress Cataloging-in-Publication Data

Hellman, Suzanne Drentlaw.
      Freedom's promise/Suzanne Hellman.
           p. cm.--(Promises, a romance)
      ISBN 1-56476-718-3
      I. Title. II. Series.
      PS3558.E47654F74 1998   98-7347
      813'.54--dc21   CIP

Dedicated

to Ngaire Kellogg, my English friend. Thanks, Ngaire, for proofreading. Thanks to the Waukegan Historical Society. Thanks, especially, to the Lord Jesus for the miracle of letting me go to England just when I needed to.

One

*I*t wasn't until the doctor pulled the sheet up over Samuel's face that Tabitha Bradford cried. Only a single tear. There were many more in her heart, but she struggled to keep them at bay until she could be alone. She brushed her cheek discreetly, or so she thought. She glanced up as Dr. Taylor left the room— and looked right into Leah Harrington's glaring brown eyes.

Leah waited till the door's latch clicked softly behind the doctor, then she spoke. "You dirty little actress." Her voice was low but venomous. "I can't believe that you've actually fooled people into thinking you cared for my brother. Your marriage was a sham and a mockery to all that's holy." With that, she made a theatrical exit.

Slowly Tabitha shut her mouth, which had been hanging open in shock and rage. How dare she! It had always been obvious that Leah didn't like her, but Tabitha wouldn't have guessed the woman could be so cruel today. Samuel wasn't even cold yet.

Her eyes went to the covered body.

At least Leah had been considerate enough to not vent her wrath in front of anyone else. She'd made a point of waiting until Dr. Taylor had left the room. At that thought, Tabitha frowned. Quite the point, actually. Leah had waited with her preposterous accusations because she knew that no one would believe her. Leah's social peers would heap scorn upon her if they heard such words coming from her mouth because, much as they respected Leah, they had all loved Samuel Bradford. They would find questioning him distasteful, even on a good day. And today, of all days, they would be appalled.

Anger and thoughtfulness combined to stiffen Tabitha's spine and dry her tears. She would have a battle on her hands, she knew, and Samuel was no longer here to fight it for her. Nor was her father. For the first time in her twenty-four years, she had to stand on her own two feet. It was an intimidating thought.

Tabitha clutched her husband's hand through the sheet. *Samuel, why did you have to leave me? I need you!* She wanted to go to him with her problem, as she had for eight years. And before that, there had been Father. Now, when she really needed someone, she was alone.

No. Not really alone. She felt a calm come over her. The One who was Father to the orphans and Husband to the widows was with her. Tabitha closed her eyes. *Lo, I am with you alway, even unto the end of the world.* And this certainly did feel like the end of the world. But dealing with

Leah would be a very small task for God, and she would leave the whole situation in His capable hands.

At the moment she had other things to do. Notify the undertaker, the newspaper, the pastor, the solicitor. Instruct the maids to dye some dresses black, for her and for Leah. There was a dreary thought—black clothing for a whole year.

The following three days were a nightmare. A milliner had to be found to make hats—black, with heavy veils. The servants and the kitchen help had to be instructed about the reception, which would be held after the funeral service, here at Bradford Hall. They had a hundred questions about what food to serve and where to haul the furniture to make room for standing guests. Chairs would be left around the walls, but the larger furniture had to be moved out of the way.

Leah didn't help with the many details. It would have been nice to have someone to go through this hard time with, Tabitha thought, but she had to admit that Leah might not be much of a comfort. It was her sister-in-law's contention that Tabitha, as the widow, had the responsibility to arrange everything.

The advantage to the situation was that she didn't have much time to think. Each evening she allowed herself a few minutes in the library, where Samuel's body had been placed after the undertaker finished preparing him for burial. He looked peaceful. As if he were sleeping, only he was pale and waxy, and dressed in a suit rather than pajamas.

It had been several months since she had seen him in a suit, actually. As his illness progressed, he had gone from sitting in a chair most of the day to lying in his bed. During the last week, he had hardly been awake at all.

What a peaceful way to die. People prayed for such a death. And Samuel was one who deserved to have a small favor like that granted by God, for he had served Him faithfully for many years.

The funeral was an ordeal. All her life, Tabitha had been scornful of the black veils of widows. They seemed like an advertisement to the world, pointing out the sorrow, proclaiming *Pity me, I've lost someone dear.* Now she developed an appreciation for them. A red nose and puffy eyes weren't a concern behind the privacy of a veil. She was safely hidden from the gawking eyes of the world.

❦

Leah stood with the other mourners in the bleak cemetery, unable to look away from her sister-in-law. Fortunately, with a heavy veil, the direction of her gaze went unnoticed. The long-familiar tentacles of jealousy and hatred made her hands tremble. In spite of the weeds she wore, Tabitha was lovely. Black was becoming on her. Only her long, slender hands showed. Her waist looked tiny, whereas Leah's had expanded with child-bearing until even the black of her own mourning dress couldn't hide the fact.

That was some satisfaction—Tabitha had not produced an heir. No Bradford would have the blood of that money-grabbing little tart. Now Samuel was dead, and Tabitha would just be a footnote on the family tree. Of course she would one day be buried here . . . *Beloved wife of Samuel Bradford.* Even that was more than the little gold digger deserved.

Leah noticed men glancing in Tabitha's direction, saw their many little helpful gestures. *Sure, help the widow. What about me? I'm the bereaved sister. Samuel was my protector and provider too.* But their attention was all for Tabitha.

It had always been so. Even before she was widowed, Tabitha had drawn their attention when they had come to visit. They had held her chair, sought her opinion, opened doors for her, while she, Leah, could have been the doorjamb for all the notice they took of her. It had been amusing, their subtle, hopeless pursuit of a married woman. Now Tabitha was widowed, and the field was wide open. Well, she herself had been widowed for more than the required year. The men wouldn't even have had to wait for her, yet she had seen no interest. *It wasn't fair!*

Why hadn't her brother waited? He had needed company, true. If only he could have known that David Harrington would have the grace to die young, leaving Leah a comfortable and youngish widow. . . . It would have been such a convenient arrangement. If Samuel had waited just a few months longer, she could have been his companion in his old age. Despite the twenty-year difference in their ages, Samuel and Leah had been close as a brother and sister. It would have been pleasant to spend their years together in the big house their father had built. But he had to go marry his beggared friend's destitute daughter. Not help her financially, but *marry her!* Now Tabitha would get everything, and she, Leah, might soon be looking for a home for herself and her son.

It was a fitting day for a funeral. Drizzly and gray, the weather ignored the calendar, which said August. The gray and the cold and the headstones and the mourners in their black couldn't have been more funeralish if it had been the set of a play. One cheerful yellow pansy lifted petal hands happily to the sky, near the grave. Tabitha bent to pick it, then held it to her nose under the veil. Leah watched, disgusted. She turned and, with her son, David, made her way to the carriage and back to the house. She had lost parents, husband, four of her five children, and now her brother. She knew more of grief than did Tabitha, yet no one offered her an arm or a hug. All the condolences were for Tabitha.

After the service, the crowd gathered at Bradford Hall. Tabitha's heart was warmed by the number of people who showed up to pay their last respects, despite the dreary weather. It was a testimony to how loved her husband had been. Some, of course, were only there to get a peek at the Hall, or from a sense of morbid curiosity about the family. Others came because they felt obligated. But most, she thought, were there out of genuine respect for Samuel and sympathy for the family.

She glanced about. The massive fireplace held a crackling fire that warmed them as it cheered the room. Flowers were everywhere, so much so that the sweet smell was nearly overwhelming. She should, she supposed, have a satisfaction from the sense of who attended, as well as how many. The room held a virtual who's who of English society. But it didn't matter. Rich or poor, high or low, there were things that all of humanity had in common—births, marriages, and deaths—and those times drew them together.

Leah, however, seemed to be a bit more impressed with the "who" of their guests. There she stood, talking to Sir James Grant, looking as sycophantic as a supplicant to the king.

Tabitha chastised herself. She shouldn't have such thoughts about her sister-in-law. But Leah wasn't an easy person to like. She had been distant and aloof the entire time she had known her, and more so in the three days since Samuel had died. David, her son, had been quiet and had spent most of that time in his own rooms. The Hall had been silent—as silent as a tomb, it seemed to Tabitha. The days had felt more like November, dreary and a bit chill, and damp drafts crept through the windows and doors. In her more fanciful moments, they seemed to be calling to her, like a voice from the grave. Or perhaps heaven was mourning the passing of Samuel.

But that wouldn't make sense. If she were fanciful

enough to believe that God affected the weather based on His feelings about Samuel, it would make a lot more sense to think it would be a sunny, cheerful day, because God would be so happy to have Samuel there with Him.

People were now leaving the Hall, making their final condolences, but Tabitha was having trouble concentrating on their words. Tomorrow the will would be read. It was an ordeal she was not looking forward to. She was afraid of the consequences, no matter what Samuel had done. If he had left everything to her, fingers would point and tongues would wag. Many people had thought she married for money, and she couldn't blame them. Her marriage did look odd. Now they would feel justified in their opinions, and she did not want to have to face those expressions of righteous indignation.

"How are you holding up?"

Tabitha forced her thoughts away from the worries of tomorrow and tried to put a name to the blue-eyed man who was now holding her hand. Lord . . . Lord . . . Lord what? Abercrombe, that was it. Lord William Abercrombe, from Scotland.

"As well as can be expected, Lord Abercrombe," she replied.

Still he held onto her fingers. "Is there anything that remains to be done? I'm in London for another few weeks, and I would be more than happy to be of assistance."

Pleased with the thoughtfulness of a near stranger, Tabitha gave his hand a squeeze before she extricated herself from his friendly grip. "Thank you! I do believe that everything has been taken care of."

"Don't hesitate to call on me if you need anything."

"I'll do that. And thank you. It's people such as you who make times like this more bearable."

He left her then, reluctantly, and sent a servant to fetch his hat and umbrella.

That evening Tabitha had a fire lit in her room and ordered up some tea. She sat there in her orchid silk gown and robe, brushing her long, gold-tinted brown hair, thinking, staring at the flames. They reflected gold and red in her hazel eyes and gave her rosy, clear skin a golden hue. The room was cozy and warm on the chilly night.

Lord Abercrombe came to mind. There were still nice people in the world. With her eyes closed, she stretched her neck to one side, then the other, and concentrated on the warmth of the fire and the full, rich flavor of her tea.

Yes, the small pleasures in life were still hers to enjoy. A crackling fire, a cup of tea. Maybe, after tomorrow, she could enjoy them more fully, without this weight on her mind. One more hideous day to get through before she could let herself rest and try to establish a new definition of "normal." Try to get used to life without her closest companion.

Any will-reading was not an occasion to look forward to, as far as she was concerned. It made vultures of them all, and she wanted no part of it. Yet she knew that it was a necessary evil. The whole concept of private property would go by the wayside without seeing to the disbursement of one's worldly goods when one was beyond needing them.

With a sigh, she finished her tea and set the empty cup on the mahogany nightstand by her bed. She blew out the lamp and crawled between the sheets. By tomorrow night it would all be over. Questions would be answered, and the whole business of death would officially be over. There would be nothing else to dread. She could begin weaning herself from thinking about Samuel and how she missed him. She could begin getting used to falling asleep without the comforting thought of him in the next room. She could think about life. For she was certain she had much of life yet to live.

Tabitha was at the head of the stairs when the bell rang, and Bates, the butler, stepped to answer it. Bates had been in Samuel's service for years. He had even been with him in India. But no one thought of his loss or his feelings. He was a servant, and as taken for granted as the furniture. And she had been as bad as anyone.

In the light from the door, when Bates opened it, stood Lord Abercrombe. Tabitha could see part of his face over Bates' shoulder. Bates stepped back to allow his entrance, but Abercrombe didn't come in. His voice drifted up the stairs.

"I've only stopped by to leave my calling card for Mrs. Bradford," he said. "Today is a bad day to come calling, so I won't bother her. I only wanted her to know that she's not alone in this difficult time. Would you see that she gets this, please?"

Bates accepted the card. "Very good, sir."

Then William Abercrombe was gone, and Bates closed the door and made his way back to the nether parts of the house.

Tabitha walked down the grand, curving stair and picked up the card that lay in the tray on the table by the door. It only had his name and title printed on it, but it was very elegant, in keeping with the impression she was forming of the man.

Mr. Mortimer, the barrister, finished reading Samuel's will. The room was deathly silent.

He looks more like an undertaker, Tabitha thought. *He fits into this dark, dreary library with its dark paneling, in this dark, dreary house with its dreary tapestries and cold, gray stone.*

Why was everything around her so depressing? And why had she not noticed it before? She thought of anything but the words Mr. Mortimer had read. For he had just condemned her. Condemned her to a long, dreary existence of sameness.

Samuel had left the house to his nephew, David, with Leah overseeing things until he was of age. Bates had received a substantial pension, and some of the other servants were also mentioned. A large sum was going to an orphanage in India. Tabitha got pin money. Pocket change, quite generous for paying cab fares or buying pretty calling cards and perfume, but pocket change, nonetheless. It was clear that Samuel had expected her to live here at the Hall, where all her comforts would be well provided for. A home, clothing, food, servants. But she would have to stay here, still dependent. Only now she would be dependent on Leah and David, rather than Samuel. She might as well have died with him.

The house seemed to close over her, suffocating her. The house belonged to her sister-in-law and her nephew. She was merely a permanent, unwanted guest.

Leah could not keep the smug smile from her lips. Vindication. The little upstart got nothing. The wages of harlotry were small indeed. What decent woman would marry a man almost old enough to be her grandfather? None. The only young, attractive woman who would give herself to a wrinkled and cold old man was one who wanted his money. It warmed her unforgiving soul that Tabitha should get no wages for her sin.

Timidly David asked, "Does that mean . . . ?" But he couldn't finish the question.

"Yes," Mr. Mortimer replied. "It does mean. This house, the lands, and a good deal of the money, is now yours." To do him credit, Mr. Mortimer looked disgusted when David grinned.

Tabitha held no hard feelings for David. What sixteen year old wouldn't be pleased to be suddenly rich? And what sixteen year old would give much thought to how it affected others? It was more difficult to forgive Leah, sitting there looking like the cat with the cream. *Oh God, how can I live with her?*

The only answer that came to her was to pray for her enemies. And Leah was her enemy. Tabitha was stuck here, under her authority.

Without a word, Tabitha rose and walked out of the library and up to her rooms.

TWO

*F*or several days Tabitha remained in her rooms, isolated and numbly apathetic.

Outside, the weather turned. Sunshine came through the windows, birds chirped, and butterflies fluttered from blossom to blossom on the purple butterfly bushes, but for once, Tabitha saw nothing of the beauty of creation. She spoke to no one until Ivy, her maid, brought her another calling card from William Abercrombe.

Leah stood down the hall from Ivy when she knocked on her mistress's door. Curiosity made her listen.

"Yes, Ivy?" asked a Tabitha who was not visible from where Leah stood. The girl remained in the hall, talking to her through the open door.

"Just brung ye this card, mum. The same gentleman what was here before stopped and said to give it to ye."

"Thank you." Tabitha quietly shut the door, dismissing the girl.

Leah frowned in concentration. Lord Abercrombe was being uncommonly solicitous. And his sympathies seemed to be directed only towards Tabitha, not to the entire family. The thought gave her pause. Could he be interested? Tabitha could end up with that fine-looking young man, and a title to boot! That certainly wasn't justice.

Tabitha leaned against the closed door and stared at the card, and her fighting spirit took a shaky breath of new life. She would not let the rest of her life be years of pointless catfights with Leah. But what could she do?

Feeling alive again, but without direction, she rang for tea and sat on the edge of the bed to think. Obviously, she had to get away. Where? How?

What did she want from life? And how could she achieve it?

What she most wanted was to get out of this house and away from Leah . . . but Samuel had not left her enough money for that. Even if she got a small cottage somewhere in the country, she could only afford to live for a few months, maybe a year, before she ran out of money. That meant she would have to work. Could she? What could she possibly do that anyone would pay her for?

Her choices were limited. She could become a governess or a companion. Both ideas she immediately rejected, shaking her head. What did she know how to do?

She could sew.

Growing up as the only child of a small landholder in the Lake District, she had done a lot of sewing, both for practicality and to keep boredom at bay. She could sew anything, and even here at the Hall, she had supervised the sewing of all the clothing that was made for her.

That was it, then. She would sew. She would go away . . . somewhere . . . and set up a sewing shop. But where? And how?

Tabitha now had energy, born from her new idea and a germ of enthusiasm. Surely she could think of some way to get started. She glanced down at her hand, and saw she still held William Abercrombe's card. "Call," he had said. "I would be happy to be of assistance." *Should I?*

Yes, she decided. She had nowhere else to turn for help. But help doing what? She had better have at least the glimmer of a plan before she spoke to him.

By midafternoon, she had decided. She would look into purchasing tickets to go somewhere, perhaps back to the Lake District. Perhaps Lord Abercrombe would be kind enough to take her to the train station so she could inquire about the price of a ticket. She could even purchase it today, if it seemed the right thing to do.

Tabitha rang for Ivy and sent a message:

Please come to call at your convenience. I would appreciate your advice and assistance. Tabitha Bradford.

It was evening when William rang the bell at Bradford

Hall. He had been out when the message from Tabitha had arrived, or he would have come sooner. He glanced round at the house while he waited. It was well cared for.

While he had been serious in his offer of help, he had not really believed she would ask. Now that she had, he was nervous. Maybe things would start going his way. Her lovely face floated through his memory, slightly red-eyed from grief. So she was softhearted. She was prettier than he remembered from the one time he had met her before the funeral. This could be his break.

Bates opened the door and showed him to the library. While he waited, Lord Abercrombe's eyes went over the dark-paneled room. A typical library. Books covered three walls, and heavy tapestries hung from the fourth, between the tall, narrow windows with their velvet draperies. There was a slightly musty odor of old books.

Not much in the house was old. There were no family portraits showing hundreds of years of Bradfords. No armor. No family crest, as he had at home. The stairs here were wooden, not stone, not worn in the centers from the passing of thousands of footsteps.

He missed his home when he was away. But he had to find some way to make the money the huge old family mansion needed for constant repairs and upkeep. In a way he resented his family home. From time to time throughout the generations of Abercrombes, it demanded sacrifices such as the one he was now contemplating. If he failed, it would nullify all of those past sacrifices. All the times his ancestors had fought for their home, all the convenient but sad marriages, would be for nothing. He could not let that happen.

Tabitha entered the library, quietly closing the massive oak doors. It was the first time she had been in the room since the will was read. This was where Samuel's body had lain before the funeral, and she almost expected to see him there and missed him afresh to find him gone. She pushed the thought from her mind.

"Lord Abercrombe, how good of you to come."

William kissed her fingers. "Of course I came," he said smiling. "I said I would. Now, how may I help you?"

He stood near a wingback chair, with one hand on the wing. Tabitha sat at the edge of the seat of its mate. "Please. Be seated."

He did so, looking nervous.

"Shall I ring for tea?"

"No. Thank you."

"Well then. Let me get straight to the point and not waste your time. I wondered if you would be kind enough to escort me to the station."

"Not leaving us, I hope?"

She smiled, and her one dimple showed. "I haven't decided. I feel I need to get away from here, and I wanted to look into schedules and prices."

He nodded sympathetically. "Train station, I assume? Victoria? Or did you mean to travel by ship?"

Ship or train . . . ship or train. Ship meant not staying in England. It was a new thought, one that left her speechless.

"Ship or train?" he repeated.

"To be honest, I hadn't thought about ship travel. Which would you say is preferable?"

It was his turn to grin. "That would depend on where one wishes to go."

"Um," she hesitated. "I had thought perhaps home, to the Lake Country. But perhaps somewhere very different would be better. France, or maybe Italy." Even as she spoke, she knew she wouldn't be going to France or Italy. Her Italian was nonexistent, and her French, while sufficient for her to locate a restaurant or a hotel, would not be enough for her to be taking customers as a seamstress.

"That would be ship, then," he replied with a friendly little laugh.

Tabitha frowned, thoughts rolling in her head. To go completely away and still speak English meant America, Canada, or Australia. So far! So intimidating.

What was she thinking? She could not even get herself to the train station without asking for assistance, and she was considering traveling—no, *moving*—overseas, to a foreign country! It was insane.

Maybe a train would be better after all, she could say. It would be easy. He would be amused by her feminine timidity. He would take her to the train station, and she would have her sewing shop here, in England, where she felt at home. But the words wouldn't come.

"So," he began, when she said nothing, "tomorrow, then? I could stop at, say, one o'clock, and take you to the docks?"

"Yes, please." Tabitha stood, wanting him to leave. She had to think.

"Tomorrow, then. I shall look forward to it."

Tabitha thanked him and showed him to the door, then leaned against the wood. The sound of Leah's footsteps approached, and she steeled herself for the encounter.

"Lord Abercrombe?" Leah asked. "Seems he's here too frequently for good taste. You are so recently widowed to be having visitors."

Tabitha ignored the barb. "Yes. I'm thinking of . . . taking a journey. He has been kind enough to offer to take me out tomorrow to purchase my ticket."

"I see. I think that would be a good idea, Tabitha. Get away from here for a while. Rest."

Yes, I'm sure you would love to see me gone, Tabitha thought. Leah's false concern angered her, strengthening her resolve to leave. She could not stay in this situation.

"Good night, then," she said, trying to be friendly. "Busy day tomorrow."

Safely in her room, she collapsed on the bed. She had to get out of here. But was she brave enough? Especially, was she brave enough to get on a ship, all alone, and go far, far away?

It wasn't final. She could still decide on a train, and remain in England. Wouldn't that make Leah happy, to know that she had become a seamstress? Surely, word would eventually get to her. Maybe she should even tell her before she left where she was going and what she would be doing. While she was sure that Leah would take a perverse pleasure in her having to work, she would also be appalled at how it would look, and she would perhaps even attempt to prevent her from going, to save face.

Tabitha fell to her knees for guidance . . . and to pray for her enemy. Even if she left, even if she went so far away that she never was to see Leah again, she didn't want the bitterness between them to continue.

Lucas Hayes bit into the dry, overdone pork chop. Amanda, his ten-year-old daughter, wrinkled her nose in distaste, but didn't complain. She knew by now that it didn't do any good. He was not a cook and never would be.

He was also not a seamstress. His pewter-gray eyes were drawn to the needle and spool of thread he had left in the middle of the table in frustration when he could not get the thread to go through the eye of the needle so that he could replace the button that had fallen off Amanda's shirt. The shiny sliver of metal accused him silently, and he reached to move it to the countertop, near the dishpan, where he couldn't see it and wouldn't have to think about it while he ate. Such a small thing to have defeated him.

Not that meals were any pleasure anyway. Hadn't been for a long, long time. One would think he would be used to it by now. The bad food didn't seem to bother Amanda. She probably didn't remember much of how it used to be. When you were ten, your memory didn't extend back very far.

"You don't have to eat it," he said.

She smiled, pushed the dry chop away, quickly finished her potatoes, and ran outside.

Luke considered his options, coming up with the same old nonanswers. He could hire a housekeeper. Except he couldn't afford to, and could think of no one, anyway. There weren't many folks around. Town was a half hour away on a good day, and what woman would want to be making that journey, back and forth every day.

He could remarry. Again, he could think of no one. Well, he supposed there were a few single females in town. Truth was, he didn't want to remarry.

Or he could go on with things as they were. Bad food. Asking Evelyn Garfield, his friend's wife, to do the small amount of sewing and mending that was necessary. She was always gracious about it, but he always felt bad asking. She had her own house and family to tend to.

With a sigh he got up from the table and began clearing away the meal. Through the curtainless window he could see Amanda running through the tall prairie grass, a lamb and a piglet following her. She wanted a dog. He should get her a dog. A dog would be useful to him, too. There were coyotes and foxes and hawks. Even an occasional wolf. And chickens to protect from them. But he couldn't work up the heart to do it. Dogs were too happy.

Bouncing and wagging. And chewing the furniture and having accidents on the floor. He didn't need that.

Amanda stopped running, and Luke watched her turn and bend over the lamb. When she stood, the lamb had a bow tied around his neck. The "ribbon" was a thin piece of cloth, torn from a rag. Amanda's action only made him feel more inadequate. He should be buying real ribbons for his daughter.

Luke realized that their life was taking on a sameness that wasn't healthy for either of them, but he felt helpless to change things. What did one do with a daughter?

The next morning he went into town to talk to Albert Garfield. The world always made a little more sense after a talk with Al. In front of the store he dismounted and reached to lift Amanda down from Dolly's back. He looped the reins to the hitching post and went in, making the bell on the door jangle.

The store was dark after the bright summer sun outside. The floors were graying from wear, and the shelves were cluttered with every item imaginable, from jelly beans to macassar oil for the slick, shiny hair of gentlemen. The jars were dusty, Luke noticed, smiling. Macassar oil didn't seem to be much of a big seller here in Waukegan, Illinois.

He saw Amanda eyeing the spools of ribbon and lace, but walked on past to the candy counter. Al was sitting on a stool behind the other counter, the one with coffee and tea and sugar and the cash register. He was reading the newspaper from Chicago, but looked up and grinned.

"Luke! How ya been? Haven't seen you for a while."

"Mostly fine," Luke said, coming up to the counter where his friend sat.

"Mostly?"

"Do you suppose Evelyn would consider fixing this?"

Albert took the bundle without further question, and without making Luke pause in his talking. "What do you suppose makes a man incapable of sewing?"

"What do you suppose makes a woman incapable of driving?" Al countered. They both knew that Evelyn could handle a wagon or carriage as well as either of them, and that Luke had been teaching Amanda, and she was doing okay with it. "Maybe it's just certain men who can't sew?" Al suggested. "Myself, I can sew a bit if I have to. But I don't have to."

Luke joined his chuckle, but asked, "How is that fair? You can sew, but don't have to. I have to, and can't."

"Sometimes God's idea of fair ain't the same as ours. Now I would say that it ain't fair for you to be so pretty like and me so ugly."

Luke smiled. "Well, even with your ugly mug, Evelyn seems happy with you."

"She's a good woman. You should have one of your own."

Luke frowned. "Can't say that I need one. Or want one." He looked to Amanda, who was edging towards the lace. "But I think maybe she does." Gray eyes sought out his friend's brown ones. "Yesterday I saw her putting a bow on her lamb. Al, what do I do with her?"

"Nothin.' Just love her."

"You think so? It seems so inadequate. She's got no one to talk to about clothes and girl stuff. And it's only getting harder."

"Plenty girls grow up with no mother and turn out fine. Don't worry so much."

He supposed Al was right. Amanda wasn't the first little girl in the world raised by a father.

"Just make sure she knows you love her. Maybe do something special with her from time to time."

He could do that, if he could think of anything special to do. Feeling reassured, he bought the supplies he needed and they headed home.

Three

*L*eah made sure she was the one to open the door the following day for Lord Abercrombe. Not having inquired of Tabitha as to the time he was to arrive, she watched the windows closely all morning. The waiting fueled her irritation with her sister-in-law, so by the time the caller arrived, she had no hesitation in carrying out her plan. Lord Abercrombe's interest in Tabitha was perfectly obvious, and she hoped she was guessing correctly about his reasons. If he was smitten by what was unarguably a pretty face, her ploy might only serve to make him feel protective of the little tart. But she had a feeling that his interest lay more in the money he expected that Tabitha had just inherited than in the woman herself.

"Why, Lord Abercrombe! What a pleasant surprise!" She beamed as she opened the door.

He stepped into the large entryway. "Is Mrs. Bradford ready? She has asked me to take her down to the Thames.

Seems she feels she needs a holiday, and I can't say that I would disagree."

"Oh, yes. She did mention something about going out today, and that she might be going away for a bit. Come in, come in. I'm sure she'll only be a minute."

As she shut the door, she touched his elbow and whispered, confidentially. "I am so glad I was able to speak to you first. I need to ask yet another favor, if you would? I've tried to talk to her myself, but she can be quite stubborn. And as thoughtless as a schoolgirl."

Lord Abercrombe raised a questioning eyebrow.

"It's money I worry about, if I may be so vulgar as to mention it. You see, she doesn't have much. Would you try to steer her away from expensive accommodations?"

Lord Abercrombe said nothing. His mind was in a turmoil, wondering what the woman meant, trying to think of a way to clarify it without being boorish. He needn't have worried.

Leah rushed on. "My brother, God rest him, had enough foresight to not leave her much. He knew that a woman just isn't up to dealing with it. No, he was wise enough to leave it to his nephew. Most of it, that is. Tabitha, of course, was left a small stipend, but she isn't the type to have a care for the future. I'm afraid she'll go through the entire sum rather quickly if she doesn't have proper guidance."

"Ah, of course," he stammered. So. She hadn't inherited all this. He glanced around with regret. Better to learn now than later.

Leah left him in the library to wait for Tabitha. He watched her leave. She was a bit on the plump side, which could be good. Her build suited her. The problem—the reason he didn't feel drawn to the woman—was her face. Her features were nice. Ordinary, not spectacular. But there was something lacking. She had a face like a snowman; round, white, and cold.

His reverie was interrupted by the sound of Tabitha's approaching footsteps. Mrs. Bradford looked lovely, even in mourning. She smiled her appreciation when he assisted her into his carriage, showing her dimple and giving his heart a lurch. With regret, he closed off his emotions. He could not afford to consider, even briefly, becoming entangled with a woman who didn't have money.

From the Hall, near Hyde Park, London was a thing of beauty. The streets had large, well-tended houses with green lawns and flower beds, and trees and sidewalks. But that began to change, the closer they got to the river. The black cloud of coal dust that constantly hung over the city was thicker, coating everything in a black, grimy layer. There was more traffic, and there were more people about. There were dogs and horses. Rotting garbage and animal droppings added to the rank odor in the air. Some of the people moved Tabitha to pity, but also made her wonder how they survived, and what unsavory acts that survival might demand of them. Unconsciously, she slid a bit closer to her escort, who didn't seem to notice.

Lord Abercrombe paid a lad to watch his carriage and

matched grays while they set out to prowl the area of the docks and see what they could learn.

The riverfront was noisy and crowded and dirty. The river was lined with gray stone and rotting wood pilings, with a layer of green on them up to the high-tide mark. The water of the Thames was thick and smelled of sewage. Garbage, bits of paper and wood, and even dead animals floated on its surface. Yet all was not bad. London had its share of grace and beauty, as well as its poverty and filth. There was a vibrancy and excitement in the city. That excitement was especially noticeable along the river. Ships of all descriptions lined the banks. Crates and boxes and burlap bags were in various stages of being loaded and unloaded on the docks, and it seemed to Tabitha that most of the voices were either foreign or had strange-sounding accents.

She stepped closer to Lord Abercrombe, who was ever the gentleman, but was more distant today than he had been. She wondered if there was something wrong, some problem bothering him, but she didn't know him well enough to be so forward as to ask. And she was feeling a bit guilty about being out at all so soon after Samuel's death. It just wasn't done. That her escort was a young, single man only made it worse. What had possessed her to ask him to bring her here? Why had she even wanted to come in the first place? The whole plan suddenly seemed ludicrous.

Lord Abercrombe guided her around a stinking, steaming pile of horse droppings, onto a quay wall. A bag being unloaded from one of the ships broke near them, bringing a string of curses from the workman, who noticed Tabitha and muttered an apology before scurrying guiltily back to work. Tabitha's eyes widened. The bag was full of wheat, and the golden grains spilled out onto the ground and onto the other bags. Hundreds of bags. Thousands, maybe.

"Is this all wheat? Where is it from?"

Lord Abercrombe glanced at the ship, from which a string of men kept unloading the bags. The flag had familiar red and white stripes, and white stars on a blue background. "The United States," he replied.

America. Tabitha regained a bit of her enthusiasm. She had never seen such a wealth of grain. Her eyes went from the wheat to the stars and stripes fluttering at the stern of the ship, then back to the grain, spilling gold before her. The grains that had fallen were ignored in the sheer quantity of the sacks.

The red-and-blue flag snapped loudly, demanding her attention. America. A land so flowing in food that it could ship this much away!

The ship was beautiful. It was long and smooth, and painted black with a wide white stripe. There were three masts. Even with the sails lowered, she was an elegant lady.

Everything seemed to fit; everything seemed symbolic, pointing the way. *This is your destiny.* The flag, the timing, the gold—not gold from California, but gold still, in the form of fat kernels of grain.

Spurning convention, Tabitha walked directly up to one of the men, who was now finishing his task of helping to remove the burlap bags. "Excuse me, sir."

The man's surprise was quickly followed by a leer, which was, in turn, quickly erased when Lord Abercrombe stepped to her side. "Ma'am?" The voice sounded flat and harsh to her ears.

"Is this ship returning to America?"

"To North America, yes, ma'am. Be going home in a couple days." He hooked a thumb over his shoulder. "Signing passengers down there."

"Thank you, sir."

The dockhand tipped his hat and walked up the wharf towards the city.

As soon as he was out of earshot, Lord Abercrombe spoke. "You can't be serious, Mrs. Bradford."

"I think I am. Quite serious."

"Just because a ship arrives loaded with wheat? It's preposterous."

"Is it? Why?"

"Because," he hesitated. The reasons were so many that he didn't know where to start. "Because it's too sudden. You haven't thought it through. And because it's apparently a cargo ship, not a passenger ship."

"He said they were signing passengers. I want to inquire." With that, she headed in the direction the young man had indicated. There was a sign, not far away, on the side of a small, booth-type wooden building. In fact, there were several signs. The building was papered in them. There were advertisements for passage, advertisements for land, all enticing people to distant ports. Mostly, they were about America. There were prices for first class, second class, and steerage, varying quite a bit from ship to ship.

Glancing back, she read the name of the boat that had brought the wheat. *Freedom*. Then she searched for the name on the advertisements. "Here it is! Sailing in a week. To Quebec." Her eyes met those of her companion in a puzzled frown.

"Quebec?" they asked, in unison, which made them smile. Lord Abercrombe, Tabitha decided, looking into his friendly blue eyes, was a very nice man.

"Quebec," said a tall man who was walking up to them, "is a main port for the central part of North America. Raw materials out—timber, minerals, grain—immigrants in. Works rather well. The ships need ballast for the return trip, and so many people want to vote. Or want land. Or just want an adventure. Never a lack of passengers.

"By the way," he said. "Name's Adams. Captain Jefferson Adams." The man's blue eyes were surrounded by creases put there by years out in the weather. His hair and beard were black, and the hair curled up around the edges of his cap. Years of experience and wisdom were carved into that face, and Tabitha trusted him immediately. She introduced herself and her companion, and then Captain Adams continued, as if there had been no break in the conversation.

"So much of the goods of America come from that region. And so many people want to go there. The biggest problem in shipping to and from the Great Lakes is the river."

"The river?" she questioned.

"The Saint Lawrence. It's a natural outlet for all that vast interior, but it isn't navigable for the whole length. Canals have helped. At least now the stuff doesn't have to be portaged. But the draft limit is only nine feet. There are several canals along the Saint Lawrence between Montreal and Lake Ontario. Then there's the Welland Canal. That bypasses the falls at Niagara." He paused. "You've heard of it?"

When she nodded, he went on. "The Welland connects Lake Ontario with Lake Erie. There's a drop of 330 feet between them. Needed forty locks. So goods—or people—have to be transferred from ocean-going ships like the *Freedom*, which is a clipper-schooner and has a draft of almost twelve feet. At Quebec City, we change ships, to a smaller lake schooner."

Tabitha liked the man. He was obviously proud of his country, and just as obviously was a knowledgeable man. He had the flat, horrible American accent, but his grammar was good, he was educated, and he knew his business.

"Where did your ship get her name?" she asked him. "Why *Freedom*?"

"Because this ship is what gave me my independence. I work for myself. I'm not under someone else's thumb."

That decided her. It would be her freedom from Leah as well.

Tabitha took a deep breath. "Might I purchase a second-class ticket for the next voyage to America?"

"Certainly, ma'am. We leave a week from today" the worker said.

🙚🙚

Tabitha would be sharing a cabin with three other ladies. Captain Adams showed her the cabin and personally escorted them on a tour of the *Freedom*. It seemed huge to her, though the captain said that some ships were nearly two hundred feet long. The *Freedom* was only a little over a hundred.

The top of the ship's three decks was planked in oak. Captain Adams explained that all the exposed wood was white oak, which was much more durable than pine. The planks were not painted, merely oiled. Tabitha liked the shine. Aft were the captain's and first mate's cabins. Down the center, between the masts, were the hatches and ladders to the lower decks. Captain Jefferson Adams made much of assisting her with the ladders.

The next deck down housed the passenger cabins. There were eight at the stern—four on each side, separated by a narrow passageway. Towards the bow were the galley and the saloon. This was where meals were eaten, and the room was also used for playing cards or whatever activities passengers could come up with to while away the hours. Captain Adams called it "social central."

The third deck, Tabitha thought, was a mess. One end was steerage, and she pitied those who would be crammed into that lightless, airless space. The captain had a lantern, but she imagined that there wouldn't be much lantern light for the passengers during the voyage. It was this deck that carried much of the cargo on the eastbound trip. The other end had what seemed miles of anchor cable and hooks in the bulkhead, where the crew strung their hammocks at night. Below that was just ballast—in this case, gravel.

While they walked, Captain Adams explained that the framing of the ship and the "knees"—the supports between decks—were made of live oak, which was very strong and didn't rot. The knees were cut in a sort of boomerang shape directly from the tree, to increase strength.

Back on the quarterdeck, the captain told them about the masts. Each was made from four poles of Douglas fir, flattened on two sides and rounded on the third, so that each pole looked, in cross section, like a quarter of a pie. The four poles were fit together and red-hot metal bands placed around them to hold them together. When cold water was poured on the metal, it shrunk, holding the pieces tightly together. The deck fittings, he said, were painted white, so that they were easier to see in the dark.

One week. Could she pack what things she would take, dispose of the rest, go to Mr. Mortimer to receive her share of money from Samuel's will, and do everything involved in making a major move in one week? She would have to. Tabitha's determination rose, and she quickened her step as she approached Lord Abercrombe's carriage.

Her escort, she noticed, had grown increasingly silent as their tour progressed, and as they drove back to Bradford Hall, she dared to asked him what was wrong.

"Part of me wishes I could go along," he replied. "I admire your courage. I don't know many men who would set out on their own as you are doing. It would be a great adventure. The other part of me is and always will be in Scotland. I'll never leave, or not for long. My home is very much a part of me."

Tabitha was touched by his compliment, though she didn't feel particularly deserving. Her daring was born more of desperation than courage or an adventurous spirit. "I wish," she said, "that I had someplace to feel that attached to. I wish I had a home."

"What about the Hall?"

"It's not really my home. It was fine as long as Samuel was alive, but now it belongs to my nephew, and I'm accepted but not really welcome. I'm an outsider."

William looked at her, wishing things too uncouth to verbalize. She was pretty, she was a pleasant companion, she needed to belong somewhere, and she wasn't the flighty, thoughtless creature her sister-in-law had made her out to be. The arrangement would be perfect . . . if only she had money.

"You're not at all what I expected," he said.

"Oh?" Tabitha looked startled. "And what did you expect?"

"Someone without a relevant thought. For instance, I figured you would book first-class passage. I was prepared to try to dissuade you. But you took second class, which is the wisest, considering."

"Considering what?"

He had said too much. Her affairs, financially or otherwise, were no concern of his, and he had aroused her curiosity.

"Well," he paused, then looked at her with an expression that was half apology and half pity. "To be honest, your sister-in-law told me of your situation. I was only following her advice, to try to keep you from extravagant spending."

What was going on? Why would Leah say such a thing? Tabitha's mind reeled, trying to come up with a reasonable explanation.

Her confusion must have shown, for Lord Abercrombe went on. "She is trying to look out for your welfare. She's concerned about you, because you've never had to handle your own affairs before, and she asked me to keep you from doing anything foolish with your money."

It was beginning to make sense. Of course Leah would find a way to let him know that she, Tabitha, wasn't rich. She probably thought Lord Abercrombe was interested in the fortune that the world must assume she had just inherited.

Was he? He certainly had shown more friendly concern than she would have expected from a casual
acquaintance. But a fortune hunter? She would need
more evidence than that to believe it. Well, she would
never have that evidence, because she was leaving.

The view from Lord Abercrombe's open carriage
revealed a rare, glorious, sunny day. Rain had cleared the
air, and a brisk breeze had helped. When they came up
the drive, Bradford Hall in the sunlight looked so wel-
coming. It looked like home.

Tabitha wavered. Was she doing the right thing? Or
was she off on a lark, unanchored? Maybe, she told herself, her place was right here, living as a witness of the
Gospel and praying Leah into the kingdom.

How could she know?

A cloud passed over the Hall, clearing her thoughts.
The Lord only guided footsteps; He did not reveal life-
times. She would take one step at a time, and trust that
He would change her heart or close opportunities if she
strayed from His path.

Four

*T*abitha wondered if she had forgotten anything. If so, it was lost to her; she would never be able to come back for it. She looked around her. Samuel Bradford had certainly given his young bride the best rooms in the Hall. From one side she could see the trees of Hyde Park, from the other a stately row of large, impressive houses marching down the cobbled street. The cobbles were rough in the middle of the street, for the horses to gain traction, with parallel lines of smooth stones cut through for the wheels of wagons and carriages. Huge green trees touched branches over the street, shading luxuriant lawns. Flowers of every size and color graced gardens and sunny spots, all meticulously tended.

The curtains in her room, as well as the rugs, bed-clothes, and even the flowers on the nightstand had been of her choosing. This place had come to mean home, but a large part of that feeling of belonging died with

Samuel. Oh, how she missed him. How many times had she wanted to go to him to discuss her excitement or her fears, only to stop and realize that he was no longer there. If he had been, she would have no plans, no reason for either excitement or fear.

The delivery of a trunk to her room had caused no ripple in the household. Leah was expecting her to take a holiday. No one knew that she would not be coming back. Tonight at supper she would tell them, and tomorrow she'd be gone.

She had packed her Bible, a few mementos from her family, her clothing and toiletries. Her black clothes were on top, easier to get to. Anything colored was packed at the bottom. Her money was in an enamel box that had belonged to her mother. There was enough for her to live on for quite some time if she had to, and it went a long way in boosting the courage she needed to move to a foreign country by herself. The trunk was full, and it held everything she needed.

A ripple of fear fluttered in Tabitha's stomach. It was time to go to dinner, but she did not feel much like eating. She took a deep breath and went downstairs to join her sister-in-law and nephew.

The three of them sat, an island of gloomy humanity, at one end of the massive table. Only the sounds of clinking glass and silver broke the silence. David had been moved from his seat at his mother's side to the head of the table. *The king is dead, long live the king!* Tabitha thought.

Leah noted that Tabitha wasn't eating much, but as she and David had been finished with their main course for some time, she ordered dessert to be brought. The supper conversation had been lacking since her brother had passed, and she did not like the long, emotionless meals. She could tell by the morose expression on her son's face that he didn't like them either. At least he ate well. But then, what sixteen-year-old boy didn't?

They could at least try to be civil. Forcing a smile, she reached for her spoon and said the first thing that came to mind. "So, Tabitha. Tomorrow you leave us for a while. I never liked summer travel. Too warm. I think I would visit Scotland this time of year, or perhaps Switzerland. You have been remiss in informing us of your plans. Of course we are interested."

David brightened visibly and looked to his aunt.

"Actually, I have some news for you." Tabitha set her spoon beside her crème brûlée. "I am going to America. I'm not coming back."

The reactions were simultaneous, but very different.

"America!" David beamed, excited.

"Not coming back?" Leah was clearly shocked by the news.

"How exciting!" David exclaimed. "I wish I could go!"

Leah ignored him. "What are you thinking? How will you live?"

"It's not the same here without Samuel. I am too young to spend the rest of my life as my nephew's ward," Tabitha replied calmly. "As to how I'll live, Samuel left me enough for a few months, until I get settled. Then I plan to take in sewing."

"Take in sewing! Tabitha, have you lost your mind?"

"I am fully in command of my mental faculties. There is no shame in earning one's way. I have not had servants and titled friends all my life, and I am perfectly capable of supporting myself."

Leah gulped air like a landed fish.

"You needn't inform your friends of my reduced status, so I don't need to be an embarrassment to you. Merely tell them I emigrated." Tabitha regretted the words meant to wound, even as she spoke, but she knew she had hit the nail on the head. Leah turned crimson and developed a sudden intense interest in her dessert.

David glanced from his mother to his aunt, then timidly asked, "Where are you going, Aunt Tabitha? America is terrible large."

"I'm not certain. I've been looking at some of Samuel's maps in the library. The ship I'll be traveling on goes as far as Quebec, and then I'll be transferred to a smaller ship that can make the passage up the river to the Great Lakes. There are many cities along the lakes: Cleveland, Detroit, Chicago. Several smaller places. I haven't decided yet where I'll stop."

"That's north, though, wherever you stop. The winters will be horrid. And if there is a war, England will side with the South, because of the cotton that we need for our mills." He grinned, enjoying the chance to show off his knowledge. "Do you think there will be war?"

Tabitha's heart quailed. War? Harsh winters? She had not given them a thought, and here David thought of them almost immediately. Were there other things as well, things that might turn out to be vitally important, that she had ignored?

"No," she answered, forming arguments to support what she wanted to believe. "I don't think there will be war. A civil war is a serious thing, and a nation doesn't make war on itself easily. Surely they will not have a war. As to winter, I am not worried about that. The people who live there apparently get through it. And they certainly have bountiful crops. It's not as if I'm moving to Siberia."

"I wish I could go," David said again.

"You must finish your studies," his mother silenced him. "Perhaps when your schooling is finished, you may tour the Continent."

David refused to hush. "Oh, posh. Who wants cathedrals and gondolas? I want to see New York City, and plantations with black slaves, and savage red Indians!"

Tabitha turned white. "I don't believe I'll be seeing New York City," was all she could think of to say. Were there Indians in Illinois? Then she calmed. She would live in a city and be on a ship up to that point. Even if there were Indians, and even if they did massacre white people, she would be safe enough.

Later that evening David tapped on Tabitha's door.

"Come in!" she called, and he peeked around the corner. They had never been close, but now, oddly, she felt that she would miss the boy.

"I really do wish I could come with you, Aunt Tabitha. Mum is so boring. She would never do something as exciting as going to America."

"She is right. You need to finish your schooling. And soon you'll be all grown."

He brightened. "Then may I come to see you in America?"

"Of course." She smiled, patting his cheek, then quickly removed her hand when she realized she was embarrassing him. "I would love for you to visit me. As soon as I am settled, I will send you my address."

David grinned, then spontaneously threw his arms around her neck. "I'll miss you!" He bolted for the door, and Tabitha's "I'll miss you too!" followed him down the hall.

Luke toyed with the edge of his linen napkin, avoiding eye contact with Miss Lillian Morton. The whole evening had been uncomfortable, and he wished for its end. It wouldn't have been so bad, maybe, if he'd had some warning.

He had readily accepted Al and Evelyn's invitation for supper. It was a routine occurrence. They always ate all together around the big table in the dining room, family style. But tonight the children, Amanda and the Garfield flock, were seated in the kitchen, and he was seated in the dining room, which had the best linen and china and candlelight. With him in the room were Al and Evelyn . . . and a Miss Lillian Morton. He'd been set up.

Al had given an apologetic shrug, then held chairs for his wife and their guest while Luke got over his shock and collected his ability to move and speak normally.

Lillian Morton was petite, slightly plump, and pretty, with honey blonde hair and blue-green eyes. And, apparently, without a will of her own. She ate what was offered, spoke when spoken to, and agreed with whatever comment was made, all the time gazing vacuously at Luke across the table.

Evelyn had stopped chattering, drawing information about Luke, which she already knew, for the benefit of Lillian. She had asked about his farm and his daughter and his plans and his interests. Likewise she had questioned Lillian for his benefit. Realizing that they were both embarrassed, she had stopped, and there had been a difficult few moments of silence before Al tried to spark conversation.

After several monosyllabic replies from Lillian about how she liked Waukegan, which church she attended and the like, he gave up and talked to Luke. Lillian finished her meal quietly.

"New state, Minnesota. Whaddya think of that? This country grows and grows. All the territories, all the way to the Pacific, will be states before long," Al said.

"Yup. But will they be free states, like Minnesota? Or slave, like they're trying to make Kansas?" Luke replied.

"Getting to be a serious question, ain't it? Can't quite believe how this country could get to the place where we could actually argue and even come to violence over whether or not we should allow folks to own folks."

Luke noticed Miss Morton's sudden stillness and changed the subject. The "peculiar institution" of slavery was a hot topic, and it could easily ruin what little was good about the evening. "Is the Tariff Act affecting your business any?"

"Hardly notice it." Al frowned. "Don't sell much imported stuff. Why?" But he didn't get an answer.

Lillian suddenly stood. "May I be taken home now?" It was the longest sentence she had spoken all evening.

"Certainly." Luke stood too. He had wanted to end the evening, but he hadn't wanted it to go this way, with the girl so upset that she left early, nearly in tears. "I'll see her home, Al. Be back shortly for Mandy. That okay?"

"Of course."

Evelyn was in a tizzy, having had her social evening ruined and not knowing why or what to say. She settled for "I'll fetch your things."

There were apologies at the door, and then Luke was outside in the warm summer night, walking Miss Morton the few blocks to her parents' house. Fireflies danced in and out of the trees. A full moon hung in the east, making it easy to see their way. Children were out playing, enjoying the lightness of the night. He could hear their running and squealing and the near-constant slamming of screen doors.

"You said you were from Kentucky, Miss Morton?"

"Um-hm."

That didn't tell him much. Folks in Kentucky could think either way about slavery. And some of them felt mighty strongly about whichever side of the argument they came down on. "I'm not sure what upset you, but I am sorry," he said.

"I don't reckon it's your fault," she replied. A rush of speech followed. "People believe what they will. Pa hates it. Slavery, that is. Zachary, that's my brother, bought a slave. He's savin' up for more. Pa said he was unchristian. Zach said Pa was a white trash cracker and always would be if he wasn't willing to do what needed to be done, and accused him of keeping me from a good marriage and him from a good education, because he wasn't willing to make enough money. So Pa packed us up and came here, to a free state. Zach stayed in Kentucky. But how can I hate my brother?"

Luke was speechless.

"Even here," she went on, "we can't get away from it. Folks arguing all the time."

"Nope. Don't suppose there's anywhere you can go to get away from the issue. And I reckon it'll get worse before it gets better."

"Do you?" There was disappointment in her voice. Clearly, it was not what she wanted to hear. "I sincerely hope you're wrong, Mr. Hayes."

"So do I." By then they had arrived at her house, so he bid her good night and headed back to Garfields'. He too hoped he was wrong, but he didn't think he was.

There had already been violence . . . the trouble in Kansas, where the settlers had wanted their state to be free, but "border ruffians" from Missouri had come in, temporarily settling in Kansas Territory so that there would be sufficient proslavery numbers to make Kansas a slave territory. The newspapers called it "Bleeding Kansas." Then there was John Brown. He and his band had killed five men. Congressman Brooks had beaten Senator Sumner with his cane, doing serious damage to the man—right in the Senate chamber, when the senator had been alone in the room.

There would be more bloodshed and more broken families, which in turn would fuel more violence. Luke didn't see how the issue could possibly be resolved peacefully.

Tabitha ran her hand down the fine, carved mahogany of her bedpost, saying good-bye to her things and to the home she had known for more than eight years. Bradford Hall had been a haven for her, and certainly it was full of creature comforts. But without Samuel, it was only a house. No. Worse than that. It was a prison, keeping her from growing, keeping her from experiencing anything of the world beyond its walls. She was right to get away.

By now her trunk was already aboard ship, waiting for

her. It was almost too much to grasp. Leaving England forever. What was out there on the edge of her horizon? Her stomach quivered at the idea of facing the unknown, but she had money to last awhile, and she had God. He would guide her and protect her.

It was time. The ship would be leaving whether she was there or not. Bates would have the carriage waiting. Having him drive her was the last thing she would ever ask of the Bradfords. Bates would be retiring soon and moving to a cottage in the country. Samuel's will had made that possible, and she was glad for the loyal servant.

Good-byes were brief. Leah showed no emotion at all. Was she glad to see her go, Tabitha wondered. Or now that it was real, did she realize what could have been? Would she miss her? Was the idea of Tabitha taking in sewing an embarrassment to her, or did she take satisfaction in the thought?

David was sorry to see her go, but anxious to have her new address so he could come for a visit when he was old enough. The implication was that "old enough" meant as soon as he didn't need his mother's permission.

Leah scowled and muttered something not quite audible about America and civilization. Tabitha hugged her anyway and wished her happiness. She then hugged her nephew, who ignored his dislike for physical affection and returned her hug warmly. Then the door closed, leaving them inside and her outside, alone, facing Bates, the carriage, and the world.

Etienne Rousseau whistled his way down the busy London street, swinging his walking stick in the warm August sunshine. It was a lovely day. He would miss London, he supposed. But there were other lovely cities. And many of them had a lot more warm, sunny days. New Orleans was a city he was considering. It was a warm city. It even had a French section. It had its culture and its luxuries. It also had its more decadent side, which also had certain advantages. Yes, he decided, New Orleans was the place for him. He hoped, now that he had decided, that he could find direct passage, but he was not adverse to taking detours. Any route could provide entertainment and diversions. The main thing was to be on his way today, now that he had decided where he wished to go.

Just ahead of him he saw a young pickpocket in the process of lifting a lady's purse. There was a bobby not twenty feet away. Stupid urchin. And the woman's male companion was just as stupid, totally oblivious to what was going on. Etienne watched the dirty lad with a mixture of pity and contempt. The woman screamed and the boy ran off, the bobby in pursuit. Etienne bent to help the lady retrieve her things, which had scattered all over the cobbles.

"Why, thank you, sir." She blushed, just enough to give her cheeks an attractive pink tint. She couldn't be called pretty, but there was a certain elegance about her.

"You are most welcome." He smiled, tipped his top

hat, and continued down the street. Without turning, he knew she was watching him. That's how it always happened. His grin broadened, showing sparkling white teeth and causing a few heart flutters in the ladies that he passed.

His finely tapered, olive-skinned fingers reached into his trouser pocket to play with a few coins. He loved the tinkle and always carried some coins, even though he was now able to carry a thick wad of bills. The sound of money was his omen. He had come far, and the world was wonderful.

Etienne booked passage on the first ship he found headed in the general direction of North America. Its destination was Quebec, which was close enough for him. The rest of the journey to New Orleans could prove interesting, and it was a nice time of year for traveling.

Five

*T*abitha took a brief look at the small cabin she would be sharing with three ladies. Her cabin mates weren't in the tiny room, so she made her way back up to the wooden deck, where she stood, watching London from the railing. A breeze diminished some of the black cloud over the city, and lessened, to a degree, the odor. But she still held a cologne-doused handkerchief near her nose.

The *Freedom* was a beautiful ship. The sails, down in port, were white, the masts strong and straight. The movement of the river passed through the timber of the ship to her feet, and Tabitha was anxious to be off.

Her memory brought up images from childhood—huge waves crashing on a rocky shore. Once a year, while her mother had lived, they had gone to the coast for a holiday. With a smile, Tabitha remembered telling her father that she wanted to cross that ocean someday, to see what was over there.

She frowned. Briefly, she'd had her doubts, considered the possibility of the ship sinking. But she had seen Captain Adams inspecting the ship, had seen the affection in his eyes for the old girl and the swat he gave her prow. She remembered that he had crossed the Atlantic many times, and her confidence in him and his ship grew.

The Thames crept by the ship, towards the sea, lapping against the siding, and Tabitha was impatient to follow the river. The crew loaded the last of the crates and trunks. Then they removed the gangway and replaced the gatelike structure in the wooden siding through which they had all come aboard.

Tabitha replayed in her mind her departure from Bradford Hall. When they reached the end of the driveway, she had asked Bates to stop, and had turned for a last look. She was glad that the sun shone brightly on the gray stone walls and the flowered gardens. It was better to remember it like that, in the sun and hospitable, rather than cold and drafty and impersonal. Then they stopped at the cemetery and together planted some yellow pansies on Samuel's grave.

The route Bates chose took them through the parks—Hyde, Green, St. James—and along the Embankment. It was a route chosen for beauty, and she had been thankful for his thoughtfulness, though it made her cry. He detoured slightly to pass by the beautiful and relatively new buildings of Parliament, ornate and majestic, with the huge clock tower and Big Ben. As they passed, it gonged the hour, saddening Tabitha. All the sights and sounds she loved, but would probably never see or hear again. She would miss London, in spite of its dirt and noise and areas of poverty.

There was the majestic dome of Saint Paul's Cathedral. Then there was the Tower of London with the crowns at the peak of each tower of the White Tower within, and the gates at the river's edge, where royalty and prisoners could enter from barges without passing through the crowds of the city. The poorest of the city's poor were in greater numbers around London Bridge. Tabitha had heard that large numbers of people lived under the bridges, whole families even, and she knew it was true, though she didn't want to believe it. The cold, the damp, the dirt, rats, and smell. How could a young child survive such a life? A few miles away, the Lord's Prayer was written in Latin, all around the base of Parliment. *Give us this day our daily bread.*

"Give *them* this day their daily bread," she whispered. A prayer from Proverbs came to mind, and it became a personal prayer for her. *Give me neither poverty nor riches; feed me with food convenient for me: Lest I be full, and deny thee, and say, Who is the Lord? or lest I be poor, and steal, and take the name of my God in vain.*

At the docks they had said good-bye, and she had presented Bates with a parting gift. She had chosen Samuel's sword from his army days, as well as his other sword, his Bible. Speechless with emotion, Bates had accepted the gifts, then left her.

Now here she stood, on the deck of the *Freedom*, truly on her own for the first time in her life. She was not as fearful as she thought she would be. A mere seven days ago, she had had to ask Lord Abercrombe for assistance to get to the docks. Since then, she had settled all her own finances and made her own arrangements. She had traveled about London as neccessary, either taking the Bradford carriage and a driver, or getting a cab.

Funny. Lord Abercrombe had been so concerned, yet she hadn't seen him or heard from him since the day he had escorted her here. Perhaps he had returned to Scotland. There was, after all, no reason for him to inform her of his plans.

Captain Adams shouted an order, and the ropes that secured the *Freedom* were cast off. There was no turning back now. The ship began to move, and Tabitha trembled and said a prayer.

There was the yellow brick of the fish market. So much history. Never again would she see it. The landmarks of London disappeared. The river widened as hours passed and the sea approached. Captain Adams paused by Tabitha and smiled down at her. He was very tall, and she had to tip her head back to speak to his face rather than his jacket front. His eyes were blue, and creased at the corners. "Everything okay, ma'am?"

"Yes, thank you."

"I have a lot to do now, but perhaps later I could show you around the ship?"

Tabitha smiled. "You already did that."

He laughed. "So I did." He touched the bill of his captain's hat with two fingers, but hesitated before continuing on his way, making her smile, inside. He was personable. Perhaps she was already making a new friend.

Etienne tossed his one small case on the bunk with a grin. Yes, things were working out. But then, they usually did. Captain Adams had insisted that he ship had no room for additional passengers, but he had proved to have his price, and now the two men were sharing the captain's cabin for the voyage. The first mate had been sent off to the crew's cabin in the lower deck, leaving the upper bunk open for Etienne. His reason ng for needing passage on that particular ship had never come up. Money spoke loudly enough.

The cabin was small, containing the tw ⟩ bunks in the wall, each with a small, inset shelf area, a chest of three drawers across the tiny floor space from a hinged seat over a box for more storage space, and a small washstand across from an equally small closet. One lamp in a sconce on the wall gleamed on the woodwork.

Satisfied, Etienne entered the saloon, ignoring the twitters and giggles of a pair of unattractive sisters. His black eyes scanned the long table, flanked by narrow benches on both sides, sizing up his traveling companions. No one caught his attention. Could be a long, tedious voyage.

Choosing a table, he joined its occupants for his first meal on the ship. The meal was a disappointment. Not horrible, but not up to his standards. He knew that before the Atlantic passage was over, the food would get worse. Well, he could live through bad food. He could live through no food. He had done it before. But he was beginning to question the wisdom of his impulse. There seemed to be no one interesting aboard, with the possible exception of the captain. Everyone else was either an uneducated sailor or an emigrant. Most, in his opinion, dull and ignorant.

After eating and chatting and joking comfortably with a couple of farmers who were emigrating to America, he rose to continue his exploration of the *Freedom*.

He located her on the deck. For a few moments, he stood and watched her, unobserved. Her hair was coming loose, and a few strands blew round in the wind. He approached and spoke, startling her. Her face, up close, was even prettier than he had expected. It was a face devoid of guile, as innocent as a baby's, and for a minute he could think of nothing to say. Such speechlessness around a woman was new to him.

Was she what she seemed? When she blushed and turned to face the sea again, he had the impression of cleanness. There were no shutters. Her eyes, her face, were completely open, and the lack of vice made him uncomfortable. Surely she had something to hide. Surely she was as human as the other women he had known. Surely she had her price—her desires. There was a wedding ring on her finger. There was also a black dress, devoid of decoration. Well, he would have to pursue this one slowly, just in case she was indeed as pure as she seemed. He would enjoy this voyage after all.

Tabitha had been standing at the railing of the ship for a long time, thinking she should go below and acquaint herself with what would be her home for the next several weeks, and the ladies who would be sharing it. But she couldn't leave. She stood at the rail, watching England go by. The hills, the trees, the meadows, the flowers. Even the haze over the green and the farmers at work in their fields spoke to her that this was England, and she would see it no more. At sea, they rounded into the channel. There were the cliffs of Dover. So much history.

Twilight came, then deepened, but she did not move, though the evening sea breeze was growing chilly. Someone approached her, and she turned, sociably. The man who stood there was very refined and very handsome. For what seemed the longest time, he said nothing, and she finally spoke. "Good evening, sir." The pause, his stare, made her blush and she turned away. There was a small flutter in her pulse.

"*Bonsoir, madame,*" he said. "It is getting cold up here on the deck. And the time for dinner is past. Pardon my forwardness, but are you feeling well?"

The man's voice was low, silky but also gravelly, and he had a decided French accent. She felt another little thrill. What magnificent eyes! Black and alive, interested in what was around him.

Afraid that her own interest would be unseemly, Tabitha turned back once more to face the sea. Decreasing light and increasing distance from land were making England fade. "I'm fine, thank you," she replied. "I just feel a bit emotional. Leaving my home. It isn't as easy as I thought it would be."

She hadn't turned away to be rude, but from a sense of self-preservation. This man attracted her, and she could easily do something foolish or make some insipid remark and humiliate herself. "I really should go below. I haven't even met my cabin mates yet. If you will excuse me."

"Certainly. I am sure we will meet again. My name is Etienne Rousseau."

"And I am Tabitha Bradford." She curtsied and left him there by the ship rail.

Tabitha's head was full of the handsome Frenchman, and she scolded herself for her rudeness in leaving so abruptly. She wasn't thinking at all about the people who would be in the cabin, and there was an awkward silence when she entered the small room.

Her cabin mates were a woman and her two daughters. The woman was round everywhere, even to the gray-streaked bun at the back of her head. The daughters had rather thin, straight hair of a faded brown, and thin noses.

"We saw yer trunk"—the woman pointed to the familiar case—"but we was wonderin' if you was showing up."

Her speech was heavily Cockney, making Tabitha smile.

"I was watching England recede," she explained. "Rather sad, isn't it?"

"Not to us. Not much behind us, and all in front. We're going t' America ta me brother. I be Mrs. Dobbins. These"—a thumb over her shoulder pointed in the general direction of the daughters—"be my girls. Martha and Margaret."

"And I am Tabitha Bradford." She shook hands around. "Pleased to make your acquaintance."

"Where you be headed?" the woman asked, going back to arranging her things in the tiny room.

"America."

"So are we all. I mean, where in America?"

"I haven't decided."

Such indecision and spontaneity seem to take the woman aback. "Then why go?" she asked.

Tabitha tried not to frown at the woman's inquisitiveness. They would be together a great deal, and it would not do to begin by being easily annoyed. "I'm not sure, really. Spirit of adventure, perhaps. My husband died recently, and it seemed the thing. Complete change."

"Ah. Change could be the thing. I 'ope you're not gener'ly so 'adventurous.' Could see 'arm goin' off on yer own like."

"No," Tabitha assured her, fighting a smile. "I am not usually so adventurous. In fact, I hope to open a sewing shop and never have another adventure in my life."

"Ah. A sewing shop." Mrs. Dobbins relaxed visibly. "I thought you was a lady," she admitted. "You know. One a the 'igh an' mighty. Was wonderin' wot you was doin' in this 'ere dinky cabin."

Tabitha made no response.

They agreed that Mrs. Dobbins and Tabitha would take the lower bunks and the girls the upper, Martha above Tabitha and Margaret above her mother. Tabitha learned that the girls were seventeen and eighteen, Margaret being the older. They complimented her on her 'loverly' dress and pretty smile. She learned that Mr. Dobbins had been dead for nearly two years, and times had been difficult for them since then. They had been saving for most of that time for the passage money to get to Mrs. Dobbins' brother, Charles Drury, in Chicago. Things would be easier there, with family, they were sure. Drury, she called him, wrote what a "loverly" place America was.

Many immigrants, he'd warned, had a hard time of it. They were tricked and cheated on arrival. So they were to speak to no one. And many had to take jobs working long hours in dark and sometimes dangerous factories. But they would be different. They would do well, because he and Mrs. Drury, who was American (her parents being from Germany), owned a small house on a nice street. It had three rooms. One could be for them, one for his sister and nieces. The bigger, central room was where they did the cooking. It had a table, but they would need a few more chairs.

Tabitha thought it all sounded a bit dreary, but at least they knew what they were getting into. She, on the other hand, was going blindly into the unknown.

In the morning, early, Tabitha was on deck again. The sky changed from blue-silver to custard yellow, and as far as she could see was sea, rolling wave after rolling wave. The sails were full, and the wind pulled at her hair, tugging some loose. There was no sight but water, no sound but wind and sail and birds. There was no touch except for wood and wind. The fishy taste of salt was on her tongue, the smell of the ocean filled her nose and lungs.

How immense it was! The vastness of water, ahead, behind, and below, gave her a small sense of the eternity of God. Rolling, rolling. The waves continued to come. Tabitha began to feel a little queasy, but it helped her feel steadier if she held on, so she stood with her face to the wind and her hand on the rail. The two masts of square sails were behind her, but the triangular foresails were above her and a bit in front. Everywhere, it seemed, there were neatly coiled ropes.

A shadow of something large and dark passed through the water, bringing to mind tales of sea serpents and monsters and mermaids. It didn't take much imagination to see where sailors, through the years, got such ideas. Who really knew what was down there? There were numerous birds, circling and calling, so she knew they were still fairly close to land.

Margaret Dobbins interrupted her musings. "Miz Bradford? Are ya plannin' on breakfast? No supper. Ya must be 'ungry."

"Yes. I suppose if I miss too many meals, this wind will fill my skirt like a sail and blow me back to England. Now that would be a waste of my ticket, wouldn't it?"

Margaret smiled at her silliness, and they went together to breakfast. "Ooh," Margaret whispered, loudly enough for Tabitha and Martha to hear, but not loud enough for her mother. "Look! There 'e is!"

Following her indication, Tabitha saw Etienne Rousseau. He saw her look. Clearly he had been aware of them first, and he winked. Tabitha blushed, and her gaze flew to her plate. The audacity!

Well, he was French. They were a cheeky lot.

Both girls giggled.

Later, in the cabin, when Mrs. Dobbins was not there, Margaret said. "Those eyes! 'Ave you ever seen the like?"

Neither Tabitha nor Martha had to ask whom she was talking about. "Aye," her sister agreed, "but the smile is better. 'E gives me the flippety-flops just ta see 'im! Did ya ever see such a man?"

"Never!" Margaret agreed.

Tabitha did too, though she didn't voice her thoughts. She was, after all, in mourning. Samuel had only been dead for two weeks. It was quite improper of her even to notice the man, much less to join in a girlish conversation making much of his attributes.

The girls were similarly aware of Monsieur Rousseau during the noon meal. They developed an interest in their food, and their cheeks took on an attractive pink. Their mother shook her head, making *tsk tsk* sounds. Tabitha was aware that he sat at the same table as the captain, and she was aware that he watched her. She tried very hard not to return his regard.

That evening found Tabitha in her usual place on the deck, watching a gorgeous sunset, thinking that the sun would soon be setting over America, the much-fabled land. It made her think of the old legends of Avalon, beyond the western sea, where everything was a paradise. *Lord,* she prayed, *I know it's just a story, but please let America be my Avalon.* She waited, still, for the voice of her Lord in her heart. The sails snapped and puffed more westward. A passage from the Psalms came to her mind. *O Lord, how manifold are thy works! in wisdom hast thou made them all: the earth is full of thy riches. So is this great and wide sea, wherein are things creeping innumerable, both small and great beasts. There go the ships: there is that leviathan, whom thou hast made to play therein.*

The Psalms were such a source of comfort and strength. She needed to make a point of reading them more often.

The clouds changed from pink to blue. A voice spoke behind here. "There is a storm coming."

Tabitha glanced over her shoulder and smiled at Etienne Rousseau. She wasn't really surprised to see him. "Good evening, Monsieur Rousseau. And how do you know there will be a storm?"

Etienne could not take his eyes off her. Not that he saw any reason to do so. She was adorable. Elegant, definitely. And charming and sweet. Or so she appeared. He wanted to know more. When she smiled, she had a small dimple. "The captain, he assures me, there will be a storm."

"Well, I suppose he would know." Her effort to remain deadpan failed, and she giggled, then quickly recovered.

"Why do you try so hard to be sober? You are charming when you laugh."

"It isn't appropriate. I am still in mourning."

"Your husband?"

"Yes."

"I am sorry." Actually, he was delighted.

"Thank you. But about this storm. Do you suppose it will be bad?"

He lifted a shoulder in a gesture that was typically Gallic. "We shall see."

It was bad. The waves got steeper and more frequent. The ship shuddered when the wind hit. It would go down, Tabitha was sure. Oh, why had she been so stupid as to leave England? Lord Abercrombe had questioned her, asking if she was sure of what she wanted to do, but she had stubbornly insisted on following her impulse. All because of some stupid wheat!

It began to rain, then rained harder. The wind howled and shrieked, and the boat, which seemed suddenly tiny and inconsequential in the ferocity of the sea, bobbed along, with the sails lashed down. Tabitha prayed for protection from the storm, then lost her supper into a bucket. It sloshed there, along with the remains of everyone else's supper. She and her cabin mates huddled miserably on their bunks. The ship pitched and the bucket tipped.

What a mess. What a smell. Again the girls were sick, then so was Tabitha. How awful it would be to clean that! Mrs. Dobbins left the cabin, clutching the ropes in the passageway to keep from falling, and located some rags to soak up the mess. When she returned, Tabitha tried to help, but it only made her sick yet again, and she was told to please not help anymore.

The next day it was still storming, but none of them had anything left in their stomachs. They lay in their bunks, hoping and praying for the storm to end. When it did, the following day, Tabitha rose on unsteady feet and washed as thoroughly as she could with just a basin and a limited amount of water.

She put on a clean dress. It wasn't quite black, but more of a charcoal gray. Technically, it was cheating, but she didn't see that it really mattered whether or not her dress was a true black.

The cabin, she thought, would stink for the rest of the journey. Not only was it thick with the odor of vomit, but the odor of insufficiently washed bodies was mounting. She had to get away from the reek for a while, and made her way to the deck.

The sea was still choppy, so she lurched and stumbled her way, but it was worth it. The deck smelled freshly washed, and the day was a bit cloudy. There was a patch of rain in the distance. It went a long way to make her feel better. During the day, all the steerage passengers from the third deck were made to come up top so that the vomit could be washed out down there, too. Many of them looked ill, pale, and dirty. In their poverty and desperation, they were to be pitied. There was nothing she could do to help them, but she did pray for them.

The trip wore on endlessly, and a pattern emerged. Each day, Tabitha would spend time in the morning and evening on the deck, unless it rained. Monsieur Rousseau would join her, and they would share a bit of small talk. Then she would return to the cabin, and the girls would ooh and ah and bat their lashes and tell her how fortunate she was to have his attention, while their mother scowled and made it clear that she didn't think much of him. For the first few days, the captain also stopped for a bit of conversation, but that soon ceased. Tabitha supposed he didn't have much time for social niceties.

She enjoyed Monsieur Rousseau's company, but she assumed that he sought her out because . . . well, frankly, because most of the passengers were of a lower class, and mostly uneducated. He spoke to her, she assumed, as a way of passing the hours. He asked her to join him for supper once, which she refused because she was in mourning and it wouldn't be right, and that was the end of that. He didn't pursue the point.

Martha and Margaret thought she was insane. No one knew, they pointed out, how long she had been in mourning, so who would care if she ate with a man, in the company of many chaperones? But Mrs. Dobbins scowled at them and shook her head, and gave Tabitha a jerky nod of approval.

The food and drinking water grew worse and worse, and the ocean never ended. It took her farther and farther away from England and all things comfortable, yet never deposited her in America. Tabitha took to spending the long hours in the middle of the day either napping, talking to the Dobbinses, or reading her Bible.

Etienne combed his hair and straightened his cravat. What he would give for a real bath! This journey would never end. Day after day, the same monotony. Eat. Play cards. Be good and not win all the crew's money. Eat. Talk to the captain, who was only conversant on the topics of sailing and the "peculiar institution"—slavery. If not for the diversion of Madam Bradford, he would lose his mind.

That gave him mixed emotions. While she was the only thing that made the trip bearable, he was not getting anywhere with her. He had thought for sure they would be meeting in secret by now, kissing in the moonlight on the deck. Or perhaps Captain Adams would accept another bribe and find somewhere else to sleep some night. There was no reason to think he would not. He had been bribed to share his private cabin when all the passenger rooms had been sold out. He had taken a rather broad hint, and five quid, to avoid the lady. For enough, surely the man would sleep with his crew on a hammock, giving Etienne some privacy with Tabitha.

He sighed. So far he had not even been able to get her to join him for the pathetic excuse for dinner that was available aboard the ship. Critically he regarded himself in a small, constantly moving mirror. He had lost weight. But he did what he could to keep his appearance up, and knew that the other females aboard would succumb in an instant. Why not this one? He shrugged. The game was not over yet. He reached for his suit coat and headed for their unofficial meeting.

"*Bonsoir, monsieur,*" she greeted him, causing him to smile, until he noticed her sadness.

"Whatever is wrong tonight?" he asked. The conversation made him uncomfortable. A woman's problems or sorrows were to be avoided. The realization that he couldn't just walk away from her frightened him a bit.

"It's nothing, really. Only the trip. Will we never arrive in America? I don't know how much more of this bobbing on the sea I can bear. I'm tired of the poor food and the lack of tea. And I'm ashamed of myself for complaining. Think of those poor people below."

"It will end. I promise."

A smile tugged at the corners of his handsome mouth, and his eyes snapped in fun. Tabitha would have to be dead not to notice his male beauty and respond somewhere deep inside. He was trying to cheer her up, and the fact that he cared enough to try accomplished the task. Who was she? Why should he be interested in her? Why would a man like him go to the trouble to seek her out every day? She was a nobody, a nothing. Yet here he was, trying to coax her out of her moodiness.

Almost magically, it seemed, the cry of "Land!" was suddenly heard. It spread quickly through the passengers, and people spilled out from everywhere and crowded the deck for a peek. Tabitha was pushed close to Monsieur Rosseau, and together they laughed at his trick of giving her the journey's end.

Tabitha sobered, staring at his eyes. It was real. She would get to America. And, she suspected, she would miss Monsieur Rousseau more than she would miss the Dobbinses.

Passengers began to think about their appearances again. Dresses were aired, hair was combed. Captain Adams laughed at them. It was still a long time yet before they would reach their destination.

" 'Ave you decided on a destination?" Mrs. Dobbins asked.

"No."

" 'Ow about Chicago? You would know someone, and we would enjoy your company now and then."

Tabitha considered. Mrs. Dobbins was right. It would be nice to know someone. "Yes," she agreed. "I think I would like that."

Six

*T*here was sadness and shock in Waukegan. The body of Lillian Morton had been found in Lake Michigan. At first there was talk of foul play, and there were a few days of nervous speculation, especially among the ladies. But Dr. Price, the new doctor from Buffalo, examined the body and found no sign of force or struggle, so suicide was presumed. The townspeople breathed easier, but Mrs. Morton wailed piteously. Murder she could understand. But to take your own life, a gift from God, when you were young and healthy and pretty? Both her children were now lost to her, and she was inconsolable.

Luke was stunned. He had known the young woman was unhappy. He supposed he had even known, and had sympathized to a degree, in her sense of not being able to escape the ugly issue of slavery, which had split her family. On every street corner, it seemed, people voiced their opinions. Loudly. No one could remain apathetic.

Of course here in Illinois, things were mostly one-sided, but there was the occasional dissenter. As far as a lot of the men were concerned, that only made the discussion more interesting.

Poor girl. Such a short life.

But then none of them knew how long they had.

He thought of his Rachel. She hadn't planned on dying that day. The familiar rage clutched at his heart, choking him, and he forced it away—forced his thoughts onto Amanda, his precious daughter, who was very much alive. Today was the day. He would quit procrastinating and do something with her, as Al had suggested. Before he knew it, she would be grown and gone, and the opportunity would be gone, too.

"Come on, girl," he said, grinning at her. "Finish up these chores quick like. I want to go to town."

"What for, Papa?" For a minute there, when she smiled and poured water from her bucket into Hamlet's water trough, spilling half of it onto the grass, she looked so much like Rachel.

"I just want to go, that's all. Come on. I'll help you." He grabbed another bucket, and in no time the animals were all watered. Both of them put on clean shirts, washed their faces, and combed their hair. Mandy helped saddle Dolly, and off they went to town.

The town itself wasn't his destination. They continued north beyond it and went to the beach. Lake Michigan stretched north, south, and east, vivid blue and glittering in the sun. Holding hands, Luke and his daughter walked the beach. Mandy examined shells and beetles and a dead fish while Luke watched her and chewed on a willow twig. Then she plopped down, pulled off her boots and stockings, and rolled cuffs in her overalls so she could wade. At the shallow edge she ran and splashed, and when her papa didn't scold, she splashed more, a little deeper.

Luke couldn't resist. He pulled off his shoes and socks and joined her, and soon they were both soaked nearly to the waist. They walked back up to the grass to dry and watch the boats, shining white out on the blue water.

"Papa?"

"Yes, Angel?"

"Why'd we come here today?"

"Because mostly we just work. Or you're at school. Life goes by so quickly, and before I know it, you'll find some young man and get married and have your own children and I'll be a lonely grandpa. I wanted to have some fun, too."

"I'm glad. But Papa?"

"What?"

"I won't get married."

"Why not?" With a grin, he watched her scratching in the sand with a stick.

"Because I can't marry my pa, and you're the only one I'd want."

Luke was very glad he had decided to take a day to play with his daughter. "That's sweet, Angel, but I think you'll change your mind."

"Never," she insisted, and he laughed.

On their way home, they stopped in town to buy sticks of horehound candy at Garfields' store. Everyone in town was grumpy and edgy, making Luke remember what had happened. He wished they had gone straight home and not ruined their day by coming around all the speculation and whispered gossip.

"I still can't believe it," Al said, as he dropped Luke's penny into the cash register. "Why ever would a young girl like that up and commit suicide?"

Luke didn't want to share his suspicions, because it would only serve to make Al feel at fault, after the conversation at his house. Besides, he didn't want to discuss it in front of Amanda.

"Pa?" she asked when they were mounted on Dolly and headed home, "what's suicide?"

"It's when somebody kills himself." He never had approved of lying to children about the harsh things in life. They would learn the truth soon enough and then resent you for not telling them.

That surprised her, and she stopped licking her candy. "Kills himself? Like when we killed a pig last fall?"

"Yep. Just like that. Only they don't always use a knife. They might use a gun, or take poison." He decided not to mention drowning. It might ruin her memories of the day, thinking about being in the same water where a woman had died.

"Why?"

"I just don't know. This girl must've been mighty unhappy."

"Was it that lady who was at Al and Evie's house?" When she had been very small, she couldn't say Albert and Evelyn, and certainly couldn't say Garfield, so she had been allowed to say "Al and Evie." Ever since, that's what she had called them.

"Yes, it was. How did you know?"

"I heard talk about Miss Morton while you were in the store. I thought that was her name." Amanda looked thoughtful. "Maybe she was unhappy because she didn't have a little girl."

"What?"

"Like I get unhappy sometimes because I don't have a ma. She shoulda told me first. Then I coulda been her little girl and she coulda been my ma, and we'd both be happy and she wouldn't be dead." That resolved, she went on licking her candy stick.

"It's not that simple." Luke wanted to explain to her about marriage, and that you couldn't marry just anybody, just so a person could have a ma or a little girl. But words failed him, and he simply hugged his daughter to him.

That was a bad night for Luke. It didn't happen often—Rachel had been dead for so long that he was used to being alone. But that night the aloneness wrapped around him. He lay unsleeping in his bed, watching the stars through the window and the darker silhouette of forest against the sky, wishing for someone to share the view with. It was the first time he hadn't wished specifically for Rachel. Instead there was only a vague longing for "someone." The realization of that fact came slowly. Maybe, he admitted, it was time to start looking for a someone.

He missed the feel of a smooth cheek under the roughness of his fingertips, or the silkiness of hair. He missed the meeting of two souls when two pairs of eyes connected in special moments. Mostly he missed just having someone to share his life with.

Probably, he thought, wadding his pillow into a ball and turning away from the window, it was only because Mandy had talked of wanting a mother earlier in the day. Tomorrow would be better. But the night was very long.

Tabitha felt settled, knowing at last where she would end up. Chicago. And the Dobbinses would be there, and she wouldn't really be alone in a strange place.

The Saint Lawrence, up to Quebec City, was huge— more ocean than river. There were many ships, large and small. Masts created a forest, with clouds of white sails, as their ship approached the port city. A large promontory of land rose from the river, and at the foot of it and all down its rear flank were buildings. It was a sizable city and, Tabitha was a bit ashamed to admit to herself, was much more civilized and sophisticated than she had expected.

Their trunks were unloaded from the *Freedom* when they reached Quebec, and the passengers went their separate ways. Some remained in the city. Some continued by train or wagon. Some chose from the boats that traveled the Great Lakes, depending on where they wanted to go. Tabitha was appalled to see the *Lady of the Lakes*, which was to take her and the Dobbinses on to Chicago.

It was a tiny ship, with just two masts. On the deck to the fore was a tiny galley where passengers ate or talked or played cards during the day, and where the small crew strung their hammocks at night. To the aft were four tiny cabins, one for the captain and three for the passengers who could pay for the questionable luxury they provided. There was only one deck below, which, she was told, hauled freight on the way to Quebec and steerage passengers on the way to Chicago.

The lower deck reeked of vegetables, and Tabitha wondered if it had carried garbage on the most recent trip. While she felt sorry for those who had to live for the next week and a half in that dim and odorous place, she thanked God that she was not among them. She had one of the Lilliputian cabins, and the Dobbinses had another. The third she didn't yet know about.

As they stepped ashore to move from the *Freedom* to the *Lady of the Lakes,* she had to pause. This solid ground beneath her feet was North America. An entire new continent. The whole, wide Atlantic lay between her and England. The idea of it—the vast distance and the vastness of her decision—was overwhelming. For several minutes she stood, rooted, looking at the trees that grew from a new continent. A continent that would be her new home and her new life.

Upon boarding the small ship, which was warped and ugly and in bad repair, she was glad to learn that the occupant of the fourth cabin was none other than Monsieur Rousseau. His distaste in discovering the condition of their new conveyance was obvious, and she laughed. "Do you think it will make the journey?"

He smiled with her, but said, "That is not so funny, Madame Bradford. She looks like the smallest breeze could blow her apart."

Etienne's tremor of revulsion, and perhaps also of fear, was honest enough. He was questioning his sanity. Why had he gone to such trouble to discover what transportation was available from Chicago to New Orleans, and then hurried to obtain the last cabin on the *Lady?* For what? He had made no progress at all with Tabitha, but somehow he couldn't give up yet. He would travel with her as far as Chicago.

The *Lady of the Lakes* picked her way up the Saint Lawrence River, fighting the current. Because of the current and watching for rocks, the sailors were more alert, and the captain was always on deck. Their mood added to the excitement of the passengers. Most of them had stayed up on the deck to gaze at the land they had waited so long to see, but then many had returned below deck. Etienne was glad to see that Tabitha stayed where she was, watching the rocky, tree-lined banks of the Saint

Lawrence. In places the banks were steep and quite high. He read her excitement in her face: *This is Canada. How can the others be so nonchalant about it?*

After the city of Quebec, the river narrowed considerably. Small towns sporadically dotted the way. Each night they tied to a pier, and early the next morning they always continued on. Captain Jules kept to his schedule. No one did any sightseeing in the ports, for fear of missing the ship. None of the passengers complained. Ship life, even on a river, quickly grew old and tedious.

Just past the town of Trois-Rivières, the river widened into a lake, then narrowed once again. Near Montreal, the *Lady* came to the Lachine Canal, the first of the many canals necessary for boats to pass the rapids and make rises in elevation. Not far up the river was the Beauharnois Canal.

On the day after they passed Montreal, they reached the United States. New York was on the left bank of the river. Captain Jules explained that they would have to stop in Erie at the customs house, and Martha and Margaret giggled at the name.

"Ooh, scary!" said Margaret. But the captain explained that it wasn't "eerie," as in scary, but a Huron Indian word.

There were four more shorter canals before they reached Lake Ontario. It was so vast that it was difficult to believe that it was a lake and not a sea. But the water was fresh, and the air no longer smelled of salt. There were lots of birds, ducks and cormorants and loons, herons and terns. It took the rest of that day and most of the next to cross the lake. Then came the Welland Canal. It was really the most impressive one, because the difference in elevation between Lake Ontario and Lake Erie was considerable. It was this canal that bypassed Niagara Falls and made river travel between the Great Lakes and the Atlantic Ocean possible.

The following day they arrived in Erie, Pennsylvania, and all the passengers had to go through customs. While they waited, Captain Jules became quite talkative. He told them about the massive, beautiful, noisy Niagara Falls and encouraged his passengers to see them if they ever got the chance. He explained that it would take them at least a day to cross the rest of Lake Erie, probably more. Then another day through the two short rivers and one smaller lake that separated Lake Erie from Lake Huron.

From there it would be clear sailing all the way to Chicago, with stops for passengers in Cleveland, Detroit, Mackinaw, Milwaukee, and a few smaller towns. Most stops would be for only an hour or so. A few would be overnight.

The captain told them that the lakes were deceptively calm. Storms could come up quickly, and any number of ships had been lost on them. Nearly two hundred years earlier, the explorer La Salle had sent his ship the *Griffen* from Green Bay to Niagara with a hold of furs. She was never heard from again.

Tabitha's appreciation of the charming lighthouses grew enormously.

"But don't you worry 'bout the *Lady*," Captain Jules said. "There's nothin' can stop her. Not even the United States Navy."

Tabitha frowned a question, curious. Why would the Navy want to stop such a pathetic ship?

Captain Jules laughed. "She has a history, my *Lady*. She started out as a pilot boat on the coast trade, but some entrepreneur bought her and used her as a slaver. Common, actually. These smaller ships could sneak in and out of places that the bigger ships couldn't. And that fact is serving us well now, ain't it?

"Well, anyway, she was a slave ship down in the West Indies. Never did get caught. Those big, square-rigged men-of-war couldn't catch her. Actually, the Navy had to copy the design of the ol' pilot boats so they could catch some. Ha!" He slapped his leg.

Tabitha was horrified. This ship had been a slave ship! She could picture the hold of the boat, and imagined what conditions must have been like in those days. They were bad enough now! But to think of being down there in chains, packed in tightly, not fed properly or given enough water, not allowed frequent toilet breaks, not knowing how to communicate with your captors. Her stomach turned, and she could not wait to be away from the *Lady* and its past. She looked at Etienne, and the expression on his face said he felt the same.

When it was her turn, Tabitha passed easily through customs. Young, healthy, and speaking English, she was not a big risk as a potential burden for her new country, so they didn't delay her long. She stood there outside the customs house and realized that her feet were on American soil for the first time. Nothing was different, really. The trees and the grass were green, as they were in England. There was a smell of flowers and fresh-cut grass. Not so different. And inside, she still had the same English blood. But now she was an official immigrant. Her feet might never again *step off* American soil—except of course for the remainder of her shipboard journey. Which, now that she thought about it, was an American ship. *Freedom* had been, too, so she hadn't been on English "soil" for some time.

Monsieur Rousseau soon joined her on the pier where she waited, reluctant to board the ship before she had to. "Any problems?" she inquired, referring to how his questioning had gone.

"No." He flashed his disarming smile, and she still wasn't prepared for the flutter in her middle.

The journey continued. Excitement rose each day as they drew closer to the end. Towns and cities ran together until Tabitha could no longer keep track of them. She only counted days, by the captain's estimation, before they would arrive. Five days, four days. In places the shores were steep, rocky cliffs. In places there were sand dunes, some huge. The coasts of Michigan and Wisconsin were heavily wooded. Each town had its mill, which they could hear before they could see the town, and its yellow dunes of sawdust. If the boat neared shore in the morning or evening, clouds of mosquitoes would come out to greet them, dampening Tabitha's growing excitement just a bit.

One more day. Tabitha stood alone on the deck. She grew nervous, wondering what lay in store. Where would she end up with her shop? Would it succeed? What was Chicago like? In a year, what would she be doing?

The old ship creaked horribly and she shuddered, looking again at the old and battered *Lady*. A cold, wet grave awaited it one day, along with whoever happened to be aboard her at the time. After more than a week, Tabitha still hadn't quite gotten used to the old boat. Sometimes when the *Lady* trembled, so did she. This time, it wasn't only the feeling of dread that caused her to shiver. Fingers of mist swirled around her, and she pulled her shawl closer around her shoulders.

The Lady had a way of crying wolf about her immi-nent demise. Much as she creaked and moaned and shook, she hadn't yet come close to sinking, even in the storms that came up suddenly on the waters of the Great Lakes. It was less likely now, when the waters of Lake Michigan were comparatively placid. But it would hap-pen someday and, Tabitha thought as she glanced around her at the warped and rotting wood of the beams and decks, that day couldn't be too far off.

My, aren't you pessimistic today? she said to herself. It must be just a case of nerves about arriving in Chicago.

Fleetingly, she had second thoughts about her destination. Why Chicago? According to the crew of the *Lady,* it was the largest grain-shipping port in the world. Even before the grain spilled, before the day Lord Abercrombe had taken her to the docks, she had been against the idea of going to a large city. So now that was precisely where she was headed. Why? Because of some wheat? But wheat didn't grow in a city. It was only shipped from a city. Because she was afraid of Indian attacks? Captain Jules claimed that was a worry only further to the west. Because of the Dobbinses? If she was truly honest with herself, she didn't like Mrs. Dobbins overmuch.

The idea of continuing west teased her. Perhaps she would go all the way to California. Wouldn't David be delighted? She could. She had enough money for her transportation, but using it on such a journey would necessitate her finding work, or making a success of her shop sooner. How brave was she?

Part of her wanted to go on. It was, after all, just a matter of getting off the ship in Chicago and getting on a train across the state of Illinois. From there, she could travel down the Mississippi River, or stop anywhere, any place that she took a fancy to. Surely the smell of a different mode of transportation would be better! Sometimes she thought that the odors of mold, dirt, unwashed bodies, and vomit would cling to her nostrils until the day she died. That was why she was up on the deck at the moment, despite the fog and cold.

Another part of her wanted the security of being near the Dobbinses and of having, not spending, her money. Practicality affirmed her decision. It would have to be Chicago.

Idly she stared into the mist in the direction of the shore, hoping to catch a glimpse of land or a lighthouse. At times there had been something to see, but more often not. Still, the lake was calmer than the sea had been, and the deck was more pleasant than her cabin.

There were less than a hundred miles now to Chicago. The ship portion of her voyage would soon be over. Only one more small port to stop at and then Chicago, and she could bid a glad *adieu* to the *Lady*.

"*Bonjour,* Madame Bradford," came a deep voice from just behind her.

She turned towards Etienne with a silent smile. While he still came up behind her and spoke to her, it was no longer startling. She expected it.

"*Bonjour, monsieur.*"

"Ah, call me Etienne, *s'il vous plait.* For days we have been together on this . . . this . . . *bateau,* and before it, the other. I do not think we need to be so formal any longer. *Oui?*"

Tabitha glanced quickly away from the sparkling white half-smile to the equally sparkling black eyes and then, just as quickly, to the water. Gazing directly at this man was not comfortable. He was too attractive and too mysterious, and it was too difficult to keep him at a proper distance. "Very well, Monsieur—Etienne." She smiled in spite of herself at how readily she had agreed to doing away with formalities. Not that it mattered. After tonight, she would never see the man again.

"The fog appears to be lifting," he remarked. He had joined her in gazing towards the shore, over the railing. He actually saw what he was looking at, though, whereas she was merely using the view as an excuse to keep from staring at her companion.

Why, she wondered, had a man of such obvious means chosen to travel on such a dilapidated ship? It was a question that had plagued her since Quebec.

"Tabitha?"

She glanced up and forced her eyes to focus on Etienne.

He seemed chagrined, like a small boy being reprimanded. "I may call you Tabitha? It is an enchanting name."

"Certainly." There. The liberty was given before she had even mulled it over. But how could she refuse such a simple request when he already looked so miserable at using her Christian name before she had given permission? She was treated to a rare but dazzling full smile, and had to smile herself at how quickly the suave gentleman had replaced the shy child when his wish was granted.

"I was just pointing out that the fog is breaking up, but I do not believe that you were listening."

Tabitha blushed and hoped he wouldn't suspect that she had been thinking about him. She let her eyes travel the direction his extended arm indicated. Low cliffs could be seen here and there, appearing and disappearing, like ghosts of promise. Patches of blue showed in the sky. Her destination was forming from the mists of uncertainty, solid and real. Or was it? She had one night to decide whether or not to stop in Chicago. Once there she would begin searching for a place to set up her sewing shop, and there would be no changing her mind.

"I believe the weather has delayed our arrival," he said. "I had hoped to be in Chicago by now."

"Yes, it was a disappointment," she agreed. "I've had my fill of boats and water, and I can't wait to be off this ship!"

"We could go ashore," he suggested. "Perhaps this small town we are coming to has a restaurant? I believe the captain has decided to remain at this port overnight, so there will be plenty of time. I would be delighted to escort you for a few hours."

"Why should the ship stay here, when we're so close to Chicago?"

"The captain has done this many times before. He says it is better to arrive early in the day, so that passengers aren't in a quandary about finding a place to stay before night."

Solid ground under her feet. Fresh air. Good food. Maybe candles at the table. Exciting company. It was tempting. But it was unwise. While she felt she knew him and could trust him, their association was unusual, and they had no chaperone. "I'm sorry, Monsieur Rousseau," she began, and he frowned in a teasing way.

"I mean Etienne," she corrected, "but it wouldn't be appropriate."

"I'm wounded!" he cried, in mock dismay. "The lady does not trust me!" The half-smile returned, this time taunting her. "If we remain aboard this grand ship," he said, with a derisive sweep of his arm, "will you dine with me?"

Tabitha laughed and gave in. What harm could one supper do? Tomorrow they would go their separate ways. *"Oui,"* she said. But that dinner would not turn out the way either of them expected.

It was almost time to meet Etienne for supper, and Tabitha was in the cabin. Whatever could she do with her hair? She brushed the long golden-brown mass, wishing for a curling iron. She may as well wish for the moon. Even if she had it, there was no stove to heat it on, and she didn't have time to create the mass of curls on the top of her head that she used to wear for special occasions back in England. That, and she didn't want to make it seem as if she'd taken extra pains with her appearance.

Deftly she made one long braid and pinned it to the back of her head in its usual coil. It was not as easy to do as it was on dry land, though she'd done it thousands of times. She had only one small, dingy mirror, and the movements of the ship added to the difficulty. Finally she got the job done and rose to go.

The ship rolled unexpectedly, and she fell, landing squarely on her bottom, catching her foot between her trunk and her bunk. Mrs. Dobbins came rushing to her, followed by the two girls.

"Mrs. Bradford! Are you 'urt?"

"No. I'm fine," Tabitha said. Actually, her backside was sore, and her pride was also injured, but she said nothing. She stood, and found to her dismay that the heel of her shoe had broken off in her fall.

"Oh, dear! Your shoe!"

"Yes, and my only pair." She sighed. "Well, nothing to do but go into this town and see if I can get it repaired."

Mrs. Dobbins looked doubtful.

"I can't go hobbling about until we get to Chicago, can I? And once in Chicago, I will be looking for a place to live and a place to set up my shop. I would rather not have to deal with the business of having a shoe repaired first." Indeed, the very thought of wandering the city on her own was daunting, and she surely didn't want to add to the stress of it.

Though Mrs. Dobbins didn't reply, Tabitha could tell that the older woman didn't approve. Well, that was too bad. Tabitha was, after all, a grown woman. Turning to fetch her purse and shawl from the cabin, Tabitha remembered Etienne. "Oh, Mrs. Dobbins, could you do me a favor, please?"

The woman nodded slightly.

"I was to eat supper with Monsieur Rousseau. Would you please tell him what happened and give him my apologies?"

Mrs. Dobbins could no longer hold her tongue. "You take my warning, Mrs. Bradford, about that Monsieur Rousseau! Don't associate with 'im. 'E's an oily one!"

An oily one? What an odd description.

Tabitha hobbled off the ship onto the pier, assured that Mrs. Dobbins would pass on her message. She was slightly apprehensive about leaving the ship. She hadn't been ashore much, and never by herself. It was, she told herself, a foreign country, even if they did speak the same language. Sort of. But now a need for her to go ashore had arisen, so she must pull together her paltry amount of courage and get the task done.

Waukegan—what an odd name—was reportedly a very small town. She would just pop into a shop and then hurry right back. And she had better be quick about it or all the shops would be closed, and then she would have no choice but to hobble until sometime tomorrow in Chicago.

The town was indeed small, and quiet looking. There was a collection of buildings along the lake shore, and behind them a bluff, with the sun setting beyond. More buildings stood up on the bluff. The closer buildings appeared to be warehouses and a lighthouse, so she walked up the bluff. There she found a general merchandise store, a bank, and a jeweler. The buildings were made of wood, not brick or stone, and the streets were not cobbled. Everything seemed more poorly made, compared to what she was used to, and carried an aura of hurry. Built fast, not built to last. And still.

Truth be told, Tabitha was disappointed. This little town seemed to be the end of the earth. But it was peaceful.

All of the shops were closed, so she couldn't go in and ask where to go about her shoe, and she had a sinking feeling that she was missing her supper with Etienne for no reason. For if these shops were closed, what made her think a shoe shop would be open? Still, she was already ashore. She may as well look. For a moment, she stood there, not knowing which direction to go. She wanted to be safely aboard her ship by dark.

The sunset was truly glorious. Clouds aflame with yel low and orange, trimmed with pink sky that faded first into an incredible mauve and finally to a deepening blue. She could almost expect Jesus to return from clouds such as those.

This was America. This was really it. This very place could be her new homeland if she chose. Not that she would stay here, of course, but she could. It was America. She toyed with the idea of staying. Waukegan was not a city. Presumably, they grew wheat in the area, considering how near they were to Chicago, that great hub of wheat shipping, and because of the flatness of the land and the farms she could see in the distance. Yes, she could choose to stay here, where it at least smelled good. But there was nothing here! Such a small town. And so new. There was no sense of anything around her being any older than she herself was. There was only a feeling of new, and raw. It was something she had not anticipated about America.

Tabitha closed her eyes and took a deep breath. There was a faint odor of fresh-cut grass in the air. America. She was here. A smile crossed her lips, and she let her thoughts wander.

What could there be about Etienne to make Mrs. Dobbins rail so against him? Her daughters certainly didn't share her opinion. Tabitha's smile grew. It was quite obvious by their expressions of girlish rapture that they thought Monsieur Rousseau was wonderful.

A hand gently touched her shoulder. Her breath caught in her throat as all her fears of dangers in strange places rushed back, and she spun to see who had dared touch her. It was Etienne, and the sudden relief made her first tremble and then give a nervous giggle. "Etienne! What are you doing here?"

"It would seem that I am interrupting a daydream."

"Not quite. I was just watching the beautiful sunset. Really, though, what are you doing here?"

"Madame Dobbins told me of your accident. I came to find you and see that no harm befalls you. What do you think you are doing, roaming these streets all alone?"

Tabitha began to defend her actions, saw that he was teasing, but explained anyway. "Look around you, monsieur. This is a sleepy little town. What could happen to me here?"

The idea that someone, and someone so handsome and masculine as Etienne Rousseau, was concerned about her made her feel good and added to her sense of contentment. A wide smile showed her dimple.

Dark eyes rested a moment on her lips. Then Etienne said, "As long as we are already ashore, we may as well have that supper in a more enjoyable location than the ship."

Tabitha suddenly found it difficult to swallow. "Yes," she forced out through a constricted throat. "That would be very nice." She took a step to accompany him and stumbled, reminding her of her mission.

Etienne was quick to place one hand on her elbow and the other at her waist to help restore her balance before she tumbled headlong into the muddy street. Her footing may have been restored, but her dignity was in tatters.

"My shoe," she mumbled. "I need to have it repaired."

"*Ma jolie,* it is evening. You will have to wait until morning. All the shops are closed."

My pretty! The quick mental translation made her cheeks a bit pinker, but inside, she felt better. Much better.

"What shall I do?" she asked. "I cannot continue to

hobble about like a peg-legged sailor."

He chuckled, rich and throaty. "Your choices are limited, and both lack dignity. You can hobble, or you can go barefoot."

Barefoot! Like a dirty little street urchin? Never! She shook her head, and with as much "dignity" as she could muster began to walk down the street, tiptoeing on the unheeled shoe.

With grace and gallantry Etienne offered her his arm, just as an elderly man passed by, tipping his hat to the man. To all the world, the gesture appeared completely normal, and Tabitha had to admit that it made walking easier. Thoughts of her companion being "an oily one" were far from her mind.

Soon they were settled at a table in the restaurant of Waukegan's one hotel. The food was good. Nothing fancy, but well prepared and made from fresh ingredients. She was so sick of stale, moldy food! Etienne had a few glasses of wine, which she declined. Fresh water was better than the finest wine could possibly be.

Everything was wonderful, not just the fresh food and water. They were eating from a table that didn't rock with the waves. Etienne was with her because he wanted to be. And the only odors were those of the food and his cologne.

This was, she thought, the type of evening she had envisioned years ago, before she learned that there would be no "season." No parties, no balls, no dinners, no beautiful new gowns, no handsome young beaus. Her social debut had been canceled because of her father's precarious financial situation. But for a time, while she was a girl, she had had governesses and finishing schools. She had naturally assumed that she would be shown to society in a flurry of silk and satin, shown off so that she could find the best possible husband, and she had spent many hours daydreaming about what it would be like to go to parties and have beaus. In all her dreams, it had been like this. This night with good food and the pleasant company of a man who was attentive, slightly exotic, and very handsome.

Tabitha woke thinking of the flashing smile of Etienne Rousseau, and stretched luxuriously in the clean, crisp sheets. He was certainly an entirely different sort of man than Samuel Bradford had been!

She turned over, enjoying the feel of smooth material against the skin of her legs. Even better than the feeling of a full stomach was the feel of cleanliness. Too bad she didn't have a change of clothes with her.

Procrastinating against leaving the warmth and comfort of the bed, she thought back over the previous evening. Finding a place to eat hadn't presented a problem, because dining out was becoming more and more fashionable on both sides of the ocean. The evening had been filled with easy conversation, in which Etienne had convinced her, insisted actually, that she should spend the night in the hotel. She would be at hand, then, when the shops opened, and she could have her shoe repaired and be back aboard the *Lady* before she sailed on to Chicago.

Yes, Tabitha admitted, it had been an extravagance, paying for a hotel room, but it had been worth it. She pulled the soft covers up to her chin and shut her eyes, to better smell the clean.

Etienne had accompanied her for a walk before taking her back to the Exchange Hotel. It was a dark night, cloudy, with a feel of rain in the air. Light spilled from street lamps in round pools. Just as they stepped into one of the circles of light, a dark creature swooped out of the black night, flying very close to Tabitha's hair. She almost screamed before realizing it was just a bat. Her heart pounded.

Etienne pulled her close. "It was only a bat. There's nothing to fear." His arms were around her. Startled as much by his protectiveness as she had been by the bat, she tipped her head back to look up at him. Those coal-black eyes, reflecting the glitter of the lamp, were staring at her lips. For a frozen moment she stood there in the wonderful, warm circle of his arms, staring at his face, watching his lips draw nearer. If she didn't move now, she was doomed. She knew that as certainly as she knew her name. Desperately, perhaps overreacting, she pulled away and began walking once more towards the hotel, which was now only a few buildings ahead. She forced a small laugh. "Silly me. Only a bat."

His laugh behind her was lightly teasing, but he fell in step with her. "Someday, lovely Tabitha. Someday you will not scurry away." It was both promise and threat, and she knew he was right. And she was very glad that tomorrow they would reach Chicago and part company.

Together, they made her room arrangement. The large, matronly woman behind the desk had glowered at them until Etienne had bid Tabitha a silky *"Bonsoir"* and left. He had insisted on that, too, saying he was returning to the ship because he didn't want Mrs. Dobbins or anyone else to think poorly of her. After that, the hotel keeper had hurried to apologize for jumping to conclusions and had gone out of her way to see personally that Tabitha was well taken care of.

Early in the evening, while they had been walking, Tabitha had smelled rain in the air. Later, lying in the comfortable bed waiting for sleep, she had heard the wind pick up and the first raindrop splatter against the glass window. It was the first rain in her new life, and she thought she had made the right choice in coming to America. The rain was still falling steadily when she fell into a blissful sleep, dreaming of Etienne.

In the morning, it was the sunlight through the lace curtains that woke her, and the smell of bacon and coffee. She preferred tea, but fresh, hot coffee would be wonderful compared to the thick, film-coated stuff she had had on the *Lady*. The thought of putting her unwashed dress back on made her wrinkle her nose, but she had no choice. If she didn't get up and get dressed, she would miss her ship, and that would be a disaster. Not that this was such a bad place, but she wanted to continue on to Chicago. It was a city, true, but she would know someone.

The morning smells coming from the restaurant immediately persuaded her to dip into her purse for another decent meal before tending to the shoe and heading back to the pier. There seemed to be a bit of excitement among those having breakfast at the hotel. The many strangers stopped talking when she entered the room, and watched her. Carefully balancing on her heel-less shoe so she wouldn't draw even more attention, she selected a small table and sat down to wait for a waitress. Whatever the big local news was, it would be something she knew nothing about, anyway.

Lucas Hayes immediately spotted the woman as she entered the restaurant, certain he had never seen her before. This was a face—and a figure—he surely would have remembered. He actually felt himself blush, and concentrated on Amanda, who was also watching the stranger. Thankfully. At least she wouldn't notice his reaction.

Why would a beautiful woman, and a stranger in town to boot, be here alone? Surely she was married. Even if not, which he thought was an astronomically slim chance, she would have a traveling companion of some sort. Time slipped by, however, and no one joined her. The fact that she dined alone gave her an air of independence. That, he didn't want to think about; she was disturbing enough.

As she ate, Tabitha's attention was drawn to the man and little girl at a table not far from her. The child was beautiful, but dressed in boy's work clothes, and her long, taffy-colored curls would benefit from a ribbon. At least she was clean and combed. Her large blue eyes gazed at the man in adoration, and she overheard, "Thanks, Papa, for the special breakfast."

The man was clearly her father. Tabitha could see his profile, which was identical to the girl's. He had a blade-straight nose, strong jaw, and wavy, coffee brown hair. Tiny lines fanned out from eyes as gray and cool as a rainy day.

The waitress came with her breakfast of scrambled eggs and toast, and Tabitha asked her for directions to a shoe shop. "One that could hurry, perhaps?" she continued. "I need to get back to the ship before she sails."

"Ship, ma'am?" The woman stepped back, wide-eyed.

"Yes, the *Lady of the Lakes*. She's down at the pier and leaves for Chicago this morning."

"The old two-masted ship that was there?" The waitress's voice had an uncertain quaver.

An apprehensive flutter turned in Tabitha's stomach. Could the *Lady* have left already? "Was?" she made herself ask.

"Yes, ma'am. It broke up last night. Wind blew it against the pier."

Broke up? She knew it wasn't in good shape, but . . . sinking? Thank God she had not been on it! But Etienne had. And Mrs. Dobbins. Not to mention all she owned in the world.

Oh, God, what will I do now?

Seven

*T*abitha shut her eyes and swallowed hard. "Did anyone . . . ?" She could not finish the question, but
the waitress understood.

"No, ma'am. Everyone got ashore all right, but there's
a lot of wood and debris floating around this morning.
Saw it myself on my way here. There's some men out trying to salvage what they can."

"I see." Yes, she saw perfectly. Etienne and the
Dobbinses were well, if the information was correct. But
there was a good chance that all her worldly belongings
were no more.

"Can I get you anything else, ma'am?"

She shook her head. "No. Thank you."

The waitress left, but Tabitha had lost her appetite
and sat staring at the food, telling herself she should eat
it. Her first instinct was to jump up and run down to the
lake, to see, to help. Help what? The ship was lost, the
passengers were saved. Still, she should be there, making

sure for herself that Etienne and the Dobbinses were all right. She had been absentmindedly pushing her food around on her plate, and now the eggs were a cold, greasy lump and the toast was hard. The coffee, when she took a sip of it, was cold. She grimaced and replaced the cup on its saucer.

Finally, she gave up toying with her breakfast. She didn't know what to do, but sitting here until she atrophied wasn't it. She needed to walk down to the lake to see what had become of her friends and to see if any of her things had been salvaged.

With all that on her mind, she totally forgot about her heel. Pushing back her chair and rising, she completely lost her balance, clutching the edge of the table to keep from falling down.

Stupid, trouble-making shoe! What else could go wrong? Then she realized that if it hadn't been for her shoe breaking, she would have been aboard the ship and gotten a cold dousing, if not outright drowning. The Lord certainly did work in mysterious ways.

"Papa!" The little girl's voice carried to Tabitha. "Can't we help that lady from the broken boat? Look! Her shoe's broke, too!"

Tabitha's eyes flew to the man, mortified to have had her stumble observed and her circumstances discussed so frankly. He looked as uncomfortable as she was at his daughter's lack of tact.

"Of course, Angel. That is, if the lady needs any help." His words answered his daughter, but he was speaking for

Tabitha's ears. His soft, gray eyes met hers, and he seemed genuinely concerned.

"No," she replied. "I don't believe so. I'll just be going to get my shoe repaired and then go to check on my friends and see if my trunk survived. Thank you." She nodded good day and walked out to the street, with the girl's question to her father about why Tabitha talked funny fading in her ears.

Later, shoe repaired, Tabitha made her way back down the bluff. There were some men climbing onto the pier from a small boat, and near the shore there were several pieces of floating wood. Not much was left of the *Lady of the Lakes.* The top of a mast with a bit of sail clinging to it stuck out from the water's surface. A large pile of things was on the beach, and people stood about looking dazed.

She located Mrs. Dobbins and her daughters, who had made it ashore before the remains of the *Lady* went under, and were none the worse for wear. They sat on one of their three trunks; the other two were nowhere in sight. Captain Jules stood staring blankly and shaking his head. He was close to retirement, and he'd never had a ship go down before. "At a pier!" he muttered, over and over.

Etienne was nowhere around. Shouldn't he be there, helping the other men?

Immediately, Tabitha told herself she was being judgmental. She had no idea where he was or what he was doing. If he was not helping the townsmen with the wreckage, he must have sufficient reason. After all, he had more to lose than they.

"Mrs. Dobbins!" She hailed the older woman. "How are you? How did it happen?"

"'Ow it 'appened, I don't know. We sure 'ad to scramble ta get out o' there, an' we only had time ta rescue the one trunk. We lost 'alf our clothing an' all our 'ouse 'old goods."

"I'm sorry to hear that. What will you do now?"

"Our trip was ta Chicago. My brother is there. I suppose we'll finish by train. After buying tickets and losing our things, we'll get there poor as church mice, but we'll get there. Thank the Good Lord we're alive an' 'ave somew'ere ta go. 'Ow 'bout you? I see ya got your 'eel repaired."

Tabitha thought she detected a note of disapproval in Mrs. Dobbins' voice, but she pushed away the idea. Probably it was just the strain of their situation.

"Yes," she replied. "I couldn't get it done until this morning. That's why I stayed on shore last night."

Skepticism crossed Mrs. Dobbins' face. "Lucky for you," was what she said. "It was a miserable night."

"Actually, it was Monsieur Rousseau's idea. Have you seen him?"

Mrs. Dobbins was utterly flabbergasted. She stood, jaws moving, but no sound came, which made Tabitha wonder what was going on. Nothing that had been said should warrant a reaction like this!

"No, I 'aven't!" Mrs. Dobbins' reply, when it came, was

indignant. "An' you would be better off if you 'adn't, either!"

So that was it. Mrs. Dobbins was overreacting to Tabitha going ashore after she had cautioned against it. Especially when she had ended up dining with Etienne, and Mrs. Dobbins had made it clear how she felt about him. But now that Tabitha understood the cause of her irritation, she found it easier to talk to her.

"After today," Tabitha said, "I'll most likely never lay eyes on the man again. However, he has treated me nicely, and I would like to know how he fared last night. Did he lose everything he had?"

"That, I certainly wouldn't be knowin' about!"

"Mrs. Bradford." Margaret, who had been sitting sullenly on the trunk, now broke the brief but awkward silence. "Did you lose your things, too?"

"I don't know yet. I only had the one trunk, and I don't yet know if it's lost. I haven't seen it." Her eyes scanned the beach, and she spotted the man who had seemed to be in charge of the small boat. She made her way over to him and described the trunk, asking if he had seen it.

"Yep. I seed it."

Relief washed over her.

The teeth he had remaining were stained brown, and twin tobacco stains trailed down his gray beard from the corners of his mouth. He lifted a gnarled finger towards the lake. "I seed it way out thar somewheres, 'n takin' on water."

Her relief turned into a gasp of dismay. Gone! She had half expected it, yet hearing it as reality was a blow. Everything she had in the world, except for the clothes she wore and a small amount of money in her purse, was gone! Her clothing, her dishes, her toilet things, her mementos. She choked back a sob. Her wedding ring, her mother's locket, her favorite books, her family Bible, her grandmother's vase. All gone! All her personal things, as well as almost all of her money.

She was in a foreign country with no family and no friends to turn to. Mrs. Dobbins was the only person she knew well enough to ask for assistance, but she was also almost penniless. Tabitha couldn't make herself a burden to her.

Oh, Lord, no, she prayed silently. *I know that you provide all things, and that You're faithful to feed even the sparrows. But God, I'm frightened! I've never been this desperate before. What should I do? How will I get on? Please, Lord, lead me. Provide for my needs. Amen.*

"There she is, Papa!"

The child's voice carried over the beach, and Tabitha turned to see the little girl from the hotel bounding towards her, her taffy curls bouncing, and her father in tow. "We came to see if you're awright!"

"I'm sorry if my daughter has embarrassed you. Again." The gray eyes held understanding of her position. "But I let her talk me into coming here. We, er, she, was concerned." The man glanced away. "Did you find your things? Will you be okay?"

Tabitha got over her discomfiture quickly, touched by his honesty and their interest in her welfare. "Thank you very much, Mr. . . . ?"

"Hayes. Lucas Hayes. This is my daughter, Amanda." He extended a hand, manlike, and Tabitha couldn't help but compare the coarse gesture to Etienne's refined continental style. Still, she shook the man's hand, with a genuine smile. "And I am Tabitha Bradford. Thank you for your concern, Mr. Hayes. My trunk has unfortunately vanished in the wreckage."

Mrs. Dobbins came puffing up beside her. "Mrs. Bradford, did ya locate yer trunk?"

Tabitha shook her head.

"We found one more, of clothes that smell of fish, but we're counting ourselves lucky. We can't afford to put up here, so we're going to 'urry to catch the Chicago train. Are you going?"

"I haven't decided yet," Tabitha hedged. She hadn't had time to think her options through.

Mrs. Dobbins glanced from her to Lucas Hayes with distaste. "I suppose this is good-bye, then. Watch out for yerself. But then, ya 'ave yer Frog. We'll be a prayin' for ya." She turned then, not one to prolong things. She and her daughters headed towards the train station, dragging their trunks.

So, she had her "Frog," hm? What was that supposed to mean? She neither "had" him, nor was setting out to get him.

From the corner of her eye, she saw Amanda tugging

on her father's sleeve. In an overloud whisper the child asked, "Can I see her frog, Papa?"

Mr. Hayes was clearly at a loss for words and turned the question over to Tabitha. "I'm afraid I don't understand, myself. It's a bit cold for frogs."

Tabitha had to laugh at their confusion. "We English," she explained, "have been at war with France so frequently that there is little love lost between us. 'Frog' is a derogatory term for a Frenchman. Mrs. Dobbins, you see, is prejudiced."

"Ah!" A wide smile curved his mouth, which, as Tabitha noticed, was far from unattractive.

"Tabitha! There you are!" Etienne called. He was just down the beach, and strolling rapidly towards them. "Where have you been, *ma jolie?*" he asked as he came up. "I have looked for you both at the hotel and at the shoe shop, but I could not find you."

So that's where he had been! Looking for her. Concerned about her. The thought warmed her. She made no attempt to stop her smile of pleasure at his arrival, but she was unaware that her eyes were shining with that same pleasure.

She glanced to Mr. Hayes to make introductions, but his coldness made her pause. The warmth had gone from his gray eyes, and his jaw was clenched steel.

Etienne gave her no time to ponder. He lifted her hand to his lips and kissed it, sending a quivering tingle up her arm.

Lucas Hayes ran his eyes over the newcomer and

formed a fist in his pocket. The man was unarguably handsome. And from the tailor-made tweeds to the beaver top hat held casually against his thigh, he reeked money. And that other woman had called her "Mrs. Bradford." Of all the world's fools, he had to take the cake! Of course a beautiful woman would not be unmarried and traveling alone. What could he have been thinking? He had told himself that before, yet he had allowed himself to be fished in, hope springing eternally. Not only did she have a husband, but he was as rich as Midas. And he'd thought she needed his help? What a dolt! Did he think he was Lancelot, rescuing the damsel in distress? A creamy complexion and wide, thick-lashed eyes had made him brainless!

He reached for his daughter's hand, and noticed that she, too, was fascinated with the dark stranger, and had no intention of going anywhere. "We must be going, Amanda," he said, forcefully. Her defection was almost more than he could stand. "The pig is hungry."

Amanda knew full well that the pig had been fed early that morning before they'd come to town. She also knew better than to question her father when he was angry. Meekly she took his hand. "G'bye, Mrs. Bradford."

"Mr. Bradford. Mrs. Bradford." Lucas tipped his work-worn hat and turned, almost dragging Amanda towards the bluff and town.

Lucas was gone too quickly to hear Etienne's incredulous "Mr. Bradford?" Then the Frenchman laughed outright, the sound booming across the beach. His laugh was rich and delightful and did horrible, wonderful things to Tabitha.

"Oh, dear," said Tabitha. "Wherever have my manners gone? I should have introduced you! He thought. . . ."

"Yes." Etienne smiled with wicked enjoyment. "He thought we were married. What an enchanting idea!"

Tabitha's cheeks were now pink and fast on the way to crimson.

"I confess," he went on, "that I am not ready for marriage. It does, however, have certain advantages." He lifted her chin, taking in the smooth skin and dark fringed eyes. "Especially when the wife is so pretty.

"But now, *ma jolie* . . ." Mercifully, he dropped his hand from her and changed the subject. "What will you do? You are going on the train to Chicago, no?"

"No." The word just slipped out, surprising her as much as it did him. She hadn't actually decided not to. She had no idea that the train for Chicago had already left, and was equally oblivious to the near-empty beach, and the fact that it had been that way for several minutes.

"You are staying here?" He was incredulous. "In this . . . village?"

"Yes, here in Waukegan."

"*Mon Dieu!* Why?"

"I don't like cities," she explained to herself as well as him, trying to reason out her sudden impulse to do something totally illogical. That much, anyway, was the truth. She hated the soot and the noise and the masses of people crammed together. A picture formed in her mind of starving, cold people living under a bridge, and she knew her decision wouldn't change.

"You were going to Chicago!" he argued in his accent. "That is a city!"

True. But if her choices were limited to Waukegan or Chicago, suddenly Waukegan seemed the better choice. If she used what money she had to get to Chicago, she would arrive literally penniless rather than just impoverished.

Tabitha swallowed her pride. "I lost all that I had on that ship," she explained. "I cannot afford to go to Chicago."

Etienne was immediately contrite. There was something about the sight of her eyes, misty and trying to be brave, that tugged at an unknown part of him. Something that drew him to her and at the same time made him want to run as far and as fast as he could. He hesitated, then suggested, "You could go with me."

Her mind swirled with relief, with uncertainty, and with questions. The questions formed more clearly, but they were not the type of questions she could ask. She could not, as a lady, even utter the words. And if she did so, she could very well insult him by her lack of trust. But what did he mean, go with him? After what seemed an eon, she stammered, "What . . . do you mean . . . ?" but she could not bring herself to finish.

Her vulnerability made him feel strong and protective, but also gentle. It was all new to him, and a little frightening. For a time he stared at her, his gaze traveling repeatedly from the question in her eyes to the slight quiver of her parted lips. *"Oui,"* he admitted. "But never against your will. You will be perfectly safe with me. I will take you to New Orleans with me, or only so far as Chicago, if that is what you choose." He gave New Orleans its French pronunciation.

Tabitha's eyes rounded.

She didn't speak, so he continued, tracing her jaw with a gentle finger. "I believe you would eventually come to me. I see the fire in your eyes when we speak. If I am wrong"—one shoulder gave an elegant shrug—"I would take you to Chicago anyway, out of . . . how do you say? 'The milk of human kindness?' "

His touch was creating havoc with her pulse. If he had had the decency to make it an honest proposal, she would have done it.

"No," she nearly choked. He was very attractive, and the thought was exciting. She was flattered that he was interested in her, a poor nobody, but at the same time she was highly insulted at what he thought of her morals. And what he was suggesting was indeed immoral!

"Thank you, monsieur, but no." She took a step back, away from him. "I cannot accept your charity, and I would not for a minute consider, shall we say, 'earning my keep'?"

"Then I am truly sorry, madame." He put more distance between them. No woman had ever before refused him, and a large part of him was indignant. A smaller but more insistent voice demanded that he not leave forever, though. He needed to see her again, both to prove the attraction was mutual, and to discover what made her different. "I really must be on my way to New Orleans," he explained, retreating. "But I will return someday to see how you have fared. Until then, *bonjour.*" He slapped his hat on his head and walked away, out of her life.

A strange emptiness filled Tabitha. Etienne might be dangerous, exciting, or merely a balm to her ego, but she hadn't realized until then how often or how fondly she had come to think of him. She would miss his flashing black eyes and effusive compliments, which never failed to make her feel better.

Slowly she looked about and took stock of her situation. The beach was as desolate as she felt inside. Everyone had gone. She'd lost her things, her money, the Dobbinses, and the dream that had just been beginning to form about Etienne, all within a few hours.

Clouds covered the sunshine, and she shivered. Usually she found cloudy days restful, but now it was just cold and gray, like the eyes of the stranger, Lucas Hayes.

Even he had offered to help her. Not once, but twice, and her pride and her dreams had gotten in her way. He was not likely to ask again. What a fool she was!

She stood alone on the beach, staring at the immense lake. Fog was forming on its surface once again, and a cool September wind blew through her. She felt chilled inside as well as out, and very, very alone. She wished she'd been able to go with Mrs. Dobbins, she wished she could have accepted Mr. Hayes' assistance. She even almost wished she had accepted Etienne's invitation. Realistically, she knew she would have made the same choices if given the same chances again, but she wished she had someplace to go. She wished she had a friend.

Slowly she turned and trudged up the muddy road to State Street.

Where should she go? What should she do? Afraid of doing nothing, she kept walking. Going north on State Street for a few blocks, she turned aimlessly west on Grand Avenue, away from the lake. Coming to a church, she went in. It was dark, but quiet and peaceful. There wasn't a soul around.

Tabitha sat in a pew towards the back. She tried to pray, but couldn't find words. The questions chased each other around inside her head. *What can I do? How do I start? Where will I live? Should I have gone to Chicago with the Dobbinses? No. Too late for that now, anyway.*

A slender, balding priest with a gentle smile stood in the aisle near her pew. "Is there anything I can do to help you?"

She had been leaning against the arm of the pew like a lazy schoolboy, and suddenly feeling as if she was herself in school, she straightened her posture.

"I don't know," she answered. Then, after a pause, added, "I don't think so."

"Have you had dinner? I was on my way to mine when I saw you here."

Tabitha hesitated. She was hungry. Breakfast had been interrupted by the news about the ship, but she didn't want to impose.

"Come along," he said. "While we eat, you can tell me about whatever it is that is bothering you. I'll help if I can, and if not, well, sometimes it helps just to talk." He walked as he spoke, expecting her to accompany him, which she did, because she didn't have a reason not to, and because she didn't know what else to do.

"Mrs. Schmidt!" he called as they entered the parsonage. "I have a guest. Could you please set another place?"

An elderly woman appeared in a doorway to what must be the kitchen. "Certainly, Father," she said cheerfully, then disappeared again.

The priest, who had introduced himself as Father Langley, waited until she had almost finished her meal before trying to get her to talk. "You were on the ship that broke up in the harbor?"

"Yes," she admitted in surprise. "How did you know?"

"I haven't seen you around town before. Then, the day a ship sinks, you turn up, looking totally forlorn."

"I see." She supposed it was obvious, now that she thought about it.

"Did you lose someone?" he asked gently.

"No. There were no . . . that is, no one aboard died. I only lost my things. Everything I own."

"How is it that you are alone? Pardon me if I seem rude, or overly personal."

"No offense taken. I am a widow."

"I'm sorry. No other family to turn to? Perhaps friends?"

"No," she replied quietly, feeling how truly alone in the world she was.

"Are you trained for anything? Teacher? Nurse?"

"No. But I do sew quite well. I was on my way to Chicago to start a sewing shop."

"You know someone in Chicago?"

"No. Only some friends of brief acquaintance. And they are not in a financial position to be burdened with an extra, friend or not."

Silence ensued while he thought. "Our Lord is sovereign," he reasoned, "so He must have a purpose in placing you here in so dramatic a manner." He glanced up from his thoughts to inquire, "You do believe in the Lord and His ways, don't you?"

"Oh, yes! But I must confess to a bit of doubt right now." Her cheeks warmed as she realized her choice of words. Telling a priest she "must confess"! And she wasn't even Catholic!

He looked amused, however, and it broke the momentary tension.

"Finish up, and then I will walk back downtown with you to ask about any available seamstress jobs."

Tabitha felt much better and ate her dessert with relish. She didn't know if there was a job waiting for her, but having someone who knew whom to ask was a definite improvement over floundering about alone.

"May I help you with the dishes, Mrs. Schmidt?" she asked when the old woman began clearing the table.

"No, thank you, dear. I dare say you have more important things to do."

Eight

*A*n hour later, Tabitha and Father Langley had visited both the town's tailors. Neither needed any help. They had also inquired of Captain Cory at the Exchange Hotel for any possible jobs as a maid, waitress, or dishwasher, to no avail. That seemed the bottom of the barrel to Tabitha, to be rejected for even the most servile jobs!

"Don't despair," said the priest. "The town is growing. We even got a new physician this year, a Dr. Price from Buffalo. Surely there is a job for you somewhere." He looked thoughtful. "Would you be interested in working for one of our merchants? Perhaps Mr. Garfield or Mr. Lyon could use assistance with customers."

"Anything," she agreed.

Tabitha threw out a silent prayer of thanksgiving when she was hired at a general merchandise store, to work from 7 A.M. to 7 P.M. doing everything from stocking shelves to cleaning up and counting money. She would work Monday through Saturday. The pay wasn't much, but at least she had an income.

Father Langley, satisfied that she could now manage on her own, took his leave to get back to his church.

"Thank you so much!" she said to the priest. "I'm not Catholic, so I don't suppose I'll see you at church, but I hope God blesses you for your kindness."

"Just part of the job," Father Langley said lightly. "I'm glad God could use me to help."

Tabitha was standing on the corner of Genesee and Washington, pondering what to do next, when a huge horse came toward her. Horses and carts and wagons of all varieties were passing all around her, and she would not have noticed this one in particular, except that she heard a child's voice piping above the other street noises.

"Papa! There's the pretty lady from the broken boat!"

Tabitha looked up to see the girl—Amanda, wasn't it?—astride a big work horse in front of her father, pointing directly at her. She colored slightly under their gaze. Mr. Hayes pulled the horse to a stop beside her. He was not in the best of moods and gruffly told Amanda not to point.

Why am I stopping? Luke asked himself. *So I can prove beyond a doubt what a fool I am?* He could say it was because Mandy's eternally soft heart wouldn't let her sleep tonight if she thought there was the slightest possibility that Mrs. Bradford was in trouble. Not likely, with Mr. Moneybags around. But he wasn't one to kid himself. He knew it was because the woman looked like a rose in a cabbage patch; totally out of place and lost. And he was a sucker.

Tabitha was beginning to feel uncomfortable. The man's cloudy-day eyes reflected the fact that he didn't think too much of her. What reason could he have for not liking her?

"Hello again, Mr. Hayes," she said, determined to be civil even if he was not. "Hello, Amanda." Gratefully, she returned her gaze to the child, who was much less disconcerting to watch.

Amanda was back to her bubbly self. After her father's reprimand, she'd been frowning and silent, but now that she had Tabitha's attention, her grin was like sunshine. "Hello! Are you lost?"

"No." Tabitha smiled at her directness. "In need of direction, perhaps, but not lost."

"Where's Mr. Bradford?" Luke asked rudely.

The words were like a splash of cold water to Tabitha. His eyes were like chips of steel and burned with anger. She had no idea why he should be angry, but she was becoming angry, too. She had not asked him to stop and had done nothing to deserve his ire.

"Dead," she said, without elaborating. She knew full well that he believed Etienne to be Mr. Bradford, but she didn't think she needed to go out of her way to keep him from being uncomfortable with his remark, if he was going to be nasty.

"I'm sorry," he said, but it was the trite phrase automatically said on such occasions. He didn't really mean it, and they both knew it. But if her husband were dead, then what of her behavior with the "frog"?

"And the gentleman you were with earlier is . . . ?" The word "gentleman" was wrapped in sarcasm, making his opinion of Etienne clear.

As if it is any of his concern! Tabitha seethed inside. The question was entirely too personal for their brief acquaintance, but she chose to answer. Leaving him unanswered would only make him suspicious, and if there was one thing she did not need, it was a bad reputation when no one in this town knew better.

"The gentleman"—she emphasized the word—"is Monsieur Etienne Rousseau. A friend from the ship."

Friend, huh? Luke remembered the glow on her face when the swine had kissed her hand. Mentally, he took a firm grip on the conversation he was having with himself. He was being downright boorish, and he felt truly sorry, though he couldn't make himself admit it to her.

"Now," she said tightly, "if your curiosity is satisfied, would you please direct me to a boardinghouse?"

Several emotions flitted across his face, and it was difficult to tell what he was thinking. She thought she detected remorse, but, as he did not apologize, she wasn't sure. Were all Americans so lacking in civility?

He sighed. "Go north here on Genesee and turn left when you get to Julian Street. There'll be one on your left a few buildings down. Not too expensive, I hear."

"But Papa!" Amanda protested. "Why can't she stay at

our house? We've got lots of room!"

Finally, something made him squirm! It would have given Tabitha a boost to see him uncomfortable and searching for a response, except that the girl's question made her uncomfortable, too.

"I'm sure Mrs. Bradford would prefer to be in town," he said.

"Yes," she agreed quickly. "I'll need to be close by. I've just been employed at a shop. But thank you for the kind offer." That last she said directly to Amanda, knowing that the idea had been hers alone, and it had been sincere. "Now if you will excuse me, I should be making some living arrangements for myself. Good day."

She left them, heading in the direction he had suggested. Luke watched, with nagging doubts that were giving him indigestion. Her dress, now that he was observing more rationally, was not fancy, and it was modest. She in no way looked like the tart he had taken her for. And, clearly, she intended to remain in Waukegan. Now there was something to consider.

Mrs. Grimes, who owned the boardinghouse, was a petite and proper middle-aged lady whose cream-colored dress abounded in ruffles and lace. She served Tabitha tea in the parlor, along with what she called "cookies"— an American sweet, Tabitha discovered, somewhat like an English biscuit. She was a garrulous woman, and before long Tabitha knew that Mrs. Grimes was a widow who had, years ago, been in circumstances similar to her own present ones—only she had started a boardinghouse instead of working in a store. Now she had a cook and a girl who helped with the cleaning. It gave Tabitha encouragement to see the other woman's success.

Tabitha also heard all the local gossip. The new doctor was only twenty-eight and single. That topic Tabitha steered around, only to learn about the beautiful new Greek Revival house on Second Street, and another big, new house just out of town if you continued north on State Street. Then Mrs. Grimes drifted onto one of her favorite topics—slavery. "And they call themselves Christian! . . . And South Carolina wants to secede from the Union and form a separate nation. . . . Preposterous! . . . What is President Buchanan to do?"

Suddenly she jumped up and looked at the watch pinned to her bodice. "Goodness me!" she exclaimed. "Look at the time! Let me show you to your room so that I can get ready for supper!"

The room was light and spacious, not huge, but ample enough for Tabitha's needs. There was a big bed with an ivory quilt that had roses on it. The two windows had ecru lace curtains and roll-down blinds. There was a braided rug on the wood floor, and a dresser that matched the bed. On the dresser were a washbasin and pitcher, and behind them a framed mirror.

Glad to have the use of the basin, Tabitha washed her face and hands. She carried the towel with her to the bed, where she sat, numbly thinking. Compared to Bradford Hall, the room was downright spartan. Compared to the cabin on the *Lady,* it was the rarest luxury. What a funny, topsy-turvy world.

But the Lord was faithful. Even amidst disaster, when what was left of her world crumbled about her, He had been there, clearing her path. She was now without a cent in the world—she had spent every bit of it on this room—but she had not missed even a single meal, except for breakfast, and that wasn't God's fault. He had provided it; she just hadn't eaten it. She had a comfortable room for at least a week, and it came with meals. She had a job, and with hard work she could soon start buying some clothing and replacing some of her lost items.

At the moment, that was as far as her goals carried her. She fell to her knees in a prayer of gratitude, as she realized what had really happened to her. The money had been her security. She had trusted in mammon, not in God. So He had removed it, forcing her to trust Him. Then He had promptly shown her that He was trustworthy.

Supper was served in a long room with windows all along one wall. Outside it was growing dark, and the trees swayed in an evening breeze, sometimes brushing the glass. Green curtains fluttered in the breeze from the open windows. In the distance a cow mooed. The table was very long, made of planks sanded smooth and varnished. Benches ran along both sides, and there were chairs on both ends.

Mrs. Grimes, at one end, ladled out beef stew and biscuits. They weren't biscuits to Tabitha's way of thinking, but they were tasty. Quite similar to scones.

Most of the other boarders were crusty bachelors who only used their table manners because Mrs. Grimes would not tolerate them at her table if they did not. They eyed the newcomer speculatively, some with idle curiosity and some with blatant interest that bordered on rudeness.

There was also a spinster with a sharp face and a severe hairstyle that made her look older than her probable forty years. She sat in the chair opposite Mrs. Grimes, and Tabitha soon learned why. The benches were difficult to get onto or off of in a dress. In the future, she would remember to be almost late for meals, so she could sit on an end. For now, she would have to wait until some of the others left the table, so she could slide to one end and get up more easily. God forbid there would ever be a fire at mealtime. Everyone in the middle of the benches would be trapped.

After supper, Tabitha went outdoors and sat on the steps. It was nearly dark now. Fireflies flew in and out of the trees and grass. Mosquitoes buzzed around her, and she thought they were a part of America that she didn't like and wouldn't ever get used to. There was forest only a few blocks from the house and scattered farms. Cows and dogs gradually quieted, and their noises were followed by those of an owl and a cat.

A breeze blew, driving a few leaves from the closest tree and delivering them at her feet. After praying for warm enough clothing for winter, Tabitha rose and went to her room. She stripped off her clothes and washed them out in her washbasin with the hand soap. Then she wrung them and draped them around the room. Perhaps she could borrow the use of an iron if she got up early enough.

She lay awake for a long time, pondering the day and all that had happened. Had it really been just that morning when she'd had only a broken shoe to worry about? So many things had happened . . . there was so much to think about . . . so much to get used to.

She felt overwhelmingly alone. The house was full of people, but none of them were hers. There was no one to go to, no one to talk with. Tabitha hugged her pillow to her chest and ignored her tears.

Where was Etienne? What was he doing? She saw his face in her mind, with his half smile and flashing black eyes. The eyes changed to gray, snapping with anger.

She pushed the image of Lucas Hayes from her mind. He was ill-mannered, and he didn't appear to like her at all, though she could not guess why. How could such a crude . . . colonist . . . have such a charming daughter? Tactless, perhaps, but it was a lack born of innocence, not rudeness. Tabitha could think of nothing she had done to offend the man, so she put it in the Lord's hands and out of her thoughts.

Her mind wandered again, but quickly returned to Etienne. She should be angry. Never had she been so insulted. Or so flattered. He was clearly not a Christian man, so she could not expect him to live up to her convictions and morals. That made forgiving him easier. He had not meant to give offense, she knew.

His smooth *ma jolie* echoed in her thoughts as she drifted off to sleep.

It was a lovely piece of cloth, and Tabitha's fingers stroked it to feel the smooth texture. She could not believe it was hers.

Her very first task in the store had been to rearrange the sewing supplies. She had taken note of the various bolts of fabric while she worked, daydreaming about the clothes she would make for herself when she had saved up enough money to buy the goods. The charcoal-gray dress she wore was sturdy and made a good work dress, but it was frightfully plain. She was still in mourning for Samuel, and she had no arguments with convention. He deserved the respect.

The whole idea was kind of silly though, she realized, following rules about what to wear and what activities were allowed for a full year. What mattered was how she felt inside, how she missed him. But if wearing dull things satisfied others that she was mourning properly, she didn't mind. And she did miss him. Sometimes very much, like last night when she had felt so alone and vulnerable.

She reminded herself again that he was in a better place now, and she would see him again. Between now and then, there were most likely many years, and she had best get accustomed to that idea.

"Pretty, isn't it?" Mr. Garfield's voice interrupted her musings, startling her and making her drop the spools of thread she was organizing. She nearly fell off the ladder in her attempt to catch them. He laughed and bent to retrieve the spools that rolled across the wooden floor.

"Yes." She smiled. Her clumsiness probably didn't instill any confidence, but she saw the humor in it. "I was just thinking that if there is any of this mauve cotton left by the time I save up some money for new clothing, I would like to get some. It would make up into a lovely skirt." Her employer knew all about her situation, and she didn't feel shy about discussing it candidly.

"My gift," he said, dropping the last spool into her hand. He smiled a lot, and the gap between his teeth showed through his straw-colored beard. "Take as much as you want to make a dress or something. Reckon you need it."

Tabitha blushed.

"No offense, please! I didn't mean to make it sound like it's a grudging gift. I know you are quite capable of working and waiting for it, but I'd like to give it to you now, just because I know you've stumbled into a streak of hard luck. Jesus told us we should be watching out for the widows and orphans."

"In that case, thank you."

"If you like, you can take what else you need now, too, and we'll figure it out of your wages later. Make up your own mind about that."

Tabitha felt truly humbled. The man was almost a stranger, yet she felt she knew him well. He was a fatherly sort of figure, and he might fill part of the void left first by her own father and then by Samuel. "Again, thank you," she said. "I'll consider it."

Mr. Garfield nodded and went back to his sweeping.

It didn't take her long to consider. She needed at least one change of clothes and some more underwear. It shouldn't take too long to work off that much. Considering what to buy took longer. By the time there was a quiet spell in the afternoon, she had decided on navy blue wool for another dress, along with the mauve, which she would put aside until it was once more an appropriate color for her, and some white cotton for her more personal apparel.

Tabitha paused at the counter, scissors in hand, staring down at the wool. She wouldn't be much past having this paid for when it would be time that she could wear something more cheerful, and she would be stuck, drab, until she could afford the material for yet another new dress.

Mr. Garfield was nearby, with a pencil and paper to figure her bill as she figured what she needed and cut the lengths. "Dress?" he asked.

She nodded.

"That yellow would look a sight prettier," he commented.

Tabitha followed his gaze to a bolt of lemon yellow calico with tiny brown flowers and green leaves, and agreed with a sigh. "I can't," she explained. "I'm still in mourning."

"Now that's a fool notion," he said. "Do you still feel depressed about being widowed?"

She considered, then, deciding she could trust him, admitted, "I never did . . . although I do miss Samuel."

"Well, if you weren't depressed before, that dreary color will make you that way."

Shocked eyes met his, and he laughed.

"I see no reason for acting like a wren when you feel like a meadowlark. Get the yellow."

"But—"

"But nothing. Nobody in this town even knows you're a widow, although that won't last. Every buck in the county will be inquiring. Still, they don't know you haven't put in your obligatory year of weeds. 'Cept me, and I won't tell if you don't."

He was right. It was a stupid custom. She didn't feel depressed and dreary, so why act as though she did? And there was no one to scandalize by flying in the face of social convention, because no one here knew. It was a freeing thought.

"I thought you would see it my way!" he announced, when her decision became clear by the look on her face.

"I'll do it!" she said, and returned the wool to the shelf.

Her thoughts over the next hour were even more freeing. She was free to go where she wanted and do what she wanted, with no one to consult except God. There

was no husband; there was no father. There were no
social matriarchs with their endless, stupid lists of "Don't
invite an uneven number of people to supper" and
"Don't let the sun color your skin" and "Wear black for a
year" or a thousand other unimportant rules. Only to
strive to be pleasing to God. The sunlight shone a little
brighter through the big front window, and there was a
spring in Tabitha's step.

In the small back room her bundle of fabric wrapped
in brown paper waited for her, and she thought about it
while she worked through the afternoon. There was
enough white cotton for a new camisole and pantaloons,
the mauve cotton for a skirt later, and the yellow calico.
There were enough buttons and ribbons and thread to
complete everything, and a packet of shiny new needles.
She could hardly wait to go home and get started.

The weather wouldn't last forever. Soon she would
need some heavy wool for a cloak, but she didn't purchase that yet. She had more than enough credited
against future wages. She would have to continue praying that the weather held until she could pay for the
cloth she would need.

Anticipating a new dress inevitably made her mind
drift back to the last new clothes she had gotten, right
after her marriage. Samuel had had enough money to
buy clothes for a queen, but they had agreed that it
would be in poor taste to spend a lot on personal decoration, so her new clothes had been restricted to a simple, tasteful wardrobe.

Samuel had been in India with the army, and the poverty, especially of children, had made an impression on him. He had sent quite a bit of his money there, and Tabitha didn't grudge it. She understood him, as he told tales of his experiences so vividly that she could picture India, with its color and poverty and sad beliefs that kept those born into poverty trapped in it for their lifetime.

Leah had never understood Samuel's ways. By now the money he had left to that Indian orphanage had surely been sent. And just as surely, it would be the last Bradford money it would ever see. If only Tabitha had had a son, the Hall and the money would be hers, and she could continue to support those children. But she hadn't, and Tabitha's failure to produce an heir was one of Leah's favorite weapons, as well as one of her amusements. That memory still had the power to make Tabitha upset, and she forced herself to concentrate on her task to keep from letting herself get worked up over it. But there were no customers at the moment, and her thoughts wandered.

The will had been a bit of a surprise, but not really. Deep inside, she had expected it. Samuel had assumed she would stay on at the Hall. Always, always, he had been blind to the friction between his wife and his sister. But there was no way on earth that Tabitha was going to spend her days under the same roof with a woman who was forever snipping and harping, making hurtful comments. That decision had led to her coming to America, which had led to her working in a store in Waukegan,

Illinois, with all of her things at the bottom of Lake Michigan. Funny how one decision could lead to so many unforeseen consequences.

That night, before she took time to begin sewing her new things, Tabitha took time to write a letter to David. It wasn't a very long letter, but she knew David would enjoy reading about her adventures. She didn't know how to tell him how things had turned out without seeming like she was whining about her circumstances, or worse yet, asking for money. Leah would take pleasure in learning of her ill fortune, which was another reason for her to gloss over things. And she certainly didn't want to mention Monsieur Rousseau. Her cheeks burned just considering putting his offer on paper. But now David would know that she had arrived and would have her address. She had kept her promise.

Nine

*T*abitha stifled a yawn. She was helping a customer, Mrs. Larson, choose some fabric, and she didn't want the woman to think her rude, but she had been rushing home every night at seven and sitting up late sewing. She'd finished her yellow dress, which she was wearing today, and she had a good start on her underthings. The lack of sleep was beginning to tell. Her eyes felt gritty, and she thought that if it weren't for the constant activity of her job, she would fall asleep standing up.

Tabitha shook herself mentally. Her customer was speaking, and she hadn't been paying attention.

". . . so much for your assistance. You've been a big help. But if it's all right, I'd rather think about it for a day or two before I decide."

"Certainly." Tabitha forced a smile. She walked with Mrs. Larson to the door, assuring her that both fabrics were pretty, and that she would be there to help her whenever she made up her mind.

She was almost back to the counter when the bell jangled again.

"Hayes!" Mr. Garfield greeted Lucas with a gap-toothed grin and a beefy handshake. "What brings you to town? And where's that pretty little girl?"

Tabitha took advantage of the men's conversation to step behind the counter and jumble up a display of hard candy, so that she could appear very busy straightening the mess. The man had been so rude and so difficult to understand before, that his mere appearance reduced her to a bundle of nerves. Even her palms were clammy! She hadn't given Luke Hayes a thought for weeks, and now look at her. She took a deep breath.

Perhaps Mr. Garfield would attend to whatever business the man had, and she would not need to speak to him. He was, she told herself, in the store to shop, not to scowl at her or say nasty things.

"She's outside petting a dog," she heard him reply to her employer. "I expect she'll be in shortly. I need some supplies," he added.

"You should by now!" Mr. Garfield slapped Luke's back. "I haven't seen you around for a while. Go see Mrs. Bradford," he went on. "She already knows this store almost as well as I do." He nodded toward the counter and Tabitha's jumbled pile of candy.

Luke followed his friend's nod. He'd heard, as had everyone in town, about the English woman working for Garfield. Remembering their earlier encounters, he had been tempted to avoid her. But Al was his friend, and he had always shopped at his store. He would not let the uneasy feeling in the pit of his stomach at the thought of seeing her stop him from continuing on as he always had.

She was even prettier than he remembered. He had to make a conscious effort to pay attention to what Garfield was saying.

"I'd help you myself," the man continued, "but I have to get back to seeing what I need to order up from Chicago."

Thank God for inventories, Luke thought, suddenly eager to speak to Mrs. Bradford.

Mr. Garfield headed toward the back of the store, saying, "Good to see you, Luke," over his shoulder.

Tabitha concentrated on the candy, aware of every step he took. Her heart was pounding, anticipating another dreadful conversation.

Lucas Hayes leaned one arm on the counter, placing himself, as far as she was concerned, much too close. "Pretty dress," he said.

That was about the last thing she had expected from him, and she looked up with a start, managing to stutter a thanks.

"Did you make it yourself?"

"Yes."

"Very nice."

"Again, thank you," she said, managing this time not to sound like an idiot.

He was close enough today that she noticed the laugh

lines around his eyes, and the color and texture of his hair, and the fact that there was a darker ring around the gray of his eyes. She found she was glad that she had on her new dress.

Tabitha swallowed hard, suddenly admitting to herself that she was attracted to the man. That was probably what had bothered her about him all along. And he was a married man!

Dear God, she prayed silently, *help me!* There was a flutter of guilt and nerves in her stomach, and she could feel herself blushing. He straightened, putting a few extra inches between them, and she immediately relaxed enough to inquire, "How may I help you today?"

"Let's see." He hesitated. "Five pounds of coffee. Fifty pounds of flour. Ten of sugar, a bag of beans, and a couple of those pieces of horehound candy you've been fiddling with. Oh, and what does a cake need to make it rise? Baking powder? I'll need some of that, too."

She forced a cheerful smile as she looked down from the ladder where she was reaching for the coffee, determined to be the perfect, friendly, small-town store clerk. "Didn't Mrs. Hayes send a detailed shopping list?"

"Hardly. She's dead."

Her hand flew to her mouth in horror at her *faux pas,* but he merely smiled, a lazy, mocking smile. "And now you know exactly how it feels to step in the same puddle I did when we last met."

"Still, I'm sorry," she said, coming down from the ladder with the coffee in hand.

"It's okay," he said. "It's been years. How about you?"

"Er, not that long." She glanced down at the yellow dress, not wanting to say that it had only been two months. Not when she was already concerned with pretty clothes.

"That was ten pounds of sugar?" she asked, steering away from the touchy subject.

"Yes, please."

Luke watched her measure sugar from a big barrel into a bag, noticing the hazel of her eyes and the smoothness of her skin. Now that she wasn't blushing, it was all a creamy ivory, with just a hint of color in the cheeks. That made him smile to himself, though he didn't let it show. Was it just embarrassment at her question that had brought her blush? Or was it him?

Ha! He had neither money nor culture, and he could not begin to compete with The Frog. In Luke's mind, that was Etienne's name. "The Frog," with capital letters. Petty, maybe, but amusing; it helped to soothe his ego.

"Where's your friend?"

Tabitha looked up. A strand of hair had worked itself loose and hung limply along her face. "My friend?"

"Yes. The Fr . . . um, Frenchman."

"Etienne?" She smiled and shook her head. She could not stay angry. He was a rogue, but a lovable one. "By now, he is likely in New Orleans, with a girl on each arm."

"He just left you here?"

"He offered to take me with him," she defended her one-time friend.

"So why didn't you go? Why stay here?"

"I didn't want to accept his charity."

"Maybe," Luke suggested, knowing all the while that what was on his mind was too vulgar to say to a lady, but unable to keep the words from coming out of his mouth. "Maybe charity wasn't what he had in mind."

Tabitha had never been so mortified. How could he know that? And how could he be ill-mannered enough to refer to it? The color drained from her face.

Now I've done it, Luke thought. He had been curious about the extent of her relationship with the man. He had been poking around for information, driven to know. Yet now that he knew, he didn't want to, and it wasn't just because it was unpleasant information. It was because hitting the bull's-eye distressed her so. That wasn't what he had intended.

"So, Mr. Hayes," Tabitha said, in a voice that squeaked a bit, "what else was it you needed?" This was one conversation she was not going to continue, and she hoped he would take her rather broad hint and quit discussing such personal things.

"I'm sorry," he muttered. "Truly I am." Then he reminded her. "The candy."

Oh, yes. The horehound she'd been "fiddling with," for Amanda.

Just then, the girl burst into the store and ran over to her father to tell him about a beautiful horse she'd just seen. Her heavy boy's boots pounded across the planks of the floor.

"Hello, Mrs. Bradford!" she beamed, spotting Tabitha.

"Hello, Amanda. How are you today?"

"I'm fine. 'Cept I got some blisters 'tween my fingers. Papa's teachin' me to drive the wagon!" Her chicory blue eyes glowed with pride at her accomplishment and with adoration for her father.

Tabitha was at a loss for words. Here was a beautiful little girl in boy's clothing, browned by the sun, and learning to drive that huge horse without even the benefit of a pair of gloves to protect her hands. It was obvious that she had only masculine influence, and Tabitha wondered why she hadn't figured it out before.

"Will there be anything else, Mr. Hayes?" Once again, she took refuge in her work, determined to keep her opinions to herself. It was none of her business how the man chose to raise his daughter.

"Don't reckon. Unless there's something you think we're lacking?"

The question was weighted with the kind of sarcasm born from being slighted, and she knew that she had not kept her opinions as hidden as she would have liked to think. Really, she hadn't meant to insult him.

It seemed that was all they did. If he wasn't insulting her, it was the other way around. Round and round, baiting each other, though mostly, she knew, it was unintentional. Amanda was looking from one to the other questioningly.

"Of course not," Tabitha hurried to say.

"Then how much do I owe you?"

Tabitha quickly tallied his purchases, and the man departed, daughter in tow, without a backward glance.

In the gathering dusk Tabitha walked home, guilt pricking her heart. How could she have been so insensitive? After all, the child was loved and kept fed and dressed and warm. Wasn't it just recently she had deemed herself free of social conventions? And here she was, judging someone else because he didn't follow them. So what if the little girl had calluses? Driving was likely a thing she would need to know, living here in America. This wasn't England, where girls were either too poor to have horses or too rich to do their own driving.

She shivered and pulled her shawl closer. It was fortunate that Mr. Garfield was almost paid off, and she could begin to save for the much-needed wool for a warm cloak. October was progressing, and rapidly. The cloak couldn't wait much longer.

That night, however, she didn't sew, but went directly to bed after supper. Staying up so often was catching up to her, and she was exhausted. Tired as she was, however, Tabitha didn't fall immediately asleep. There was too much on her mind.

She had almost forgotten Lucas Hayes in the weeks since she had arrived in Waukegan, yet when he came into the store, she'd been as nervous as a schoolgirl. It had been quite a shock to discover, and admit, that she found the man attractive. And she had made such a fool of herself! Both in how she had learned that his wife was dead, and again, just before he left. Truth was, she was ashamed of herself.

With jerky motions, she rolled over and roughly plumped her pillow, hoping to get comfortable enough to fall asleep, knowing it would be some time still before she did.

Oh, and how she had blushed and fluttered when he'd said her dress was pretty! Whatever must he think of her? And if she was going to begin stuttering and getting sweaty palms in the presence of a man, why did it have to be *him?*

Etienne was equally handsome, but handsome in a different way; he was more polished, more charming. Luke was rough and rugged. Etienne was more fun, more comfortable, suave, wealthy, and chivalrous. She preferred him in every way. So why did she see gray eyes in her mind, when she closed her eyes and tried to sleep?

Heavens! Neither man seemed to be a believer, though she wasn't sure about Luke. She had no business lying awake thinking of either of them. She was not being still and trying to hear her Lord's voice in her heart. She was not seeking Him first. In fact, she had been so busy just getting along, just living, that she hardly gave God a thought except when she was in church. She knew that all these "things"—her need for companionship, cloth-ing, and all the things she was striving after—would be "added unto her," but she hadn't been living it. She had been seeking things, and had been losing her closeness with the Lord in the process.

It's a good thing, she thought, that salvation is free. If one had to earn one's way, no one would make it. I certainly wouldn't.

The second length of flannel was added to the one already folded on the counter when Mr. Garfield folded his apron and headed toward the back room to figure the day's cash book before going home. If Tabitha wasn't finished cleaning before he was done, he would just leave. After two months, he trusted her completely, and left her to close up before he went home. He even called her Tabitha now, instead of Mrs. Bradford, although "Albert" didn't come easily to her, and she continued to use "Mr. Garfield."

The flannel on top was white with tiny blue flowers, and the bottom one was solid pink. Both were for nightgowns. At last, she was getting the things she considered essential, including an iron for her clothes and a curling iron for her hair. The curling iron had yet to be used, as she had not seen any point in taking any pains with her appearance. Lately, she'd begun simply folding her hair into a hair net and letting it hang past her shoulders. She was not aware that it looked smooth and shining and heavy, and was very attractive.

She wanted a third everyday dress, but knew it would be a while before she spent any more money on clothes. From now on, every cent over her basic living expenses would be saved toward her own sewing shop. It was going so slowly! Her small wage didn't go far. Still, she supposed she was fortunate that in two short months she had gone from having nothing to having clothes and a few little extras. It only seemed like such a long time.

The bell on the door rang, and a very excited boy ran in, waving a piece of paper. "Mrs. Bradford! Mrs. Bradford!"

Curious, Tabitha looked up from her work and took a few steps to meet him. He handed her the paper and said, "A telegram! All the way from England!"

Albert joined them, wiping his hands on his pants. "From England? Imagine that!" He looked over her shoulder. "I'd heard that cable was finished, crossing the whole Atlantic, but just think—messages from Europe to here in one day! What's it say, Tabitha?"

It didn't strike her as odd that he would want to hear. This was big news in a small place like Waukegan, and by now the Garfields and Tabitha were quite close friends. She read aloud: "RECEIVED LETTER STOP DAVID MISSING STOP PRESUMED COMING TO YOU STOP LEAH." One hand clutched the paper, the other went to her heart. Her wide eyes stared at Albert Garfield.

Missing!

Albert tried to calm her. He said David was an old enough lad to take care of himself. He was probably fine. There was nothing she could do but wait.

Everything he said was right. But it didn't make it better. David was missing.

Several unpleasant thoughts went through her head—things that could have happened to him, awful things. And it was her fault. If she hadn't come, he would not have followed. Or had he followed? Apparently Leah wasn't sure; that was just her best guess, because he had disappeared soon after receiving her letter, telling him where she was.

Did Leah have detectives trying to find him? Surely she did.

For days, Tabitha could think of little else. Even as time passed, the thought was always in the back of her mind. Where was David? Was he coming here? Or had something horrible happened to him?

Weeks passed with no word. Life slowly returned to normal, and Tabitha forced herself to think about and do other things. There was nothing she could do about David. Perhaps now that she was done with her own sewing, she could do some for others, in the evenings. Tomorrow she would ask Mr. Garfield if she could put a card in the window to advertise. She needed the extra money, and the extra work would give her hands something to do in the lonely, quiet evenings. It would keep her mind occupied.

Thanksgiving came soon after the telegram. It was a new holiday to her, and she thought it an excellent idea—to have a holiday for families to gather and give thanks to God. But she didn't feel up to celebrating anything, so when Albert asked her if she would like to join them for their feast, she declined. If she went, she would only dampen everyone else's enjoyment of the day. Instead, she remained at the boarding house with Mrs. Grimes and the other boarders who had nowhere else to go.

The men, glad for a day off, talked, mostly war talk, and played checkers. Miss Patricia, the other female boarder, sat knitting. Tabitha tried to draw her into conversation, with little luck. The woman was beyond shy; she was downright unfriendly. Small wonder she had never married. Or perhaps her lack of a spouse had produced the bitterness Tabitha now saw. Either way, Miss Patricia needed prayer.

Tabitha was spending more time talking with her Lord . . . though it seemed none of her prayers would ever be answered. There were still hard feelings between Leah and her. Probably more so now, with the David situation. Then there was David himself. How long would it be before she should stop watching for him? He certainly hadn't had time to make the journey yet—it might be a month or more—but the time was dragging. Every day she prayed for Etienne, and for her own needs.

Beyond the window, all was blackness. Christmas was nearly upon them, but each happy child Tabitha saw and each carol she heard only served to depress her further.

She remembered the Christmases of her childhood back in England. Even after her mother died, her father would bring in holly and mistletoe, and they would decorate. They exchanged gifts, and they kept a big pot of wassail hot for carolers or visitors. Often, it had been Samuel Bradford who had visited.

Then, when she had married and moved to Bradford Hall, Christmas had taken on an even more special meaning. She had been a Christian since before she could remember, but from Samuel she learned that Christianity wasn't just a belief, but a way of life. It was knowing Jesus, trusting Him, and making all your decisions, from the large to the small, based on what He would do, or what He would think of it. At the Hall, they had also exchanged gifts, but her favorite part of Christmas had become the services at church to worship the Lord for coming to Earth that man might be saved.

Here in Waukegan, she knew no one well enough to make it really feel like Christmas. The Garfields hadn't asked her to join them, and as time passed, she assumed they would not. So a bigger-than-usual meal at the boarding house was all she had to look forward to, in celebration of this season of joy.

Her life lately, despite the season, had consisted of plodding through one day after another, reaching for that sewing shop that never seemed to get any closer, and worrying about David.

Luke and Amanda had come into the store that day. They came in from time to time, or sometimes it was Luke by himself, but since the day Amanda had shown her her blisters, the conversations had been strictly business. That, Tabitha thought, was probably for the best. Given time, she might stop thinking about him, and stop getting the flutters when he walked in or even when his name was mentioned. Thankfully, that didn't happen often, but he was a friend of Mr. Garfield's, and it was a small town, so she was bound to see him occasionally.

Tabitha sighed. It was getting late—past time for her to be going home. Mr. Garfield had already left, and there were only a few things left to do. What she needed was a friend. Someone to talk to, to pray with, to ease the loneliness. Once more, she prayed that God would bring someone into her life. The floor was finished, so she started toward the back room to put the broom away.

The bell over the door tinkled, though it was after closing, which could only mean that she had forgotten to turn over the "closed" sign. Now she would have to deal with a late customer, and be polite, so that she would not lose future business.

"Bonsoir, ma jolie," said a voice she would know anywhere. She nearly dropped her broom in her quick swing around to face Etienne and verify with her eyes that he was actually there.

"Etienne!" she said, too surprised to move or say anything more.

"So how do you like this *petit* town, eh?" he asked. "And how do you live in this horrible weather? Why don't you come back to New Orleans with me, where it is warm?"

She laughed. He was as flattering and absurd as ever.

Ah, it was good to see him! And, she reminded herself, she'd been entirely too sensitive about his suggestion when they'd last met. He wasn't sober-minded enough to propose something as serious as marriage. She should just be appreciative that he thought she was pretty and that he liked to be around her, without getting outraged by insults that were never meant.

"Which question would you like me to answer first? And what are you doing here?"

"I must have been completely mad to venture any further north than Baton Rouge this time of year! But I felt I must see for myself how you are."

He strolled around her, noting the change of dress and hairstyle with obvious approval. "You are *tres jolie*, Tabitha! You have acquired a beau since I left, no?"

"No." She blushed crimson under his scrutiny.

"In that case, am I too late to take you to dinner?"

"No, you are not too late, and I would love to go!" Tabitha collected her new gray cloak and her purse, blew out the lamps, and locked the store. They stepped out into the dark street.

A thought occurred to Etienne. "Who usually sees that you get home safely?"

"God, I suppose," she replied with a shrug that said that she hadn't worried about it.

Etienne, however, knew more of the ugly side of the world, and was concerned. And his concern in itself was enough to scare him. He hadn't actually cared what happened to someone else since . . . he could not remember when. And this woman's naive trust in her God was both irritating and charming. A vapor of the mind, he thought, yet finding someone childlike enough to believe in it was refreshing.

"Isn't there a man in this town who is not blind?" he asked, determined to keep the conversation from getting too personal, too honest. Last time he had only angered her, and he did not want to do that again. Not after traveling so far to see if his memories of her beauty and integrity were accurate, or if he had been deceiving himself. "Can they not see that there is a woman who is walking alone after dark? Is the world devoid of chivalry?"

Tabitha's reaction was to defend the local men. Many of them she saw frequently at the store, and she knew them to be, for the most part, hardworking, honest, and patriotic. She'd heard enough about Lincoln, Douglas, slavery, and secession to last her a lifetime. They talked about the preservation of the Union more than any other single subject, with the possible exception of the evils of slavery and Harriet Beecher Stowe's book, which proved how bad it was. Of course, those two subjects were almost always part of the same conversation. It was tedious to hear the same facts, or opinions, over and over, but it did show that the local people were sincere in upholding their ideals.

"I'm a big girl," she said, instead.

"*Oui, madame,* I can see that," he said in a way that could not be misunderstood. He was back to his not-to-be-taken-seriously, flirting self, which made her laugh.

"Let me carry that for you."

That, she certainly didn't expect. The only thing she was carrying was her purse, and his carrying it for her would be taking chivalry to a ridiculous extreme. She giggled and held up the bag. "This? Wouldn't you feel silly carrying a purse?"

"*Moi?* Silly?" He smiled in his slow, lopsided way. "Well, perhaps a bit. But I wish to treat you like an elegant lady. As you have no packages or books, I will have to make do with what you do have."

She humored him, handing him the purse. Lighthearted as she hadn't felt for some time, she put her arm through his. "You may not feel silly, but believe me, monsieur, you are."

If Tabitha had been lonely before, it was nothing to what she felt now. Etienne had come and gone in one day. He had taken her out, and they'd eaten a wonderful meal, laughing and talking. Then he had walked her home early, saying he had to catch the early train for Chicago so he could tend to some things before a trip he had scheduled to New York. Because of that trip, he said, it would be quite a while before he would be able to make it back to see her. Several months. Maybe spring.

So, while yesterday morning she had felt a vague dissatisfaction, a need for a friend, she now felt utterly alone. And Christmas was only three days away.

Etienne said he would be back. It would be a long, lonely time, but he would be back. She clung to that thought, not realizing how much her attitude toward him had changed. The contrast between her everyday life and the laughing enjoyment of life that she shared with Etienne was night and day. Living her life, between now and his return, seemed a bleak prospect.

With a sigh she forced her hands back to their task of dusting shelves, but such a mindless job didn't do much to keep her mind off the Frenchman. Why had he traveled so far to spend only a few hours? It was a question that had plagued her all through the long, sleepless night, and she returned to the same answer she had come up with then. He must have had some other reason for coming, such as business in Chicago, and had only squeezed in a visit because he was nearby. It was the only thing she could think of that made any sense. But why hadn't he said anything about it?

Probably, she told herself, it was because he was one of those gentlemen who thought that discussing business with a lady was ill-mannered. That explanation would fit his character, and it satisfied her questioning mind. Her dust rag moved a little more enthusiastically, and her lips curved up at the corners.

Her reverie was interrupted by the arrival of Amanda, who wandered into the store with an unhappy expression on her face. The girl walked aimlessly around the store, looking at this and that.

Tabitha reached into a candy jar and pulled out a horehound stick, remembering that it was the flavor the child had chosen before. Amanda regarded her uncertainly when she held out the candy to her.

"My treat," Tabitha said.

"Thank you, Mrs. Bradford." She slipped the candy into the large front pocket of her overalls.

"Aren't you going to eat it?"

"I don't feel much like candy right now."

Tabitha didn't have much experience with children, but the girl had come here, maybe to seek her out in particular, so she had to at least see if she could help. "Is there anything I can do, Amanda?"

Sadly, the child shook her head no.

Tabitha prayed silently for wisdom, then commented idly on a spool of satin ribbon. "Isn't this pretty? It's the same color as your eyes." Maybe talking about inconsequential things was a good way to begin.

Amanda perked up a bit, showing interest in the ribbon by reaching out a finger to touch it.

"What would you think about a length for your hair?" Tabitha asked. "That might cheer you up!"

"No, thank you. Papa doesn't like them."

"Doesn't like ribbons?"

"I wore one once. He didn't say anything, but he looked at me funny, like it made him sad."

Lucas Hayes was a subject Tabitha would rather not pursue, so she tried to think of something else cheerful to talk about. "Christmas will be here soon," she said.

"Won't that be wonderful?"

Now the tears fell. "I miss Mama most at Christmas," Amanda whispered. "She used to bake cookies and let me take some to school. That was when they liked me."

Tabitha's heart was breaking for the girl. "Who doesn't like you?" she asked. "The children at school?"

Amanda nodded.

"Why do you think that?"

Amanda looked away, chewing on her bottom lip.

"Can you tell me?"

She gestured angrily at her clothes. "They say, 'Mandy, Mandy, shoulda named her Andy'!" She mimicked the teasing voice of children worldwide.

Tabitha went to her knees and put her arms around the child. There was nothing she could do. Not without pushing her nose in where it didn't belong, telling Mr. Hayes how to raise his daughter. "I know it's not much," she said, "but if it will help, I could bake some cookies for you to take to school."

"No, thank you, Mrs. Bradford." Amanda sniffed and pulled a dainty lace handkerchief out of her pocket to wipe her eyes and blow her nose. The letters *RH* were embroidered on the corner.

"Where did you get that, Amanda?" Tabitha asked. "It's very pretty."

"It was Mama's. See?" She displayed the initials. "RH. That's for Rachel Hanson. She used to say it was a good thing she married Papa so she didn't need to buy new hankies." Her eyes widened. "You won't tell Papa I have this one, will you?" she pleaded.

"You're not supposed to use your mother's things?"

She shrugged. "That part's okay, but it's girl stuff. He doesn't like girl stuff."

Through the window, Luke could see Tabitha Bradford on the floor hugging his daughter, who was blowing her nose on that silly hanky she always hid from him, and his stomach sank. The emotional episodes of raising a girl left him feeling inadequate, and it would only be worse to have an audience. And why, of all people, did it have to be *her?* The lovely Mrs. Bradford could make him feel a fool at the best of times. Steeling himself, he opened the door, and the noisy bell turned two sets of eyes to him.

One pair of eyes was red-rimmed and puffy, and the other pair appeared often in his dreams, looking just as they did now, filled with thoughts he couldn't put a name to and lined with unbelievable lashes that fluttered with modesty and innocence, despite her age and widowed status. At times, in his dreams, those eyes needed him. Eyes frightened and helpless, making him feel like he could conquer the world. Until he woke up and merely felt like a buffoon. Other times, in his dreams, those eyes smoldered, yearning for him. Then he would wake up and be snapping and churlish, not liking himself very much, yet feeling helpless to change the way he acted.

Now those lashes dropped to veil their owner's thoughts, and pink crept up her cheeks.

When Luke entered the store, Tabitha quickly got to

her feet and made her way behind the counter, angry with herself. Every time that man walked into a room, she blushed. It made her furious. He was probably laughing at her, panting after him like a lovesick puppy. Most likely one of many puppies following him, tongues hanging out, drooling. *Oh, dear God, what must he think!*

Another thought came to mind, one that brought a chilling shudder to her soul. Just moments ago she had been "drooling" after Etienne. What was she becoming?

The answer was there on the heels of the question. She was a normal, healthy woman. She was twenty-five years old, with longings for a mate and children. Samuel had delayed the longing for a time by providing friendship and security. They had talked for hours about everything, sometimes staying up all night.

Now she hadn't even the benefit of a female friend to talk to. She was frightfully lonely, and knew suddenly that she had been reaching out to both men, grasping and desperate. Thank God that it had only been in her mind, and she had never actually done anything to humiliate herself . . . except for the infuriating blushing.

While she heard Luke asking Amanda if she was all right, she was praying desperately for a friend. *Please, God,* her heart cried, *Send me a friend before I really do something to embarrass myself and reflect poorly on You.*

"Yes, Papa," Amanda answered her father. She gave a rather sickly smile and held up the golden brown stick of candy. "Mrs. Bradford gave me candy. See?"

Luke smiled and ruffled her taffy curls. "Well, then, if

you're done with your visit with Mrs. Bradford, why don't you run out to the wagon? I'll be along in a few minutes."

Amanda ran from the store, her tears forgotten.

Ten

*J*abitha felt in the way. What she had just witnessed was a private moment between father and daughter, and she was touched with the degree of gentleness he had displayed.

"I'm sorry if she's been any trouble," he said. "Thank you for taking time for her."

"Well." She pulled down a corner of her mouth. "I don't think I was any help."

"What were the tears all about?"

If she had wanted a chance to tell him she didn't approve of the way he was raising Amanda, this was a golden opportunity. But she could see that he loved his daughter and was doing the best he could. Besides, with her English upbringing, she was not cheeky enough to advise him in family matters. And what did she know of child rearing, anyway? Virtually nothing.

Still, the girl was hurting, and he had asked.

"Maybe I should ask Amanda," Luke said.

Yet Tabitha hesitated.

"Mr. Hayes!" Tabitha called as he put his hand to the knob. He turned to face her again.

"I'll tell you, because I don't think she will. I hope you don't think I'm sticking my nose in where it doesn't belong."

He nodded, giving her permission to continue. She thought for a moment how best to phrase the criticism. No delicate words would come to her, and finally she blurted the question, "Why do you dislike the idea that Amanda is a girl?"

"What? That's absurd. Where did you get that idea?"

"From Amanda."

Luke stepped closer, and suddenly seemed much larger than Tabitha. She shouldn't have been forced into such a personal conversation in the first place, and she felt uncomfortable. She walked behind the counter to put some distance between herself and Luke, but he followed and leaned toward her, palms flat on the countertop. Tabitha couldn't back up any further; there was no place to go.

"What gave her that idea?" he demanded.

Tabitha's discomfort turned to anger. She hadn't asked for this. He had. And he had no right to raise his voice to her. She looked directly into his thundercloud eyes. "You can be assured, Mr. Hayes, that I did not. Perhaps you would be so kind as to refrain from yelling at me."

His breath came out in a rush, and he straightened

and ran a hand through his dark hair. "Sorry," he muttered. "But do you know why she thinks that?"

"Not exactly. She did say that you looked sad when she wore a hair ribbon." Confusion clouded his expression, but she could not enlighten him more.

"What do you do with a girl?" he asked, half under his breath. Then, to Tabitha, "That's it? Just out of the blue, she decides I don't like girls and comes crying to you? That just doesn't make any sense."

"Well . . . ," Tabitha hedged.

"Well, what? Do you know anything that could shed a little light on this?"

She turned up her nose and said in a childlike taunt, "Mandy, Mandy, shoulda named her Andy."

As the meaning soaked in, Luke began pacing the floor, running a hand through his hair. "Why didn't she come to me with this?'

"Because she loves you! She thinks you don't like the fact that she's a girl, and she's trying her best to be what you want."

"And she does well," he conceded, sorting through his thoughts aloud. "She can drive the team, chop wood, and muck out the barn. But she can't sew or bake a pie. When Rachel died," he continued, "I had no idea what to do with a girl. So I did what I do understand. Hope I haven't done too much harm."

"I doubt that. She adores you."

"Tabitha," he asked, a sudden light coming to his eyes. "Do you ever sew for anyone else?" He didn't even seem to realize he had used her Christian name.

She fought sudden flutters. "Why, yes, Mr. Hayes." She wiped her sweaty palms nervously across her skirt. "In fact, I have a card in the window to advertise."

"Would you make a couple of dresses for Amanda? For school? And whatever other foo-foo things she'll need?"

Tabitha smiled broadly. "I'd be delighted!"

"Then let's get this situation rectified!" He went to the door and called, "Mandy! Come back in here for a minute."

In spite of it being December, it was a warm, sunny day, with snow melting into muddy puddles in the street. Amanda had been crouching down, sharing her candy with a wandering dog, but when she heard her father call, she sprang up. She came in with muddy boots and knees, and dog hair stuck to her candy-coated fingers.

"We can dress her up, but can we make a lady of her?" Luke asked with a grin.

"Certainly," Tabitha laughed.

"What do you mean?" Amanda asked, looking suspiciously from one to the other.

"I've been waiting," her father said, "for you to change into a lady, like a butterfly from a cocoon. But I'm tired of waiting, and I've sweet-talked Mrs. Bradford here into giving you a little push. She's going to make you some dresses."

Amanda didn't say anything at first, but they could see a hopeful spark in her eyes.

"Dresses," she said at last, "for me?"

"Yes, ma'am."

An excited squeal rang throughout the store. Amanda ran to her father, hugged him fiercely, then ran to Tabitha and hugged her, too. "Thank you! When?"

Luke glanced to Tabitha for the answer. She hated to be the one to dampen Amanda's high spirits, but she had to say, "It will take a while, I'm afraid, because I can only work on them in the evenings. But I can get started tonight."

Amanda tried to hide her disappointment, and almost succeeded.

"First," Tabitha said as she led the way to the store's north wall, where bolts of fabric were stacked on shelves, "you need to choose what we'll make them out of. Then I'll take your measurements."

Amanda went straight to the yellow calico that Tabitha had used for her own dress. "I want one just like yours! Don't you think it's beautiful, Papa?"

"I sure do!" Luke winked at Tabitha, and she didn't know whether that meant he agreed with his daughter's choice or if it was intended to include her in a mild amusement.

Tabitha was warmed by the compliment, yet strangely humbled. Imitation was the purest form of flattery; it was a weighty thing, having a young girl trying to emulate her. Regardless, the yellow was a poor choice for Amanda. "Thank you," she said, "but if I may make a suggestion?"

Blue and gray eyes turned to her. "Yellow and brown wouldn't be your best colors, Amanda. Pink or blue would suit your blonde hair and fair skin much better."

So Amanda chose the same print, but in a powder blue with pink flowers. She also insisted on the same style. Tabitha was glad she had chosen a pattern that wouldn't be too grown-up looking on a child. She would hate to have to make another change in what Amanda wanted. She helped her count out twenty-six pink buttons and choose the thread and ribbon she would need.

"Now," she suggested, "how about something special for Sundays?" Her hand rested on a bolt of fine lilac-colored wool. It would be perfect.

"That won't be necessary," Luke said.

Tabitha had been feeling on top of the world for several reasons. She had a customer, she was enjoying the company of people she was growing to appreciate more and more, and she felt she was really being a help. But the chill in Luke's voice, the iciness of his voice and of his gray eyes, put an abrupt damper on her mood.

"Just another school dress," he said in a way that didn't invite argument.

They picked a solid shell pink, and enough white cotton and lace for the girl's undergarments, but for Tabitha the joy was gone.

Luke lay in bed staring at the ceiling. There was only silence from upstairs, telling him that Amanda had fallen asleep. Who would have thought that something as simple as a dress could make such a change in her? He couldn't remember her bubbling so with happiness since before her mother had died.

She needed a mother—a feminine influence. That point had been driven home today! And, of course, the lovely Tabitha Bradford came to mind as the most likely prospect. If anyone could teach Amanda how to be a girl, and do it without being weak and simpering, that woman was the one.

He found himself wondering about Mr. Bradford. What had the man been like? How had he died? What had he looked like? It was a puzzle. Tabitha acted like a real lady, but as far as he could tell, she was nearly destitute.

Their earlier meetings replayed in his head. He pictured her ,eyes snapping with barely contained fury. Or blushing suddenly and looking away. He could just as easily imagine her standing in his kitchen, smiling a greeting just for him when he came in the door. Again her image came to mind, blushing, eyelashes fluttering down.

Why did she blush so much? Could it possibly be because she found him attractive? A wide grin broke his face, and he rolled over onto his side.

But what about her husband? Surely, she was still mourning him. Or that French fellow? If she was interested in a man, wouldn't it follow that she would choose one with dashing good looks and money? One so suave and refined that he seemed to drip honey? Of course she would. *And I,* he thought, *have the most overworked imagination in the state of Illinois.*

Tabitha wasn't sleeping, either. She'd stayed up late, wanting to finish Amanda's things as soon as possible. When she was too bleary-eyed to see straight, she'd crawled into bed, expecting to fall immediately asleep. Snatches of remembered conversation kept going through her mind, keeping her awake. She thought of Luke's breath on her cheek. She could even remember his smell.

The butterflies came back, just thinking about it. She hoped, with a kind of sick dread, that he hadn't noticed. Then his face floated in her mind's eye as clear as if he was standing there, with ice in his eyes when she'd mentioned a dress for church.

She needn't wonder any longer about whether or not he was a Christian. He clearly was not. The realization made her sad for him. To live without Jesus seemed an existence bleak beyond her scope of imagination. It also made her sad on her own behalf, because she knew that she had begun to dream about him, and a someday, maybe. But that would never do. She could not consider an unbeliever for a mate, even momentarily. It would be hard to cease thinking about him, though. He was so handsome and so gentle, yet so strong. Easily she could love him, without even half trying.

Instead she prayed, both for her own moral strength, that she could be faithful even in the small things, such as thoughts that no one would ever know about, and for his salvation. Not only did she fervently wish for his eternity to be secure, but she wished for him the comfort and joy that she sensed he desperately needed.

Finally she drifted off, unaware that it was the first time in months that she hadn't fallen asleep with thoughts of Etienne on her mind.

Where could it be? Tabitha took her purse off the coat rack where it hung under her cloak, with new determination to find that dime.

Amanda's camisole was nearly finished, and she thought that a pink bow at the neckline would be the perfect finishing touch. She wanted to add the ribbon as a sort of gift, a little added femininity, but she had to find that dime!

Money was something Tabitha had learned to be very careful about, and she knew it had to be in her purse somewhere. She walked over to the counter and dumped the contents. The coin wasn't there. She turned the bag inside out.

Aha! There was a small tear in a seam in the lining.

She felt the cloth, trying to locate the dime. Sure enough, between the purse and lining, there it was. Working it out the same hole, she told herself to repair the seam that evening. How, she wondered, had she managed to tear her purse in such an unusual place?

She pushed her belongings back inside, and then cut a length of narrow, pink satin ribbon to make the bow she wanted.

"Tabitha?"

She glanced up to see what it was that Mr. Garfield wanted. "Yes?"

"Do you have any plans for Christmas Day?"

She frowned slightly. "No. Except I believe that Mrs. Grimes is planning a special meal."

"Evelyn and I have a tradition, of sorts. It's just the six of us here, the relatives being back east, so we have a big dinner for Christmas. Any of our friends who have no other plans—family or anything—come over. We'd love to have you join us, if you would like to. Sorry it took so long for me to ask. I sorta assumed you'd be coming. Then when Evie asked if you were coming, I realized I'd never mentioned it."

Tabitha beamed. Now that sounded more like Christmas! "Thank you! I'd be delighted! Is there anything I can bring?"

"If you want. Don't have to, though. I'll tell Evie."

Tabitha hummed a carol as she went through the rest of the day's work.

What should she contribute to the festivities? She was

sure Mrs. Grimes would let her use the kitchen, especially if she made enough for the boarding house, too. How about a plum pudding? She would have to get her ingredients tonight before she went home. Tomorrow being Christmas Eve, the shops might be closed.

She sewed for a while that evening, anxious to finish Amanda's clothes as soon as possible. Perhaps she could have them ready when school started again after Christmas.

The following day the store was closed, so Tabitha didn't have to work. She enjoyed the day off, more so than she had enjoyed her last day off, on Thanksgiving. True, there was still no news of David, but the idea was growing easier to live with. If he had come to a violent end, there would surely have been news by now, so she was fairly certain that he would show up here sooner or later. She slept late, cleaned her room, and took a bath, then did some sewing on Amanda's pantaloons. Too bad the sewing wouldn't be done for Christmas, but the girl wouldn't be needing them for church, so she didn't suppose it mattered much until school started again after the holiday.

Mrs. Grimes had agreed to let her use the kitchen, and everything was in order for the following day. That night when she crawled between her sheets, she was humming "The First Noel."

The next morning, as soon as she was finished in the kitchen, she tidied up, leaving an extra pudding for the boarders. Then she ran upstairs and dressed in her mauve skirt and the white blouse with all the tiny pleats at the shoulders. She curled her hair and piled it up on her head, leaving a few small ringlets loose. Her mirror showed her a pretty, stylish young woman, and she smiled. It had been a long while since she had felt attractive.

There wouldn't be anyone there she knew besides the Garfields, so she didn't question her motives. It was Christmas, and she was happy. That was motive enough. Grabbing her cloak and purse, she headed back down the steps to collect her pudding and make her way to the Garfield home, which was on Magnolia near the edge of town.

Robert, who at eleven was the eldest of the Garfield children, answered the door. He looked as polished as the silver, and cheerfully took Tabitha's cloak and led her to the kitchen so she could deposit her pudding.

Johnny, the two year old, was playing in the hall, and had to move to let Tabitha's hoopskirts pass. He, too, wore his best, and Tabitha could tell that at some point earlier in the day he'd been scrubbed and combed.

"Oh, thank you!" Evelyn Garfield said when she brought the pudding into the kitchen. "It smells heavenly!"

"Thank you."

"Just set it over there." She pointed a wooden spoon to indicate a table laden with pies and cakes for dessert.

Tabitha could see that her contribution was about as needed as a couple of buckets of water in the Atlantic.

She sighed. Looking around, though, she observed that anything she might have brought would have been so much extra baggage. The mouth-watering odors belonged to a clove-studded ham and a crisp, brown turkey. A cloud of mashed potatoes was melting a generous scoop of butter. Chunks of bacon floated in steaming green beans, canned from the summer's garden. Buttery, sugared squash sat beside corn pudding warming on the stove top. Two loaves of white bread and two loaves of dark, all still warm from the oven, waited in cloth-covered baskets. Steam wafted off a gravy boat. Various sauces and relishes completed the feast.

Evelyn, a short, plump woman whose soft brown hair was beginning to show streaks of gray, was stirring the stuffing.

"Is there anything I can help you with?" Tabitha offered.

"Not right now, dear. I'll let you know if I need you. Why don't you make yourself comfortable and enjoy your day off?"

Albert Garfield entered the room to hear that last. "Don't count on it," he grinned. "This kitchen is Evie's domain, and it isn't often any one else is allowed to lift a spoon." The woman chuckled and shooed them out.

Albert offered her a cup of hot cider. Mug in hand, she wandered around the house. In the dining room she saw that the table was set for twelve, and wondered who else had been invited. The room was large. There was a wood floor, with the wood laid crisscross in a herringbone pattern. The furniture was delicate, with claw feet. The arms of the cherry wood chairs were carved, and the seats were needlepoint. There was a glass-front cabinet, also of cherry wood, but it was now nearly empty, because all the good china was on the table.

A long hall bisected the house downstairs. When she stepped into it to cross over to the parlor, she saw Robert opening the door to admit Chester MacDonald, one of the town's bachelors. Mr. MacDonald had washed and combed his hair, for a rare change. Still, his graying red hair stuck up at the back of his head.

That answered one of the five questions. Four more unknowns would be seated around the table set for twelve.

Robert took the man's coat and hat and ran up to a bedroom to deposit them, then returned to position himself on the third step to await the next arrival. He plopped down with his knees up and his elbows resting on them. His chin was propped on his hands, and he looked about as thoroughly bored as a boy could be.

Chester MacDonald had seen Tabitha standing down the hall, so she stepped forward to greet him.

"Happy Christmas, Mr. MacDonald!"

"Merry Christmas to you, too, Mizz Bradford. That's a right purty dress."

"Why thank you! You look nice today, too."

"Think I'll git some o' that cider. 'Scuse me."

"Certainly."

Another knock sounded, and Robert jumped up to

answer. Two more of the questions were answered in the form of Jesse and Sarah Miller. They were a young couple, fairly new to Waukegan. Tabitha had never met them formally, but knew them by name.

Jesse was tall, with dark, brooding eyes, a narrow face with hollow cheeks, and a shock of straight, black hair hanging on his forehead. Sarah was a tiny thing, obviously with child. Her strawberry ringlets hung over her shoulders. She would have been quite pretty, but for protruding teeth.

"Hello. I'm Tabitha Bradford." She extended her hand to Sarah. "Merry Christmas!"

"Yes, we know who *you* are!" Sarah Miller ignored Tabitha's hand and turned her moss-colored, green-brown eyes to her husband.

Jesse, ignoring his wife's rudeness, shook Tabitha's hand. "We're the Millers. I'm Jesse, and this is my wife, Sarah. Pleased to meet you."

Robert was waiting to take their coats. They handed their wraps to the boy, then headed for the parlor. Tabitha had been near the front door for the arrival of three people so far, and was beginning to feel like the official greeter. Turning, she spotted Charles Garfield parked halfway up the stairs. His nose, as usual, was in a book. He was seven, and ever since the magic world of books had been opened to him, he was never without one.

"Hello, Charles," she said. "I didn't see you before. What are you reading?"

"Rip Van Winkle."

"Is it a good story?"

"Um-hm."

The boy wanted to read, not talk, so Tabitha decided to leave him alone.

Robert clattered down the stairs and headed for the kitchen rather than resume his post by the door. The other two unknown guests must have already arrived, either before her or while she'd been in the kitchen. She followed the Millers into the parlor. The parlor had a huge rug and was filled to bursting with small tables, lamps, knickknacks, and candles. Double doors shut it off from the passageway and the rest of the house, and Tabitha knew that it was only used for guests. She opened the door.

Anna Garfield, in a ruffled and ribbon-bedecked blue dress, sat on a sofa. Her hair, a pale brown, almost blonde, was pulled into a blue bow at the back of her head. Her lower hair was left in loose curls around her shoulders. On the sofa next to her was Amanda. Tabitha's heart gave a little jump. That meant that the other unknown guest was Luke!

Of course. She should have figured that out. Her fingers clutched her mug. So where was he? Taking a sip of cider and trying to look nonchalant, she glanced around the room. Mr. Garfield and Mr. MacDonald stood by a crackling fire, chatting. Sarah Miller was whispering angrily to her husband, and Amanda looked stiff and uncomfortable. Anna, beside her on the sofa, seemed bored. There was no sign of Luke. Tabitha turned her attention back to the two girls.

Anna was a year older than Amanda. The two were friends, but Amanda seemed to be pouting, and not interested in playing. Tabitha wondered if Anna's appearance made Amanda feel self-conscious. If she could help it, Amanda would never have to face another day like today, at least not for lack of a dress.

"Hello, Amanda. Anna. Are you enjoying your Christmas?"

"Oh, yes, Mrs. Bradford," Anna replied, perking up at someone to talk to. "I got a new doll! Her eyes really close!"

Tabitha had seen the doll when it had arrived at the store. It was indeed a special doll, and she couldn't blame Anna for being excited about it.

"Would you like to go see her, Mandy?" Anna asked.

"Okay," Amanda agreed and got up from the couch to follow Anna upstairs, though she didn't sound very thrilled about it.

Tabitha felt out of place when the two girls left the room. She had always felt awkward butting into conversations already in progress, and it seemed that her two choices today included yet another diatribe of the South or a marital disagreement. Even more reason for finding something else to do. She decided to go to the kitchen again to see if she could help.

Luke came in from the stable after making Dolly comfortable. She would be out there for several hours, so he had rubbed her down and given her some water and hay. He came in the back door, as was his usual habit, stomped the snow from his boots, and hung his coat on the latch from the porch to the kitchen. He went back a long way with the Garfields.

"Mm." He swiped a sample of ham. "This is great, Evelyn! You aren't planning on making us wait much longer, are you?"

"Not much. Although I dare say very few of you would perish if I did."

They exchanged a grin, and Luke headed across the hall to the closed double doors of the parlor, thinking about the problem that a few days ago he hadn't known he had. Now it was growing worse. As soon as they had stepped into the Garfields' house, he had noticed how Amanda had taken one look at Anna and immediately had stiffened up and lost her smile.

Why hadn't he seen it before? Amanda was in a clean shirt and new trousers, but there was a marked difference between her and Anna, who was all girl from the tip of her freckled nose to the toes of her shiny slippers. If he had noticed just a few days sooner, Amanda could have had a dress for today, and he could have spared her this embarrassment.

If *he* had noticed. *Get that!* Tabitha Bradford had rubbed his nose in it to make him see. Giving himself a mental kick, he opened the doors and almost walked smack dab into the woman.

If ever there was someone who was "all girl," she was

it! His gaze traveled from her huge skirt to her small waist to her light brown eyes, flecked with gold and green. Had carousing with The Frog put that glow on her face? He squelched any thoughts of Etienne Rousseau.

Tabitha steadied her mug, keeping the cider from sloshing over the edge, and took a step back from the wall that was Lucas Hayes's chest.

"Yet another pretty dress," he said, but she just stood there, speechless and blushing, feeling like a dumbstruck fool. Chester MacDonald had just said almost the same thing, and she hadn't thought anything about it. So why should the words coming from Luke set her pulse fluttering?

"Thank you," she finally managed to say. "I was just on my way to the kitchen to see if I can be of some assistance, which I've been informed is unlikely. And to get a spot of cider to warm this up."

Years of manners and, she suspected, some divine assistance, gave her the strength to ask, "Would you like some?" in an entirely normal voice.

"Yes, thank you."

"Excuse me." She detoured around him and made her way to the kitchen. This was terrible. If she intended to avoid him as much as possible, she was off to a bad start. Now she would have to take him his cider. Talk to him again. Hand him the mug. Their hands might touch. The very idea made her quake, and she paused to take a deep breath and try to gain some control of herself.

What she would do, she decided, was hand him his

mug, then ask the others if they wanted a refill, too. It would cut any conversation short, as well as cover her from seeming to do anything special for Luke. Could everyone see that he made her a nervous wreck? She sincerely hoped not.

"Anything I can help you with?" she asked once she reached the kitchen.

"Oh, no, dear. We're about ready to eat."

"I'm offering refills of cider. I hope you don't mind?"

"Of course not. It's a great help. I guess I'm falling behind in my hosting."

"Oh, Mrs. Garfield!" Tabitha smiled. "How can you be expected to coddle everyone when you are in here preparing a feast fit for royalty? I assure you, everyone is doing just fine."

"Thank you, dear." She went back to slicing the bread.

With both mugs filled, Tabitha returned and gave Luke his, making sure that she didn't allow her fingers to "accidentally" touch his hand. Not that it mattered. They touched. It truly was an accident. Or his doing. Again, her breath left in a sudden, quivering rush, and she turned away quickly.

"Would anyone care for more cider?" she asked the room.

"Yes, please," Jesse Miller answered.

Tabitha set her own mug on a table and bent to collect his. "Be right back."

As she left, she heard Sarah's loud whisper. "You'd

stoop to anything, wouldn't you?"

It took only a few moments to fill the cup. Jesse murmured a tight thanks, and Sarah looked pointedly away. Tabitha was confused. Clearly Sarah Miller didn't like her. Couldn't stand her, seemed more accurate. It disturbed her, because she could think of no possible explanation.

"Don't let it bother you. She's just jealous." Luke's voice came from just behind her right shoulder, loud enough for her ears alone.

"Jealous?" she turned to ask, also speaking quietly. "Of what?"

"You."

"Me?!" Shock made her speak louder, and now everyone in the room was looking at them. In the sudden silence, she couldn't even ask why without everyone hearing.

"Excuse me." She stepped out into the hall and leaned back against the closed parlor doors. She didn't even know Sarah Miller. How could the woman be jealous? And for what reason? Luke must be wrong. After all, Sarah was the one who had a husband and a home, and would soon have a baby. How lucky! Tabitha wished it were she who was expecting a baby. Jesse seemed to be a nice enough fellow. Good provider. Not bad looking. What could the woman possibly be lacking?

"Tabitha, dear!" Evelyn Garfield interrupted her confused thoughts, shaking a spoon at the parlor door. "Would you please tell them that it's time to eat, while I round up the children?"

Tabitha took a deep breath, feeling a bit like she was stepping back into the lions' den. She opened the door.

"Are you all ready to eat? Mrs. Garfield just asked me to call you to the table."

Evelyn seated Tabitha with Chester MacDonald on her right and Jesse Miller on her left, with Sarah next to him. Directly across the table from her was Luke, with Amanda on his left.

This was just lovely. If Luke's theory was correct, then her sitting right next to Jesse could only make things worse. And Luke right across from her! Her appetite was decreasing steadily. Of course, the Garfields couldn't know the position they'd put her in.

Albert Garfield said a blessing, and then an endless stream of bowls and platters was passed around the table. Luke plopped a mound of mashed potatoes on his plate and formed a crater to hold the gravy. He sure was sick of his own cooking, but he could've enjoyed the food a lot more if he could change some of the company.

Take Sarah Miller for example. She should stop glowering at Tabitha. It wasn't Tabitha's fault that she was pretty, and it wasn't her fault that Jesse noticed. Frequently. Then, on top of that ugly situation, they had to put up with the obnoxious Chester MacDonald. He, too, had been casting hopeful glances at Tabitha. That is, between taking huge forkfuls of food. At least it kept him from talking. He was one person who really taxed Luke's cordiality.

How could a woman be so blind to the male attention she drew? Must be every man between sixteen and sixty smitten, to a greater or lesser degree. The pity was that the recipient of all that attention had eyes only for The Frog, who had to be about the most unworthy man she could choose. He was shiftless and a snob.

Or was that envy talking?

Luke's own rebellious gaze kept flicking across the table. She sure was pretty. He was as smitten as the rest. Maybe more.

Amanda tapped his arm. "Would you please cut my ham, Papa?"

"Anything for my angel." He gave one of her curls a tug and smiled at her.

Tabitha's heart warmed at the sight. If only Amanda could see. If she would stop thinking about dresses and her lack of them for long enough, she would know that she was better off than Anna. Anna was, to be sure, loved. But she didn't have a father who doted on her as much as Luke did Amanda.

"Tabitha," Evelyn addressed her. "I hear you had company. Your friend from France?"

A blanket of silence settled over the table, and all eyes focused on her. "Yes." She felt the pink crawling up her neck. "He was here for one day last week, but now he's on his way back to New Orleans."

"He came all the way for a one-day visit?" Albert asked. "That's incredible."

It was rather incredible that she was important

enough to him that he would go so far out of his way to visit her. A man like Etienne, interested in her, Tabitha Bradford. Hard to believe. A small smile curved her lips.

"Is that the nice man with the black eyes?" Amanda asked.

"Yes," Tabitha smiled at the first description she'd heard of him that wasn't negative. "He's the nice man with the black eyes."

Another moment of heavy silence engulfed the table. Tabitha chewed quietly for a moment, then, to fill the uncomfortable silence, asked Amanda what she had gotten for Christmas. The girl beamed. "A dog! Papa got me a dog! He's brown, and he's about this big." She demonstrated his size with her arms. "And his name is Sinbad!"

That led to a few minutes of talk about dogs and, with the silence broken, Evelyn asked if they were ready for dessert.

"Would you help me please, Tabitha?"

Tabitha rose to help, and Sarah also began to get up from the table.

"No, dear." Evelyn put a hand on Sarah's shoulder, gently pushing her back into her chair. "You just let that baby rest."

Tabitha made several trips to the kitchen with the remainder of the food and all the dirty plates, while Evelyn started a pot of coffee. "I asked you to help because I wanted to talk to you."

Tabitha paused in her collecting of clean plates, forks, and cups.

"Will you forgive me if I'm rather blunt?"

"Of course," she replied, not sure if that was a completely truthful answer.

"How serious are you about this fellow from New Orleans?"

Here we go again. Why is everyone so interested in my relationship with Etienne?

"I don't know," she replied, honestly. "I suppose I could become serious, but I don't believe he has a serious bone in his body."

"Good."

Tabitha said nothing. Her expression was quite enough.

"Luke Hayes has been a friend for years. He's been very lonely since his wife died. I've been praying and praying for a wife for him, and I think you would do."

Shock and insult combined to make Tabitha's mouth drop open. Evelyn chuckled and patted her hand. "Just be nice to him, and we'll see if anything comes of it." With that, she turned and began to carry the desserts into the dining room.

She would do?! What did that mean? She wasn't quite the answer to Evelyn's prayers on his behalf, but close enough that they would settle for what they could get?

Tabitha took a deep breath. She knew that the insult had not been intended—it was merely a poor choice of words. Still, she was upset. She resented interference in a most private part of her life. And all she had to do was "be nice to him"?

Her whole being rebelled at the idea. If there was anything in the world she did not want, it was another marriage of convenience.

She had had a taste of the excitement a man could cause to course through a woman, and she wanted to know more. She wanted to be loved. She did not want to be a stand-in for any other woman, living or dead, there merely to stave off loneliness. She was lonely, too, but she would never be *that* lonely.

Carrying a stack of dessert plates into the dining room, Tabitha began setting one at each place. *Be nice to him, hmm?* she thought when she came to Luke. She almost threw the plate at him before turning on her heel and stalking off to fetch the coffee and cups.

Luke was stunned. But when MacDonald sniggered, his surprise turned to embarrassment and a bit of anger.

"You must all try this plum pudding," Evelyn was saying. "Tabitha made it." She began dishing it out and passing bowls down the table.

"No, thank you," Sarah Miller said. "We would prefer the pumpkin pie."

"No," Jesse said through clenched teeth. "I would like to try the pudding. I *like* plum pudding."

Tabitha had taken about all she could take. Sarah's little dig at her by way of the pudding was the last straw. As soon as they finished dessert, she was going home! She finished her cake in record time, then stood. "Let me do those dishes." This time it was not a polite offer. She was going to do the dishes. She couldn't, she realized, set down her fork and immediately leave, but neither could she remain at the table another moment.

In the kitchen, she put water on the stove to heat and began to stack plates while she waited. Her solitude was short-lived, as both of the other women came in to help.

Tabitha rolled up her sleeves and plunged her hands into the hot water, washing plates and rinsing them before passing them to Sarah to dry. When they returned to the parlor, where the men were drinking coffee, she wasted no time.

"Thank you for your hospitality and the good food, but it will be dark soon, and I should be going."

Opportunity knocked, and Luke didn't hesitate to take advantage of it. He stood, setting his cup on an end table. "It's too cold to walk that far. Let me drive you." Perhaps he could discover what she was upset about, he figured, and what it had to do with him. And, he admitted to himself, spending the extra time with her was no hardship.

Eleven

A few minutes later, Luke brought the wagon for Tabitha and Amanda. Evelyn Garfield, slyly grinning, handed a basket full of leftovers to Luke, and, while he placed the food in the back, she nodded meaningfully at Tabitha.

No sooner had they pulled away from the house than Luke asked, "So would you like to tell me why I was playing dodge-plate?"

Tabitha couldn't help but laugh at his choice of words. "It seems kind of silly now."

"What does?"

Tabitha glanced at him, noting the dark, wavy hair, blown by the wind around the edge of his hat, and the friendly, totally unthreatening look in his eyes. She thought she could speak freely. Perhaps he would find it amusing. "Mrs. Garfield asked me to be nice to you. She's worried about you."

"Is that right?" His eyes twinkled. "Then, of course,

the next logical step is for you to get mad at me."

Tabitha laughed with him, then sighed. How could she explain that the other woman wanted to see them wed? She didn't want to get anywhere near that subject. "I wasn't angry with you so much as I was just angry," she said. "I'm afraid I only saw it as interfering, and I didn't take it too gracefully.

"Now," she went on, not giving him time to pursue the subject, "if you will kindly explain your earlier remark about Sarah Miller? After her eagerness to sample my pudding, I could almost give your ridiculous theory some credence."

He chuckled merrily, clearly enjoying that particular topic. "Sarah Miller is the jealous type. She'd be jealous of any woman who so much as looked at Jesse. She's especially jealous of you because you're pretty."

Tabitha felt a glow inside at his words.

"You added enough fuel to the fire today! Poor Jesse won't ever hear the end of it."

"What did I do that could possibly be misconstrued?"

"I count three sins. One: You brought him a mug of cider."

"And her. And you."

"Two: You sat by him."

"My choice entirely."

"And three: You're also a good cook, if your pudding is any indicator."

"Thank you," she murmured. There it was again, that pleasurable confusion, knowing he approved of her in some way. After a confused moment of staring at him stupidly, she turned to Amanda. "Did you like Anna's doll?" Her ideas for conversation with Luke had evaporated.

Amanda looked utterly dejected. "Even her doll has a pretty dress."

Tabitha's and Luke's eyes met over the child's head. She could tell he felt bad that his oversight had caused Amanda any pain. He more than made up in love for any mistakes he made, and he didn't deserve any mental anguish over this.

"I'm almost finished with your underthings," Tabitha said, "and I believe I can get at least one of the dresses finished before school resumes. How would that be?"

"That would be wonderful!"

"It must be difficult," Tabitha went on, feeling a little queasy inside at what she planned to say, "for your father to raise you by himself." She knew he would remember that as his own explanation. His face turned slightly towards her, with one eyebrow raised.

She flashed a conspiratorial smile and winked at him, unaware that she was accelerating the rhythm of his heart. "I'll bet he doesn't know much about dresses and, um, 'foo-foo' things."

Now he was close to laughter.

She had heard several compliments from him, so why was it so difficult for her to return one? *Come on, Tabitha, just say it!* "Other than that, I think he's doing a wonderful job, don't you?"

Gray eyes darted to her, while Amanda threw her

arms around Luke's neck. They had just pulled up to the boardinghouse.

"Yes! My papa is the most wonderful papa ever!"

Jumping down from the wagon, Tabitha fetched her pan from the back and thanked Luke for the ride.

"Tabitha!" he called as she walked away. She turned.

"Are you going to?"

"Going to what?"

"Be nice to me!"

"Why, Mr. Hayes!" Her teasing grin dimpled her cheek. "I try to be nice to everyone!"

The bell on the store door tinkled, and Tabitha looked up to see, to her astonishment, a very cold and frightened Martha Dobbins. "Martha!" she cried, "what on earth are you doing here?"

"Oh, Mrs. Bradford! You must 'elp me! In all of America, you're the only person I know!"

"Of course, I'll do what I can," she said as she closed the door behind the girl. The cold, gusty wind was blowing snow into the store.

"First let's get you warm, then you can tell me all about it." She pulled a chair closer to the potbellied stove for Martha to sit in, and put a kettle of fresh water on for tea. Mr. Garfield kept both tea and coffee handy, so that when it was cold and there were no customers, he and Tabitha could enjoy a cup.

"Mr. Garfield," she said, as he came out from the back part of the store, "this is Martha Dobbins. She was with me on the ship from England. Martha, this is Mr. Garfield, my employer and friend."

The two said their hellos, Martha through chattering teeth.

"How is your mother?" Tabitha asked. "Is she hurt or ill?"

"She's fine, ma'am."

"And your sister?"

"She's fine, too, ma'am. Getting married in the spring. Mum says she's too young, but 'e's a fine chap. Only twenty and already owns 'is own 'otel. Right down close to the lake and the depot, so 'e does a good business. Margaret's a lucky girl."

Martha accepted the tea gratefully and wrapped her cold fingers around the hot cup before taking a sip. Her teeth gradually stopped chattering, and she was able to speak normally.

"How did you find me, Martha?"

"I knew you were in Waukegan, so when I got off the train, I asked. The first person I asked knew who you were and directed me here."

"Martha," Tabitha began, "if your mother and sister are well, then what is the problem? What is it that you need me to help you with?"

Martha hesitated uncomfortably, her gaze shifting uneasily to Mr. Garfield.

"That's all right." She patted the girl's hand.

Whatever the problem was, it would wait until they could speak privately. "I'll be off work in an hour, and we can talk about it then."

Albert was not insensitive to the situation. "Not too busy today," he put in. "Why don't you run along, now, Tabitha? I'm sure you've arrangements to make."

Oh heavens! That was something she hadn't thought of—Martha would need lodging and meals, and she wasn't sure there was room at the boardinghouse, or how to pay for it if there was.

Well, they would just trust the Lord. He would work it all out.

"Thank you, Mr. Garfield!" She collected her things and led Martha back out into the blowing snow.

An hour later, they were seated in their room with the pot of coffee and several slices of fresh bread and butter Mrs. Grimes had sent up. Supper was still nearly an hour away, so they had some time to talk.

Mrs. Grimes had agreed to let Tabitha share her room for a small extra fee, and to let Martha wash dishes and do odd jobs in the kitchen to pay for her meals.

That was a load off of Tabitha's mind, and a solution for which she was grateful. Martha, however, wasn't satisfied. "Surely," she said, "there must be something I can do to pay for my board, Mrs. Bradford. I know it's not much, but still it is a drain on you. I don't want to cost you a farthing."

The idea came to Tabitha quite suddenly. "Do you know how to sew?" she asked.

"Not well," was Martha's downcast reply. "I never took enough of an interest to learn cutting or fitting or anything fancy. Straight seams are about all I can manage."

"Oh, but that's perfect!" Tabitha clasped her hands together as her idea took root and grew. "I just put a card in the store to advertise to sew for people. You could help me in the evenings! The work will go twice as fast! You see, I hate doing long, straight seams. They're frightfully boring."

"Oh, yes!" Martha was catching on to the possibilities, and was eager to earn her own way. And Tabitha was hoping that the sewing shop would be much nearer in her future than she had previously dared to hope. Martha's appearance was beginning to seem a blessing.

"So now," she reminded her. "To what great tragedy do I owe the arrival of my new sewing partner?"

Martha dropped on the edge of the bed with an unladylike plop. "It's sorta embarrassing. Everything is working out so well. But I didn't know where else to go or what to do. And," she went on ruefully, "Mum would 'ave an attack of the palpitations if she knew I'd come to you."

"Why?" Tabitha asked. She had a sinking feeling. Something had plagued her in the back of her mind for a long time, about Mrs. Dobbins' attitude towards her. She sensed that she was about to discover why, and she suspected that she wouldn't like it.

"She thought of you almost as another daughter, I think. Somewot responsible for you. Till the night the *Lady* sunk."

"What about that night?" Tabitha frowned.

"When Mr. Rousseau followed you ashore. Didn't neither one of you come back. Not that I blame you none. 'E's an 'andsome one." She glanced at Tabitha with a thoughtful expression. "I don't suppose Mum ever knew that sort of temptation, so she wouldn't be understanding any who'd fell to it."

The implication sank in, and Tabitha sprang to her feet while the color left her face. "What?!" She began to pace, angry at being too swiftly judged and found lacking. And what about Etienne? "That can't be!" she began, remembering his words about returning to the ship to protect her reputation, to avoid this very possibility! "He said he—"

"Then it's not true?" Martha interrupted.

"Of *course* it's not true!" Tabitha glared at the girl. "I don't know where he went, but he did not stay with me!" Tabitha took a deep, calming breath. The people at the Exchange Hotel knew that. So Martha's mother and sister were the only ones who thought . . . oh, it was just too horrible! Why had Etienne not returned to the ship as he said he would?

Tabitha forced herself to calm down. It could have been worse, and there wasn't anything she could do about it. And, she realized, they had once again gotten sidetracked, and she still didn't know why Martha was here. "Enough of that," she said. "Tell me why you came to me."

"Jeremy Briggs," Martha said with a furious blush. "A

stable boy at the livery next door to Uncle Drury's 'ouse. 'E's right 'andsome, too." Unshed tears made her eyes bright. "I guess I behaved rather common. 'Avin' been married, you know what it's like to 'ave your insides do flippety-flops at the mere sight of a man, and 'ave your common sense take wings and leave you."

Tabitha was familiar with the feeling, though not to the extent of taking leave of her senses, and not in connection with her late husband. She blushed herself, and hoped that Martha didn't notice.

"I went out to the stable, pretending to just be takin' 'im an 'ot drink on a cold day, but truth was I wanted to see 'im. . . . I may as well tell you the 'ole story. I need to tell someone." She sighed, then said with a rush, "I let him kiss me! It weren't no peck on the check, neither, and it was wonderful! That's wot's so terrible!"

"Luckily, the owner of the stable came in, and Jeremy quickly stepped away from me, and thanked me for the coffee, all normal-like, and nobody ever knew." Martha giggled guiltily. "Course by then there was only about 'alf the cup wot hadn't been spilled." Then she grew serious again. "But after that, he kept trying to find me alone, or get me to go off with him somew'ere. Like I was a trollop!" Even now, she was clearly indignant.

"Mum thought 'e was a jolly good fellow and said I should marry 'im."

"Why didn't you?"

"You don't do the askin', mum. An' 'e wasn't the type to ask me. Ever. 'E's an 'andsome, fun-lovin', bad sort.

Not the marryin' and settlin' down sort."

"I see." Tabitha was embarrassed once again. It seemed this girl knew a great deal more of life and love than she. Uncomfortable with her inadequate, ignorant feeling, she changed the subject.

"We're going to be spending a great deal of time together, and I'm only a few years older than you are, so why don't you call me Tabitha instead of 'ma'am' all the time. You make me feel like an old lady."

"Certainly, Tabither. So anyway, I 'ad to get away." Martha turned the conversation back to its previous course as if she had never been interrupted. "I know myself, and I knew that eventually I would give in to 'im if I stayed around there."

There wasn't anything Tabitha could say to that. She supposed that under the circumstances, Martha had been right to run away. "Let's go eat our supper," she said instead. "Then later we can get started on our business venture. I know a little girl who is very eager to get a new dress."

The next day presented a problem Tabitha hadn't foreseen. Amanda was supposed to stop by to check on her clothes, but Tabitha had made no arrangements for fittings. The child couldn't very well try on her things in the store, and Tabitha couldn't leave work to take her to the boardinghouse. Her room there would never work anyway, should she ever have a male customer. She needed her own shop.

"How are the dresses coming?" Luke asked, stepping into the store, grinning at Tabitha and sending her heart into "flippety-flops." "I've got a little butterfly here who is eager to spread her wings."

Tabitha smoothed the sides of her yellow dress, wishing for another. She didn't like wearing the boring gray dress, and she was tired of always wearing the same thing.

"Just fine, Mr. Hayes!" She was pleased with the progress, and happy for Amanda that her wait wouldn't be so long. A wide, happy smile showed even, white teeth and her dimple. "I've acquired a sewing partner!" She brought out a sack with Amanda's partially finished order and laid the "foo-foo" things out on the counter, trying not to show her embarrassment. Raised in the England of Victoria, where one didn't even say "leg" of chicken, but instead "dark meat," it was difficult for her to display pantaloons and camisoles in front of Lucas Hayes. At the same time, she realized that while modesty was a virtue, it could go too far. She didn't want to pass her notions on to Amanda, who seemed totally oblivious to the situation.

"I wish there was somewhere you could try them on," she said to Amanda, "but I'm sure they'll fit. You can take them today, though they won't do you any good until you get a dress to go with them. If there's a problem with the fit, let me know."

Then she unfolded the unfinished dress. "We've got a good start on the first dress." The skirt was gathered and sewn onto the bodice. The side seams were closed, and the collar was finished. It still needed buttons, sleeves, and a hem.

"It's lovely, Papa!" Amanda was bouncing with excitement. She turned sparkling eyes to Tabitha. "How much longer?"

"A day or two. In a week, we should have the other done also."

The bell rang again. "Who's the sew-er?" a bearded old man bellowed.

"If you'll excuse me?" Tabitha nodded to Luke and made her way to the man.

His words followed her. "Take your time. I need a few minutes to remember what else it was we needed to buy."

"But Papa! You said we weren't going to buy anything today!"

"I thought of a few things," he said tersely, not wanting to be questioned by his daughter, unsure of how he could explain something he didn't understand himself. Or how she would react if he could explain.

Tabitha rejoined them as soon as possible, happy with her new order for five flannel shirts. "Did you think of what it was you need?"

"Ten pounds of flour and a pound of coffee."

Amanda stared, wide-eyed. They had enough coffee, and lots of flour! Why was he buying more? She soon forgot his strange behavior, though, when he ordered her two hair ribbons—one pink and one white, to go with her new dresses.

"Will there be anything else?" Tabitha asked, pleased with his interest in his daughter's problem.

"Not today, thanks."

"Then I'll see you in a week for the dresses?"

"Papa," Amanda whined, gazing up at him with her best pleading look. "She said a day or two for the first one. Do we have to wait a whole week?"

Luke looked to Tabitha. There was something in his eyes she couldn't read. Then he said, "We'll see, Angel."

Mr. Garfield walked behind the counter where Tabitha stood as Luke and Amanda left the store. She could see him lift the girl onto the back of the giant horse, then swing up onto its back behind her before turning the beast into the street.

"I believe I've seen Hayes in here more in the past two months than I have in a year." Albert gave Tabitha a look of total innocence. "Wonder what the attraction could be." He wandered off about his business, leaving her speechless, but with plenty of food for thought.

Could it be? No. That was absurd. Luke really didn't like her much. Or did he? There were times, she recalled, when they had been quite comfortable to-gether, like during the wagon ride home from Garfields' on Christmas. But there were also times when he defi-nitely seemed to dislike her, and those times seemed more frequent. If he was in the store more, it was just because of Amanda. Most likely, Mr. Garfield was in on his wife's conspiracy to get lonely old Luke married off.

That evening while they sewed, Tabitha told Martha

about David. It felt good to tell someone how she and her sister-in-law didn't get on well, and how it made her feel guilty. They talked about where the boy could be, and wondered aloud if he was, indeed, on his way to Illinois.

Martha's views reassured her. She insisted that if Tabitha had been as nice to the woman as possible, she had no reason to feel guilty that it hadn't developed into a close relationship. True, Tabitha had never done anything to antagonize Leah, but still, she'd had many less than pleasant thoughts about her. But how could you avoid unwanted thoughts?

They did not discuss Samuel. Tabitha thought Martha might be avoiding the subject to keep her from missing him and growing sad, but she didn't pursue it. Her odd relationship with her husband was something she didn't think she would ever be able to discuss with anyone. Few understood how she could be content, if not completely happy, with a man thirty-five years her senior. She hated the looks, the ones that made her feel like a freak in the circus. She could see people speculating, wondering about the more personal aspects of the marriage, though none were rude enough to ask. Still, she did not like to be the object of such speculation, and avoided the subject whenever possible.

Later, when the town was quiet and only moonlight came through the window, they were still awake, discussing the need for a shop.

"Why couldn't we?" Martha asked. If she could continue to work at the boardinghouse for wages instead of meals, and if Tabitha could cut down on the number of days she worked at the store, they could still support themselves while building their business. If they could answer those questions, then the next step would be finding a small house to rent.

Martha was like a breath of fresh air. She didn't easily say "It can't be done." Tabitha knew it would've been a long time before she would have been brave enough or secure enough on her own to try such a venture. She was glad that Martha had shown up.

Tabitha was excited at the prospect of starting a real sewing shop, yet anxious about it. There were too many ifs. The world was a scary place, and she was not a particularly brave or daring soul. She'd survived in it so far because she'd had to, and she knew Who was watching out for her and guiding her steps. Still, this was a big step, and she was glad she had someone to go through it with. Someone to encourage her, and that she could encourage in turn.

Their friendship was deepening, for which Tabitha thanked God profusely. Without the presence of Mrs. Dobbins, they both felt free to be themselves. After only a couple of days, she felt closer to Martha than she had after the entire voyage from England. Finally, she had the friend she had prayed for. Loneliness was still there, in the still hours of the night, but now it was pushed to the back of her mind, tormenting her less frequently.

It would be even better, she thought, to be able to go through the trials and daily routines of life with a husband. Some of the advantages of having a husband, she knew. Samuel had been someone to talk to, a shoulder to cry on when she needed one. They had shared common goals. These advantages she knew. The one she did not know, but wanted to, was not affection, but love.

Martha slept peacefully, but Tabitha's mind continued, robbing her of the rest she needed. Briefly, she marveled that Sarah Miller could be jealous of her. That is, if such a ridiculous idea could be true.

Etienne came to mind. Dashing, handsome, rich. With him, she wouldn't have to sew or worry about the rent. He was good for her, and fun.

Then she thought of Luke. He too was handsome. And hardworking, and loving. At least where Amanda was concerned.

She was being an utter fool. Neither of the two men had any interest in her! Not seriously. And even if they both did, neither would do her any good, because both were at odds with God. One had some unexplained anger towards Him, and the other thought of Him more as some sort of benevolent fairy tale than as the Creator of heaven and earth. That was something she couldn't and wouldn't accept.

The Word said not to be unequally yoked with an unbeliever. God did not tell His people "do" or "do not" to be the ultimate spoiler of fun. His words were wise beyond anything she could ever hope to understand in this life, and she knew that a marriage between a Christian and a non-Christian would be incredibly foolish. They would argue about money and children at every turn, each having a completely different viewpoint and set of priorities from the other. So, to keep a marriage stable, and for the benefit of the children, God had commanded believers not to be "unequally yoked." Two could not become one when they were essentially different beings. She would not allow these foolish romantic fantasies to grow, and she firmly pushed the thoughts from her mind. Then she said a little prayer for the strength to keep them out.

e did it!" Martha squealed, crushing Tabitha in a hug. "I love it!" She waltzed around the bare room. "We can use this front room for sewing, and put a screen in that corner to use as a changing room! And a big table over here to cut on! Oh, Tabitha, isn't it perfect? I knew we could do it!"

Tabitha was still rather dazed. Last night they'd been sitting in their room at the boarding house, sewing and talking. Now, not twenty-four hours later, they were here in what would soon be their sewing shop.

Martha had made working arrangements with Mrs. Grimes before breakfast. Then it had been Tabitha's turn to approach Mr. Garfield. It was not an easy task. He'd done so much for her that she was loathe to ask him for anything else. She had stammered through her request, then held her breath, half expecting to be refused or even fired. She had expected at least an angry outburst because she was letting him down, and she knew it would not be easy for him to train a new assistant.

Instead he grinned and replied that her request was an answer to prayer. It was time, he said, to begin training Robert to help in the store. He hadn't wanted to cut her hours, because he knew the financial strain she was under. They decided that she would work at the store Monday through Wednesday, then have Thursday through Saturday for sewing jobs.

In the early afternoon, Martha had come running into the store. A man had come by the boardinghouse to see if any of the boarders would be interested in renting a house at the edge of town. Not wanting to miss the opportunity, she had told him yes.

So here they were.

Tabitha supposed she should be angry with Martha for making such a decision without consulting her, but she had to admit it was a cute little house. Who could remain angry with Martha, anyway? Now, in her joy, her plain features were beautiful. She was so full of the love of life.

Tabitha walked into the other, smaller room at the back of the building. The first had been empty, but sunny, due to three large glass windows. This room had two smaller windows and the back door. There was a wood stove, above which were shelves.

The weight of what they had done rolled over her like a great wave. There was so much to do! The house was clean, but it needed furniture and curtains and Martha's screen, and more shelves or cupboards, and pots and pans, and food. The list went on and on. *Dear God, where will we get so many things?*

"Tabitha," Martha said, "what's the matter? Aren't you happy?"

"Aren't you hungry?" Tabitha countered. "We make enough money to pay the rent and buy food. Not much food. Anything else we need, even a candle, will have to come from sewing. Look around. We don't even have a pot to cook in! I don't mean to sound cross, but it's all a bit overwhelming."

Martha was crestfallen. She looked around with new eyes.

"I suppose," she said at last, "that it will be rough at first, but we'll get more orders, and things will gradually get more comfortable."

"Martha, you're wonderful!" Tabitha hugged her, grateful again for the girl's unquenchable spirit. "Mr. Jeremy Briggs doesn't know what he let slip away."

Tabitha had frequently heard her in the night, awake and restless, and she suspected it was because her feelings for Jeremy went deeper than she let on. She also knew that she didn't like to discuss him, so she quickly brought up something else.

"Actually, it's not quite as horrible as it seems. I was saving to start this shop, you know. It's a meager amount, but at least we won't starve or freeze in the next week or two, before the sewing starts to pay."

It wasn't much later when someone knocked on their door for the first time. It was Patricia, bearing a gift from

Mrs. Grimes, consisting of two Cornish style meat pasties, with a jar of canned peas from her garden and a thick wedge of apple pie. Tabitha knew that Mrs. Grimes had a soft spot for women who had to make it on their own, and told Patricia to be sure to thank her for her kindness.

"I'm sorry I don't have anything to offer you for a refreshment," Tabitha apologized while Patricia stood just inside the door casting her eyes about the room. "We're not settled yet, and we don't have much here."

"Oh, that's quite understandable." Patricia gave a tiny smile, as if she was unfamiliar with the muscles of her face.

Tabitha smiled widely in return. Perhaps the woman was opening up a bit at last. "Would you like to see the other room?" she invited. "There's only the two. It's a small place, but I believe it will suit our needs."

Uncertainly, Patricia followed her across the front room and into the kitchen, where Tabitha and Martha explained what they planned to do with the place. After that, Patricia stood for a long moment, unsure of what to say, then said she should be getting back. Tabitha invited her to come again for tea when they were more settled.

No sooner had the woman left than there was another knock on the front door. Martha lifted the roll-down blind to peek out, and saw a young man leaning unsteadily against the doorjamb. Calling Tabitha to come, she opened the door.

"Is my Aunt Tabitha here?" the man asked, his voice quavering.

Tabitha, entering the room from the back, recognized David at once and was shocked by his condition. Momentarily her hands went to cover her gasp before she collected her wits and drew the boy in. "David! What is the matter? Are you ill? What are you doing here?"

"I don't feel so good."

"Martha," she instructed, "go fetch a doctor." Martha left at a run, and Tabitha lowered David to the floor where he could sit, propped against the wall. What on earth was she to do? There wasn't even a bed to put him in. And she would have to let Leah know immediately that he was here.

All she could do while they waited was get him a drink of water and a damp cloth to wipe his brow, which felt very warm to her. Worried, she began to pray.

Martha soon arrived, though it seemed an age, with Dr. Price in tow. After a brief look at the boy, the doctor decided that he needed to take him back to his office where he could keep a closer watch on him.

Tabitha and Martha both helped get David to the doctor's office, then Tabitha gave Martha money and sent her off to send a telegram to Leah. A transatlantic cable would not come cheap, she was sure, but it had to be done.

It took an eternity for Dr. Price to give David a more thorough examination. While she waited, Tabitha looked idly around the room, unable to concentrate.

There were two shelves against the white walls. One was loaded with bottles and jars, the other with books. In the back was a white curtain in the door to the next room. The front door faced the street, and in the glass window next to it, a sign said "Dr. Price." The letters were backwards from where she sat, inside looking out.

Finally Martha returned and handed her the receipt for the cable: "DAVID ARRIVED STOP ILL STOP WILL WIRE AGAIN STOP TABITHA." Another wire, another expense. Well, it would have to be done.

Dr. Price came back into the front of his office. His face clearly said that the news was not good. "The boy has pneumonia," the doctor announced.

David had caught cold somewhere between England and Illinois. He had been chilled, traveling during the winter, and hadn't had enough food or blankets. Then he had pushed himself to continue, instead of resting and seeking medical help when he reached New York.

Tabitha sat with him for a little while. Dr. Price wouldn't allow a long visit. Then he sent them home, saying there was nothing they could accomplish by remaining in his office. Tabitha headed home, after assuring David that she would be back in the morning, and wondering if he had even heard her.

Tabitha and Martha slept on the floor that night, using their cloaks and body heat to keep warm . . . though not warm enough to be comfortable. Tabitha dozed now and then, but didn't sleep well. Her dreams were full of David.

In the morning, Martha went to work at the board-inghouse, and Tabitha went to check on her nephew. He was about the same, feverish and pale, not breathing right. From there, she did some shopping and tried to drum up some sewing business. She returned to their new home a little later with blankets, candles, a pot for cooking and one for washing, and paint to make a sign in the front window. A man was to deliver coal for the stove later.

Mr. Garfield had ordered himself a thick wool coat, and a nightgown for Anna, insisting that it wasn't char-ity. He would've had to get them somewhere, so it might as well be from her. Evelyn, he claimed, hated to sew.

First Tabitha painted the sign, then she arranged the blankets on the floor in the back room where someday there would be a bed. She had to walk back to the store then for food shopping. She hadn't been able to carry everything in one trip.

In the afternoon, with a fire going in the stove to warm the house, she swept the floor clean with a rag, then set to work sewing, sitting on the floor in a most unladylike position. Amanda would be expecting her dresses, and might stop by tomorrow. It would be a pleasant surprise for her if both of the dresses were ready by then! But she couldn't just sit there and sew, so she returned to Dr. Price's office. David had taken a turn for the worse.

He was having more trouble breathing and lay thrashing on the bed. Dr. Price didn't look hopeful.

Tabitha stayed, praying. Within a few hours, the boy was dead.

Dr. Price tried to be helpful, assuring her that he was in no hurry for payment and that the illness wasn't highly contagious. Tabitha cared little if she caught the disease. She cared that her nephew was dead, and she cared that she would have to notify his mother. In a state of shock that didn't allow a show of emotion, she made her way to the telegraph office and sent the message, then went home to cry herself to sleep.

Thirteen

A knock sounded at the door. Tabitha opened it to find Luke standing on her doorstep. "I was wondering if I had the right place," he said.

It took a moment for her to find her manners and invite him in. She'd half expected him to come by today, but he was earlier than he'd ever come to the store, and Amanda wasn't with him. It was the first time she had ever been alone with him, but her mind was elsewhere and to worry about propriety never occurred to her.

"Thought I'd surprise Mandy and have her dress when I pick her up from school. Is it ready?"

"Yes. Actually, both of them are." She said the right things, but she was only going through the motions. She felt horrible—sad and guilty about David's death—and she probably looked horrible, too, pale and red-eyed.

"Wonderful!" Luke looked around the room, and Tabitha felt her cheeks warm.

"We, Martha Dobbins and I," she explained, "just

moved in here yesterday. I'm afraid it will take a long time and a lot of sewing before we can fill it with furniture and all the other things it needs to feel like a home."

He considered for a minute. "Tabitha?"

She looked up, pleased with the ease with which he used her Christian name. She'd thought of him as "Luke" rather than "Mr. Hayes" for quite some time, but hadn't formed a comfortable way to approach the topic of names. She supposed Americans were less formal about such things.

"Is it okay if I call you Tabitha? It seems a bit senseless to carry on with this Mr. and Mrs. nonsense when Evelyn is trying her hardest to get us married."

Tabitha wanted to laugh at his attempt to cheer her up, but she couldn't.

"That's fine," she replied lifelessly. "I prefer Tabitha."

"And I prefer Luke. Never did get used to 'Mr. Hayes.' Always seems they're talking to my father. Course, he's back in Pennsylvania." None of his light banter was working. Something was seriously wrong. "Tabitha, what happened?"

"My nephew," she started to explain, but couldn't. Luke's kindness brought the tears back, and before she knew it, she was in his arms, sobbing, unable to speak. He stood patiently, holding her, letting her cry. When the worst had passed, she stepped back and blew her nose on her handkerchief. "I'm sorry," she apologized.

"No need to be."

"My nephew, David, was thrilled by my adventure in

coming to America. Apparently he followed me as soon as he learned where I had landed." She paced nervously as she told the story. "Only he picked up pneumonia on his way. He died yesterday, down at Dr. Price's office."

"What about his family? Do they know yet?"

"He only had his mother. And she only had him. I had to send her a cable with the news. He's dead, and it's my fault."

"How could it be your fault?"

Her gaze met his, wanting to believe in her innocence, but unable to accept it. "If I hadn't come to America, he wouldn't have followed me, and he would still be alive."

"How could you know he would follow? And how could you know he would get sick if he did? No, Tabitha, it's not your fault at all. You didn't do anything you should feel guilty about."

"But he's all she had!"

"Sometimes life works that way. It doesn't make it your fault."

Feeling a little better, she had more room in her mind to be embarrassed about her tears. "I suppose you're right. And I'm very sorry about crying on you like that. Your shirt is a mess."

Holding her while she cried had changed the focus of his thoughts of her. He might be lonely and need someone, but it felt good to be needed, too. It was a feeling he had long forgotten. He looked again around the empty little house, and used it to get her to think about something besides her nephew.

"What would you think," he said, "if we made a little bargain? If you like, I could pay for Mandy's clothes by making you some furniture. Come to think of it, I could use a couple of work shirts, too."

"That would be marvelous!" Tabitha beamed.

Luke returned her smile. "What do you need the most?"

Tabitha flushed scarlet and turned away from his gaze, but she didn't let it sway her from telling him that the piece of furniture she wanted most was a bed. The floor was frightfully hard and uncomfortable.

"What else?" he asked.

"More? I think if you made us more than that, you would be getting a poor deal."

"I don't expect some simple furniture takes a whole lot more work than the sewing you're doing for me. Unless you want fancy stuff?"

"No, no. Plain and simple is just fine! It will be so nice to sleep in a bed after this hard floor!"

"So what else?"

"If you're sure, then I guess a kitchen table would be next on my wish list."

"A bed and a table in exchange for two shirts, two dresses, and a passel of little girl underthings. When do you expect to finish the shirts?"

Tabitha frowned. "Mr. Brown and Mr. Garfield should get their things first. And now there will be funeral arrangements to make. I hope it won't inconvenience you? I don't expect there will be much of a delay. I'll want to be working a lot to keep me from thinking so much."

"No. Give me more time to work on the furniture. Now, I better get over to the schoolhouse and get Mandy, or she'll be halfway home."

"Let me get you her things, and oh, I almost forgot, I need to take your measurements for your shirts." She tried hard to sound businesslike. Not for anything did she want him to know the turmoil the thought of performing the task brought her.

Luke stood obediently while she used her tape to measure his chest, neck, and sleeve length, and wrote the numbers in a notebook. "There. Now let me get Amanda's dresses for you." Tabitha turned quickly away to wrap the girl's clothes in paper and tie the bundle together. While taking his measurements, she'd studiously avoided letting her eyes wander to his face, but she'd caught a definite twinkle when she turned from him. Was he laughing at her? Was her distress that obvious?

As he was leaving, he turned to say, "Tabitha, I really am glad I was here when you needed me."

Her lashes lowered to conceal her feelings.

"Maybe someday you can return the favor, and I'll cry on you."

That made her smile, albeit weakly. He had removed any remaining embarrassment, and for that, she was grateful.

The next day was Saturday, and Tabitha sewed until her fingers and back ached and her eyes refused to focus on her stitches. Martha helped for a few hours each evening when she got home, and they had gotten a lot done, but there was still a great deal of work to do.

The funeral was on Monday. It was so different from Samuel's. The church service was much less formal, and none of David's friends were present. Samuel's funeral had been crowded with friends and business associates. Here, there was no one other than herself who even knew David. The few who stood around the grave in the cold wind were friends of hers. The cemetery was small. Just a few graves. Poor child, lying in a frozen grave far from home. Tabitha couldn't help weeping.

On Tuesday, Tabitha got a new order. If business continued at this rate, she could afford another dress soon. She was lucky, she knew, that she had as many as she did, but even when she was married to Samuel and her dresses had been simple, she had at least had several of them. This wearing the same thing almost every day seemed a greater hardship to her than sitting on the floor to do everything.

It was the following Saturday afternoon when a wagon stopped in front of the shop. Tabitha looked out the big front window and saw Luke and Amanda—and a bed. There were also a couple of men from town, recruited to help move the bed from the wagon to the house.

The three men quickly had the bed placed against the wall Tabitha designated in the back room. The other two took their leave with a friendly good-bye to Luke and a respectful nod to her.

Tabitha ran her hand over the bed frame. It had a plain, squared post at each corner, a wide board between the two posts at the head, and a narrower one at the foot. It was all sanded satin smooth and varnished to a gloss. Ropes stretched from side to side to support the straw tick. She examined the stitches, which were uneven but sturdy, and she could tell by Amanda's proud expression that they were her handiwork.

"It's beautiful!" she said. "Thank you so much! I'm sure this is worth much more than Amanda's dresses." She turned to the girl. "And you are beautiful, too. Quite a young lady." Indeed, she had undergone an astonishing transformation. Her curls were tied at her neck with a pink ribbon, and she wore the blue-and-pink calico that looked like Tabitha's own dress. She even had girl's shoes and stockings.

"Yes, she is," Luke agreed, giving proud approval of his pretty daughter. "How are the shirts coming?" he asked.

"They're finished." The only other remaining order, for kitchen curtains for a house on Julian Street, was nearly finished, too. Then what would she do? Tabitha pushed the thought from her mind. The Lord would provide.

Two weeks passed. It was now the middle of February, and the days were getting longer, although it was hard to tell lately. It had been cloudy so frequently. Tabitha longed to see the sun. Winter in England had never been like this! Dreary for days or weeks, yes, but never so much snow or so bitterly cold! Truth was, she was homesick.

She put down her quilting square and walked to the window. They'd had a few jobs, but not the rush they had had at the beginning. She had acquired a lot of scrap material already, and had been using her spare time to work on a quilt to cover their beautiful bed.

She would be grateful to Luke forever for that bed. He'd never come back about the table. In fact, she hadn't seen him at all. He had clearly either forgotten or figured they were square. Either way, Tabitha did not feel shortchanged, although the idea that he may have simply forgotten was depressing. Or perhaps her behavior at their last meeting had made him more uncomfortable than he had let on.

She should be glad she hadn't seen him. No matter her prayers, no matter her good intentions, she still was affected by his presence in a way that she knew was not appropriate. But she also knew that her prayer for the strength to be pure in her heart and thoughts as well as her actions would be answered. There would come a time when she either ceased to think of Luke and Etienne in any romantic way, or the circumstances would change, so that it was no longer out of her Father's will. For she had found several scriptures about the old saints and their pleas to God for the same thing. Like David, in Psalm 19: "Let the words of my mouth, and the meditation of my heart be acceptable in thy sight, O Lord." Yet David was the apple of God's eye, even with his imperfections. Therefore, while she knew her thoughts were frequently less than God's best, she also felt less guilty about it. That would come.

Walking the floor with a sigh, she thought about Luke. It should not bother her in the least that he had not come back. She should be relieved and happy. But knowing that in her mind didn't go very far toward removing the heavy lump of disappointment in her heart.

Tabitha sat again, on the edge of the bed, and picked up her sewing. Why did she feel such dissatisfaction with her life? She had come to accept David's death, and the pain was lessening. She had the friends she had prayed for, the main one being Martha. She had the shop she had prayed for. She was in America. She had her own life. She was independent and wasn't accountable to anyone but God. She had everything she had ever dreamed of.

Except a husband.

Used to being honest with herself, Tabitha had to admit that that was exactly what was wrong. She was twenty-five, and while no one would call her an "old maid," that was really what she was. She knew she wasn't one of those the Bible talked about who could be happy to remain unmarried and devoted wholly to God.

And the bigger problem was that somewhere along the line she had begun to wish for and dream about Lucas Hayes. What she really wanted, deep in her heart, was to see Luke sometime when "Five pounds of beans" or "Are the dresses finished?" were not part of the conversation. But what could she do about it, beyond pray for strength? Her whole life was now wrapped up in this town, and she couldn't just run away, as Martha had done when she'd had a similar problem. And she couldn't avoid him. Not in such a small town. She was bound to run into him in Mr. Garfield's store, if nowhere else.

But wait. Maybe she was praying for the wrong thing. She should pray that God would bring a man into her life whom it was all right to let herself love. Then her thoughts would naturally fall into the proper order.

Oh, why couldn't she just be content with her life and wait patiently on the Lord? Disgusted, she tossed down the quilt square once again, walked to the window, and leaned her forehead against the cool glass.

Snow lay in heavy drifts and weighed down the tree boughs. The street was packed down to a sheet of ice, and there were narrow paths on either side, snow compacted to a slippery sheen by many passing feet.

"This is nothing," the old-timers claimed. "Should have been here in '43!" That, she knew by now, had been a particularly hard winter. She'd heard more times than she cared to recall how much wildlife had perished, how many fish had frozen in the lakes.

Would spring never come? How she longed to see a flower or a leaf! Even a little blue sky would be a relief, and she wouldn't feel so trapped and desperate. Why had she ever come here?

She was wallowing in self-pity. England hadn't been so wonderful, either. At least here, when the sun did shine, she could see the blue sky, and not the gray shroud that hung over London. Here she had friends. She would be even lonelier, most likely, if she had stayed. She was glad, she decided, that she had come to America.

Movement caught her eye, and she looked out to see a wagon slowly making its way up the icy street. As it drew closer, she could see that the driver was bundled against the cold, and a canvas tarp covered the contents. Her pulse quickened as the wagon came to a stop in front of her shop.

Her depression vanished, and she ran toward the door, but caught herself before she threw it open. Luke would think she had missed him . . . was delighted to see him . . . if she came running out the door looking as excited as Amanda had been about the dresses.

Was she? How far did her feelings go? And if she had feelings for Lucas Hayes, if she did indeed love him, why? Why had her heart chosen someone who was still in love with a memory, and who definitely was not in love with Jesus?

The seriousness of her questions made her noticeably thoughtful when she swung wide the door. "Hello, Luke," she said, feeling falsely calm and unnatural, but knowing it was more fitting than greeting him with the bubbling joy she actually felt.

"Luke!" he mocked her quietness. "How are you, and how is Amanda?"

"I'm sorry," she said, taking his point. "I didn't mean to be rude. I was just thinking."

"About?" he inquired, closing the door behind him.

"People. People who die and leave others behind." As Rachel had left him. She was purposely probing for a reaction.

Luke sobered. So that was it. That was what made her seem so withdrawn and—he searched for a word—tight. Her movements, her expression, and her thoughts all seemed to be tightly controlled. And that was why. She was grieving, remembering her husband, missing him. The realization brought with it a fierce streak of jealousy. He had had the impression that she didn't miss the man overmuch, but it appeared he was mistaken.

"I'm sorry if I've caught you at a bad time," he murmured. "I'll leave you with your memories in just a few minutes."

Oh dear. He thinks I was missing Samuel! Now what can I say? She could think of nothing that didn't either sound like she was flirting with him or being disrespectful of her deceased husband. "That isn't necessary," she said at last. "I wasn't particularly sad. Just thinking." She put a smile on her face that, while it wasn't exactly sunny, was nonetheless sincere. "So how are you, and how is Amanda?"

His answering smile was more natural than her own, and dazzled her. "We're fine. Sorry I took so long with the table."

The table! She had seen the wagon and the tarp on his arrival, but she had been so excited just to see him that she had forgotten.

"Be right back," he said, slipping out of the door. He returned momentarily, hefting the heavy table. It was lovely, and she started to say so, but he held up a gloved finger to stop her. "One minute." Again, he disappeared out the door, and returned with two chairs. "One more trip," he said, before she got in a word.

Stunned, Tabitha looked at the table and chairs. They were beautiful. She felt the smooth finish and thought of the amount of time and caring that had gone into them. It brought a tear to her eye, and also a question. Was the attention to detail because he was a craftsman and did everything carefully? Or was it because it was for her?

When he came in again with two more chairs, he shut the door firmly and began peeling off his gloves. "Now," he said, "where do you want these?"

"This is too much!" she protested. "They're lovely, but I couldn't possibly accept so much! Our bargain was for a table, and I thought even that was unfair to you!"

"Nonsense. I made them because I wanted to. Accept them as a gift, if you think it's an unfair trade." He knew they needed them, and he was glad he could do something for them. No, not for them. For her, for Tabitha. He would remember the look on her face when she first saw the unexpected chairs for the rest of his life, and it warmed his heart.

"But it's too much!"

"I insist." He picked up the table and headed for the back room. "Show me where."

She indicated a spot a comfortable distance from the stove, but didn't give up on her protest. "Then let me do something for you."

Luke gave an exaggerated sigh. "Don't you know how to accept a gift?"

"Don't you?" she countered.

He couldn't help his smile. He knew when he was beaten.

And Tabitha knew when she'd won, and matched his smile with one of her own. The urge to run to him was strong. She was waging a mental warfare with her arms, to keep them from reaching for him. They seemed to have a mind of their own. "What do you need?" she asked, clenching her fingers tightly together. "Any more clothes? How about for Amanda? Or maybe curtains? Or—"

He held up his hand to stop her flow of suggestions. "Actually," he said, "Mandy's been pestering me for a pink work shirt, of all the crazy things! She said it would make her feel more like a girl while she helps me outside."

"One pink shirt. What else?"

He thought for a couple of minutes. "I suppose I could use some curtains in my kitchen. There's no one out there to be lookin' in, but they might cheer the place up."

"What else?"

"Don't you think you're overdoing this?"

She shook her head.

When he didn't immediately suggest anything else, she said, "Would you like a cup of tea while you're thinking? I'm dying to try out my new table."

"Sure. Thanks." While she put some water on the stove, he brought in two of the chairs and draped his coat over the back of one.

She stopped him before he brought in the other two, and placed them at an angle to each other in the front room. Someday, she hoped to have a small table to place between them. "Martha and I can sit here to sew," she explained. "Decided yet?" she asked, walking back to the kitchen and putting the tea into the hot water to steep.

He followed her and took a seat. "Decided what?"

"What else I can make for you. These chairs are a little piece of heaven, and I really want to repay a kindness. I haven't known such comfort since England. Of course, our table there was absolutely huge, and very old. It had been in Samuel's family for years. But I think I prefer this one. It's, um, cozier. It fits this place. It fits my life here."

"Your husband was rich then? What happened? Debts?"

"Hardly. Samuel Bradford was one of the most virtuous men on earth. No, he didn't leave debts. But we had no heir, and he left Bradford Hall to his nephew. A lot of money went to an orphanage in India." She took a sip of tea, then, with a thought to how her words sounded, rushed on to add "with my consent."

Luke knew that it was none of his business, but he didn't really care. He had to know how a man could leave money to orphans he had never met, and leave his wife a pauper. "What about you?" he asked, not bothering to hide the growing anger he felt for the dead man. "Did 'one of the most virtuous men on earth' leave his wife nothing? So she'd have to work until she's bleary-eyed just to have enough to eat and a roof over her head?" His voice was rising, but he didn't care about that, either.

"No," she explained calmly. "He left me some money. Quite a bit, actually, for a society lady with nothing to spend it on but her own entertainments and vanity. He assumed I would remain in the family home and not need anything more. But what money I had was in my trunk and is now at the bottom of Lake Michigan."

Luke calmed down and asked, "So why didn't you? Stay in the family house, that is?"

Why was she talking so freely to him? Tabitha wasn't certain why, but she did know that it was nice to have someone besides Martha to talk to. Then she remembered wishing she could talk to him about more personal things, instead of shopping or sewing, and the knowledge shook her. Was God answering prayer? Or was she manipulating circumstances to her own liking?

It was nice to be sitting here with him, hearing the crackle of the stove and seeing the shine on the top of the new table. It was a cozy, comfortable feeling she could get used to very easily. *Help me, Lord,* she prayed silently. *Guide me. Don't let me fall.*

"Let's just say," she said aloud, "that there are easier people to live with in this world than my sister-in-law, Leah Bradford Harrington. And to be completely honest, I wanted to do something different. I could not see myself rotting away in that musty old house for the next fifty years, letting life pass by without ever knowing anything beyond its walls."

"Do you miss him much?"

Tabitha met his gaze slowly. Why should he care about that? Her heart fluttered briefly. Could he feel, even slightly, the kind of jealousy she felt when she thought of Rachel?

She shook her head slowly, stirring her tea and contemplating. But having come this far, and being so comfortable with him, she decided there was no advantage in refusing to talk about it. "Samuel was more than old enough to be my father. It wasn't a starry-eyed, romantic marriage. My father was dying, and he knew it. I would be soon thrust into the world with no training and no marital prospects, at the tender age of sixteen. Samuel was his friend, and my friend too. He was a very nice man, and everyone who knew him, I suppose, considered him a friend. The three of us stayed up late one night, discussing the dilemma, me in frightened tears, I admit. That was the solution we came up with. I needed a home. Samuel needed a wife—a companion. I got a home. He got a wife. Father died relieved of his worries about me."

Luke could see the logic of it. He could understand the desperation of the decision. He could also envision Tabitha in the arms of a decaying old man, and he felt sick. Some "most virtuous man." From where he sat, it seemed the old pervert had gotten by far the better end of the bargain. "So," he said, trying to keep his revulsion to himself, "he wanted a wife. So he got one. Like you get a puppy when you decide you want one."

Tabitha chose to overlook the sarcasm. Luke wasn't the first to fail to understand. "I thought myself fortunate," she argued. "My other options were worse. And Samuel was very good to me. One of the best friends I've ever known. We enjoyed the same books and music. We talked about everything and anything. My father was a gambler. He had run up considerable debts, which Samuel paid, gracefully. I had no dowry, no season."

"Season?"

"Balls. Parties. Meeting people. Being shown to society, to meet the most eligible bachelors and try to make a good match. I didn't have that."

"That's barbaric."

She laughed. "There was a time, not too long ago, when I thought you colonists were barbaric."

"And now?"

Again she was thoughtful. "I love it here. America is big and exciting. It's growing, and the people are more free. I don't mean the voting kind of free. I mean the social rules. I wouldn't go back to England if I could." It was true enough, but it was a shock for her to realize.

"We've been talking about me until our tea is cold. You've had plenty of time to think now. What will it be? What else can I make for you to thank you for all this lovely furniture?"

"Maybe I should have a new good shirt."

"For church?" she asked, her breath catching on a hope she hardly dared hope.

His face clouded. "Definitely not for church."

"What is it you have against God?"

"Why should I worship Him? He took Rachel from me and left me alone here to run the farm and raise our daughter."

"How about the air you breathe? How about your health, or your daughter's health? How about the food on your table? Aren't any of those things worth even a small thank-you?"

"Everyone has air to breathe, so I won't even answer that. As to our health and our food, we have them because we work hard. We earn the food on our table, and working to raise it keeps us in good health."

"And I suppose you earned being born healthy and whole in the first place? Or what about the strength to do the work that keeps food on your table? What about your God-given ability to appreciate music or trees or a sunset? Or the physical ability to see your beautiful daughter and put your arms around her? Don't you think those are good gifts? Maybe you could worship God just because of who He is—Creator, Redeemer. The One without sin."

Luke rose to his feet. "Thank you for the tea, Tabitha. Perhaps if I leave now, we can avoid escalating this into a shouting match. I don't think I'll ever agree with you that God is worthy to be worshipped. Because I think He holds all the cards, and He doesn't play fair. He treats us like His puppets."

He hadn't stopped talking all the while he was putting on his coat and making his way to the door. "I think I'll be just in time to catch Mandy from school and give her a ride home. By the way, she loves her dresses and says thank you. She feels much better about going to school now, and she is even making some friends." Then he was gone.

Tabitha leaned against the closed door. She had wanted to discover some clue about how he felt about Rachel, and if he still missed her and loved her. Now she knew. He still loved her very much. So much so that he would turn on a loving God and lash out, blaming Him for his wife's death. She was competing with a ghost.

Competing? Is that what she was doing? That was insane. Lucas Hayes was clearly wrong for her, not what God wanted for her. So why did it feel like a large part of her world had crumbled?

Quiet tears rolled down her cheeks.

Fourteen

The March sun was shining, reflecting blue sky on puddles of melted snow. Crocuses were peeking out of the dirt along the fence. Luke was wearing his "good" shirt and his best pants, simply because he was tired of always looking like a farmer when he came to town for supplies. That was his only reason. He had, as always, purposely chosen a day when he knew Tabitha would not be working for Al.

He heard the voices of the men before he saw them. Voices raised in anger. Several men stood in a group, arguing. He didn't need to hear the words to know what the disagreement was about. When he was close enough to distinguish words, they proved him right.

"How can you say slavery is immoral? It's in the Bible! You know that!"

"Yes, it is, but—" The voice Luke recognized as belonging to Isaiah Douglas, a preacher, was interrupted before he could get his argument formed.

"Darn right it is! An' the Bible don't say it's wrong! It only says that a slave should obey his master an' not try to run away!"

"So you agree that it's acceptable to *own* people? To force them to do your labor? To whip them? To use their women for your own lustful purposes?"

"Now, I never said nothin' about that being right."

"But you think that when one of them runs away from conditions like that, we should return them to it, because the Bible says that slaves should obey their masters?"

"They have a lot of money wrapped up in those slaves," another voice chimed in. "They wouldn't be able to get in their crops without 'em. You think we should insist the Southerners give 'em up? Force 'em to? It would destroy the entire economy of the South!"

"And how would you feel if your horse that you needed to do your field work went to your neighbor's property, and that neighbor refused to give him back?"

"You are equating a human with a horse. I refuse to dignify that with an answer."

"Oh, don't you go gettin' uppity and righteous, just because you're a preacher!"

"If I am 'getting righteous,' it's not because I'm a preacher! It's because I'm a Christian, and what I see happening in this country chills my blood."

That, Luke could agree with wholeheartedly, except about his indignation stemming from being a Christian.

"Do you want war? Is that what you're after?"

"Do you? You're the one who wants to change things."

"This disagreement ain't about slavery!" That was yet another voice. Luke stood, listening to the heated discussion, unable to keep track of who was speaking. "It's about the rights of a state to make their own laws! All the states entered the Union freely. Why shouldn't they be able to leave freely?"

Many voices chorused agreement. But one man countered the argument calmly and effectively.

"This issue dividing our country is not about slavery, and it's not even about the rights of a state to govern itself. It's about the strength of the Union and the validity of the Constitution. If any part of this country can simply withdraw when they don't agree, then the Constitution isn't worth the paper it's written on, because it would only carry weight on the passing whims of men. I find it a frightening prospect, to face living in a nation with no agreed-upon framework that all laws must fit within. It is worth fighting for, and if South Carolina, or any other Southern state secedes over this, then I would have to enlist, to save the Union and all it stands for."

The man was clearly well educated, and just as clearly knew what he was talking about and had given it much thought. The other men were silenced, at least for the time being. With a shudder at the thought of the war clouds looming in the future, Luke walked past the group towards Garfield's store.

"Hey, Hayes!" Two men had been leaning against the building, listening to the discussion, as he had, without participating. "All slicked up to see the Bradford widder?

Don't ya know she don't work here on Fridays no more?"

It was Chester MacDonald. His buddy, Bert Palmer, joined in the fun. "He's right, Hayes. Why don't ya jist go on over to her house an' order yerself some new shirts? I'm sure ya must need more by now!"

"We heard ya made that widder woman a bed! An' big enough fer two, too!"

"Mebbe if ya make her a writin' desk or somethin' real fancy, she'll find a way to say thank you that's bet-ter'n shirts!"

At first Luke had intended to ignore the men. But they had gone too far. He would not have Tabitha talked about in such low and disrespectful terms. Without a word, he grabbed both men by their shirt fronts and banged their heads together, then dropped them and walked into the store, leaving them rubbing their heads and cussing. Maybe, he told himself, he had needed a release for his own fears, after hearing those men talk, and knowing with growing certainty that his country would go to war. Whatever the cause of his little explo-sion of temper, he felt better for having indulged it.

❦

Tabitha ran satisfied eyes over the little house. The quilt was finished and lay on the bed, giving a colorful, cheerful atmosphere to the room. She'd found four wooden crates, three of which were now stacked in the kitchen to hold their dishes, cans, and other things, with the dishpan on top. The other crate had been upended between the two chairs in the front room and served nicely as a table. Mrs. Grimes had gotten a new dining room table, and had given Martha a good price on her old one. It was now their cutting table. And last night, Martha had surprised her by nailing together a frame for a changing screen, and tacking fabric of lilac and yellow flowers on a green background on it.

Tabitha decided that the perfect finishing touch would be a curtain for their crate cupboard, and window curtains to match. And a tablecloth for the improvised end table. She grabbed her purse and hung the "closed" sign in the window. She should check the post office, too.

She froze when she entered the store and saw Luke standing by the counter, talking to Mr. Garfield. She'd only seen him once since the day he had delivered her table and they had argued about God. Luke had stopped by for only as long as it took to pick up his shirt and Amanda's pink work shirt. Amanda had been with him, and he had been brief and businesslike. She thought he might be putting distance between them, and she knew that it was for the best. Knowing that did nothing to make it easier to breathe, or to make herself close the door calmly and walk towards the two men.

"Hello, Mr. Garfield. Luke."

"What are you doing here today?" Luke asked.

That answered that question. He had picked a day to do his shopping when he knew she wouldn't be here, was indeed deliberately avoiding her. Though she knew it was better this way, it saddened her. She was aware of the paradox of her feelings. She liked him a lot. Too much, considering the circumstances. The mere sight of him could make her stomach do flippety-flops, as Martha would say, and, while she hadn't done anything senseless, she knew what it felt like to want to. But she knew it wasn't to be, and she held firm to her conviction to obey her Lord. It was indeed better if Luke avoided her. Maybe someday it wouldn't even hurt.

At least now she knew exactly how Martha had felt when she had fled Mr. Briggs.

"I just came in to pick out some fabric to make curtains for the shop," she explained. "And as long as I'm here, Luke, why don't you choose some, too? I seem to recall that I still owe you a pair of curtains."

He quickly selected a sunshiny yellow, and Tabitha was already conjuring up images of ruffles and white piping, with white tieback bows. Suitable for a cheerful kitchen.

While the men talked, she picked her own fabrics out and carried them to the counter. "One more thing I need," she said, turning to address Luke. "Your window measurements."

He told her the size of the window, and then she asked what the room looked like, so she would have a better idea of what kind of curtains would fit in.

"I'm sure that any description I gave would be hopelessly inadequate. Why don't you just come to look for yourself?" The suggestion came as a bit of a shock to him. He had never intended to invite her to his house. But his shock was nothing compared to hers. She was speechless.

Luke found that he liked the idea of having her in his house. "Sunday would be best for me," he said. "Say, a week from this Sunday?"

"I'm afraid I could not," she replied. "It would be completely inappropriate for me to come to your house."

"Why don't you bring Miss Dobbins with you? Would that be acceptable?"

Tabitha felt terrible. While he had, in a way, invited her out to his house, he had done it in a way that was disagreeable, making no secret that he was issuing the invitation against his wishes. She thought she might cry. That would never do. "Thank you," she said. "I'm sure Martha would enjoy that."

"Sunday then? About eight?'

"I can't. Church lasts until ten." Let him make what he would of that. She would not back down, and she would not argue.

"Church? Why don't you skip it?"

"I can't."

"Can't or won't?"

"Won't, then."

"Why not?"

"I prefer to have fellowship with other believers whenever I can, and to hear the Word taught, and to sing God's praises. I will not miss it for curtains."

Disgusted with her, and with himself for walking right

into the stupid argument, Luke collected his purchases and stalked out. "Ten, then," was all he said, leaving Tabitha close to crying, and Albert trying to stifle a laugh.

His best luck, Luke realized, would be his worst luck. If he could convince her to marry him, he would hear "God this" and "Jesus that" all his life. He stopped in the middle of untying the reins from the hitching post. *Marry him?!*

Tabitha tried to get her mind to function, to figure out how much yardage she needed, but it wouldn't work. All she could see was the disgust on Luke's face. He felt she needed to see his kitchen to do a good job on his curtains, but he'd made it plain that needing her for anything was exactly what he did not want. He did not want to spend time with her in any way. Or, more accurately, he did not want to spend time with her God, even secondhand.

He did want to spend time with her. At times, the look in his eyes left no doubt in her mind that he was interested, and she had felt the exciting charge in the room between them. She did not doubt that it was mutual. She knew she could have him. She could easily marry Lucas Hayes and have everything she had ever wanted in life . . . except for his whole heart. That, she knew, was still part Rachel's, and probably always would be. He was the type she could laugh with, work with, cry on, talk to, or snuggle into. All she would have to do is give up God. Stop going to church, and stop talking about God and pushing Him on Luke. It was not a trade she would make, though it cost her dearly.

Albert Garfield, oblivious to her turmoil, was grinning from ear to ear. "Looks like Hayes needs some lessons in courting. Does he ask you on a picnic, or to an ice-cream social, or even to a political debate? No. He asks you to measure for curtains! Well," he went on, talking more to himself than to her, while he wrapped her purchases, "maybe he just hasn't realized yet that it's courting he's doing."

Tabitha's mouth felt dry. "I assure you, Mr. Garfield, that whatever he is doing, Lucas Hayes is not courting me."

"Oh, really?" Albert raised a straw-colored eyebrow. "Then I suppose he walked out without saying good-bye to his friend because he forgot I was here?" He chuckled at her astonished expression. "Well, my dear, that is exactly what happened. He did forget I was here, because his mind is full of you!"

Tabitha swallowed hard. Could it be? Wasn't he in love with his memories of his wife? While she had admitted that she could get him to marry her, she had never considered that it was something he was pursuing, or even something he wanted, beyond realizing on an intellectual level that being married would be advantageous for him and drive away the loneliness. She hoped Mr. Garfield was right, but hated herself for having the hope. She would not go against the counsel of an all-wise God and yoke herself to an unbeliever. Even if she had to run from the temptation as Martha had.

She was committed now to measuring his windows for curtains, but her behavior would be most circumspect. She would act with the utmost care and discretion. And never let Martha leave her alone with him, not for a minute. She would not wear her hair any differently than she did every day, and she would not make a new dress. From now on, she would be courteous but distant with the man. It was clear to her that she, at least, could no longer maintain the friendly terms they had reached and not want more.

This was Friday, she thought as she walked slowly down the street with her bundle. More than a week before the dreaded day. It seemed so far away, and yet so close.

She was anxious about it. Was Mr. Garfield right? Was Luke courting her? "Oh, what difference does it make?" she asked out loud. "If he's not, you'll be sad because you wish he was, and if he is, you'll be sad because you can't respond. You, Tabitha Bradford, are a hopeless mess."

There was another shock for her at the post office—a brief letter from Leah. It said only how Lord Abercrombe had helped her through her grief, and what a wonderful man he was. She was very happy. They would be selling Bradford Hall and moving to Scotland, which was fine with her. She had always loved Scotland, and the Hall held too much silence and too many memories. Tabitha picked up the newspaper clipping that had fluttered to the floor when she opened the letter. It was a wedding announcement. For Leah Bradford Harrington and Lord William Abercrombe.

Leah and William? That was truly astonishing. It was absurd. She must be five years older than he was, and she was not attractive. He was a titled lord. The pieces began falling into place. She remembered Leah's insinuation that he had only been after Tabitha's supposed fortune when he had been so helpful after Samuel's death, and Tabitha had pooh-poohed the idea. But here was evidence! He had married a stodgy middle-aged woman with the tongue of a serpent. Right after her son had died, leaving her Samuel's estate. *Oh! Thank God, thank God!* When she had not inherited much from Samuel, she had been protected from the mercenary intentions of Lord Abercrombe!

But Leah knew! It had been she who had warned Tabitha of this very thing! How could she be trapped by the man?

Unless she hadn't been trapped. Unless she went into the arrangement with her eyes open and considered it a fair trade for a young, handsome husband and a title!

Oh, Leah! How low can you stoop? Tabitha's heart grieved for her, for she would never know the sheer happiness that Tabitha now knew was possible. And she knew that no amount of money in the world, no title, no amount of respect in the world was worth the trade. *Pray for your enemies.* She would, surely. But Leah was no longer her enemy. Leah was someone to be pitied.

No sooner had Tabitha deposited her package on the cutting table and hung her shawl than there was a knock on the door. She did not want to see anyone or do anything except talk to Martha, both about Leah and about her problem with Luke. Martha would understand, if anyone did. Yet they couldn't afford to turn away business, so she opened the door.

"Etienne!" She could hardly believe her eyes. "What are you doing here?"

He stepped in, uninvited, and closed the door behind him. "Need you ask, *ma jolie?*" He raised her hand to his lips. "I've come to see the most beautiful diamond in all of America!"

She had forgotten the deep, velvety quality of his voice, and her memory had dulled his handsome features, so this vivid, living reminder was a bit overwhelming. She withdrew her fingers and smiled at his outrageous flattery. "Only here for one day?"

"Actually"—one side of his mouth curved up in his appealing lopsided grin—"the weather here is becoming almost bearable, and I have no immediate plans pressing me. I thought I would stay a few days."

"Here?" she asked, in a tight whisper.

He laughed, a low, silky laugh. "No, my sweet. Not here. Much as I would prefer it, I did not think you would agree. I have a suite at the hotel. Could I persuade you to dine with me tonight?"

Martha walked in just as he said that.

"Martha?" Tabitha said. "You remember Monsieur Rousseau, don't you? He was on the ship with us."

Martha nodded, a bit overcome by all the male good

looks and elegance in their tiny establishment.

"Etienne? You also remember Martha Dobbins? She is my sewing partner now."

"*Mais certainment!*" He bowed and kissed her hand as well. "I am most pleased to meet you once again, Mademoiselle Dobbins. Now I have two lovely ladies to dine with. If you would be so kind as to let me escort you both to dinner?"

He was a suave one!

Later that night, Tabitha and Martha lay awake in the dark, talking.

"To think me mum prides 'erself in bein' a judge o' character! Jeremy, according to 'er, was a 'jolly good fellow,' yet 'e wanted to seduce me in a stable! An' your Mister Etienne, she said was a bad 'un. Why, I've never seen a better mannered gent in all my days."

"That he is," Tabitha agreed. "But he's not my Mister Etienne."

"Could be, though, if you gave 'em any encouragement," Martha argued.

A bit later, Tabitha whispered, "Martha?"

"Hmm?" came the sleepy response.

"Never mind. Go to sleep." She wanted to talk about Etienne. And Leah. And Luke. Mostly Luke. But it wouldn't make any difference anyway. All the talk in the world would change nothing.

"Why, Mistah Jones!" Etienne said in a falsetto, mimicking a Southern belle. "Ah would be awnawed to have this daynce."

Tabitha giggled softly, looking up at him briefly from where she sat sewing in the next chair. Her face was bathed in the yellow glow of the lantern, and he was enthralled. He had known many women who were easily as beautiful, and certainly more sophisticated, but there was something about Tabitha that was different. There was a serenity in a room when she was there. Even this mean little room held an attraction for him. He would rather be here, in this pathetic little town, than in the fanciest saloon in New Orleans.

He had tried everything the world had to offer. Rich surroundings, fine food, beautiful women, gambling, drinking—everything. And he had enjoyed it all immensely.

Yet all this woman had to do was sit near him and sew, and laugh politely at his impersonations, to make him realize that he had been on a dead end. All those other things were getting him nowhere. Here he felt as though he actually mattered. Just because he would tell a ridiculous tale and she would laugh and smile up at him and make him feel like a king, encouraging him to tell more stories just so she would smile again.

"Me 'n Bessy," he said, using his tongue to form an imaginary wad of tobacco in his lower lip, "that's m' mule, Bessy. Me 'n Bessy ain't niver bin up that thar hill afore. Nope. It's a steep un, it is."

Tabitha laughed again; Etienne grinned at her approval and from knowing it was he who was amusing her. It was too simple.

He had seen too much evil. He had done too much evil. The world was a bad place, and everyone had ulterior motives. They were all out for themselves, first, last, and only. What was her game? Surely she could not be as simple—as clean—as she appeared. He would have to think of a way to test her.

There was a knock on the door, and Tabitha jumped up to answer it. Martha was busy washing up the supper dishes, because Etienne had, for once, allowed them to feed him, rather than going out to a restaurant.

She opened it and found a young man with auburn hair, pale blue eyes, and a cleft in his chin standing on the doorstep. He was of medium height, and had a build that was perhaps slightly less than average. His face was what held her attention. He was as pretty as a girl! Beautiful, actually, yet there was nothing effeminate about him.

Tabitha glanced from the young man back into the room when Etienne's movement caught the corner of her eye. He'd stood and was now coming towards the door. That's when she noticed the irritation written on his face. It was clearly not jealousy. He seemed more like a boy whose toys had been mishandled.

"Evenin', ma'am," the young man said. His Irish accent was thick. "Name's Jeremy Briggs. I'm lookin' for a Miss Dobbins, and I was told to try here. Do you know where I could find her?"

Jeremy! No wonder Martha had felt the need to flee temptation. But would she want to see him now? Tabitha hesitated. It was altogether too rude to just leave him standing there, though, so she collected her manners and the use of her tongue, and asked him in. Just as she finished introducing the two men, Martha walked into the room, holding a teapot in one hand and three empty cups in the other.

"Jeremy!" The tea cups began an ominous rattle, and Tabitha took them and the pot and set them on the cutting table. "What are you . . ."

"Martha!" he cried at almost the same moment she spoke. "Where have ya been, and whatever did ya just up an' leave for? And your ma frantic with worry! Not so much as a fare-thee-well, and I've had an awful time trackin' ya down! Now will ya come back with me, and give her back some peace o' mind?"

"I . . . I can't," she stammered. "Tell me mum I'm fine. Tell her ya found me, an' w'ere I am. But I can't go back."

"Why?" Jeremy came further into the room, but made no attempt to go close to Martha. He showed confusion and frustration, and a lack of sleep. "I thought things was fine with us, and then ya up an' leave, and now ya say ya won't come back with me. Well, I'm not leavin' until ya at least tell me why."

"But," Martha protested. "I thought, I mean, people said you were . . . that is, I didn't think you would . . . " She stopped in the middle of her incoherent sentence, as red as the flowers on the teacups. "I was afraid," she admitted finally, then tacked on " . . . of me." Then she gave up trying to explain.

Sudden understanding cleared Jeremy's face like the sun coming out after a rain. "Gossip, bah! I thought your ma, at least, woulda stood up for me. She's a smart lady, and she knew I was on the up 'n up."

Martha's eyes darted to Etienne, and Tabitha noticed the look, knowing what she was thinking. Well, it seemed Mrs. Dobbins had been right about Jeremy, but she was still wrong about Etienne. She stole a glance at him and smiled. Perhaps she wasn't entirely wrong. He wasn't the most serious man she'd ever come across, but he didn't qualify for the adjective "oily," either.

Jeremy Briggs was not a stupid man, and when Martha unwittingly confessed to being afraid of herself, his self-confidence returned.

"She did," Martha admitted. "She said you were a 'jolly, good fellow.' "

"Is that all she said?" he asked, knowing full well there was more.

"No, that isn't all." Martha's face, which had returned to its normal coloring, became once again a deep shade of pink. "She said I should marry you." As she uttered that, her voice grew progressively quieter and quieter, and she couldn't meet his gaze.

"And I suppose," he said, "no one ever taught ya ta mind your ma?"

Her eyes widened, searching his. "Are you saying. . . ?"

"Yes, I am."

"Oh, yes, yes!" Martha ran into his arms, and he kissed her even more thoroughly than he had before. Both of them had forgotten the presence of Etienne and Tabitha.

Etienne cleared his throat. "Forget the tea," he said, when the pair self-consciously jerked apart. "This calls for more of a celebration than tea!"

And so the four of them went down to the hotel to have a bit of an impromptu party.

Tabitha sat on the edge of her bed in a daze. Here it was, Saturday. Tomorrow Luke would be picking her up after church. She had to take a bath and see that her clothes were clean and pressed. Not that she was doing it special for Luke; she always did those things on Saturdays. But instead of doing them, she sat thinking on the bed. So much had happened!

Etienne's visit had been less whirlwind than before. He had taken them out several times, and he had been to their house several times. Those times, Martha would find some excuse to be in the kitchen, leaving her alone with him. He had seemed different this time. Not serious, by any means, but more like he had a purpose. She could still close her eyes and see his handsome face, watching her so closely, smiling whenever she looked his way. She still had to smile, remembering how he would make up stories and tell them, using different voices for all the characters he made. He'd had her laughing until she couldn't keep her stitches straight and had to set aside her sewing and just listen to him.

Tabitha had never heard accents from Boston or the South, so she didn't know how accurate he was, but he was funny. Then, when he had returned to his normal voice, she got chills down her back. When he called her *cherie* and took both her hands in his, she trembled, and she knew that she was very attracted to the man. Not just because he was devastatingly handsome, either. There was, lately, something more compelling about him, something that drew her.

So where did that leave how she felt about Luke?

Tabitha got up and walked to the back window and gazed blankly out of it, rounding up her thoughts, trying to make a plan for her life in the immediate future. Martha's future, it seemed, was settled. Which would leave Tabitha alone again. Tabitha was very happy for her friend, and how it affected her had nothing to do with it.

In the two days that Jeremy had been in Waukegan, sharing a hotel room with Etienne, who had been very gracious about it, a lot had been decided. The wedding was set for June, and Jeremy had gone home, eagerly waiting for the week or two it would take Martha to help Tabitha with a sudden influx of sewing orders. Then Martha would be gone, and Tabitha would be on her own again. She feared it now more than she ever had.

Tabitha had suggested to Martha that she choose

either the table and chairs or the bed, because they had both worked on the sewing that had been traded for them. Martha had refused, saying, "He made them for you! The man is more than a little in love with ya, Tabby. Are ya blind?" So Tabitha had tried to pay her for her work, but she had only accepted train fare back to Chicago. As far as Tabitha was concerned, it was a ticket that would be used much too soon.

Then there was Etienne. At least he would no longer be around to plague her thoughts. Not after what had happened last night!

Fifteen

*E*tienne had asked her to go for a walk, and Tabitha agreed, in spite of Martha's meaningful smirk. They walked east, all the way to the lake. When they got to the beach he gave her a hand, because her shoes were not meant for walking in sand. There was something on his mind, she knew, because she had never seen him so serious. They walked, mostly in silence.

Then he stopped and pulled her to him. "Tabitha, *ma cherie,*" he said, and put his arms around her. He kissed her hair.

She could hear the sounds of the water lapping on the sand and his heartbeat, where her head rested against his chest. She could feel the warmth of his hands through the back of her dress. He smelled good. He looked good. He was fun. He was comfortable. Was he what she wanted?

She sighed contentedly and felt his arms tighten around her.

"Tabitha," he said. "What is it about you that touches my heart? What is it that keeps me coming back?"

"I don't know." She smiled into his shirt, too shy to flirt more directly. "Why do you?"

"In part"—he pulled away far enough to see her face—"it is to discover what it is about you that is different."

"If there is anything different about me, it must be God."

"God?"

"Yes, God. Anything I am that is good is because of Him."

"You really believe that?"

"Of course!" She was surprised that he would even ask.

"To me," he said, facing the water, but leaving an arm around her waist, "you are good. You are clean, not dirtied by greed and selfishness. But I think I am too far from that to be clean and good. Not ever again."

Tabitha was curious now, and afraid of whatever terrible thing lurked in his past, but also she was anxious to assure him. "No," she replied. "You are not hopeless. Jesus died for the sins of all. There is nothing that God can't forgive, and He can make you clean again. Just admit to Him where you've been wrong, and ask forgiveness. Then you can take Him as your Savior and start a whole new life, without whatever it is that hangs over you and makes you feel that you are not good or clean."

He said nothing, but pulled her back into his arms.

Tabitha prayed, silently and wholeheartedly. If he became a Christian, his life would change. He would be happier, more fulfilled, and his life would have some direction. And, she admitted, her prayers were not entirely selfless. For if he became a Christian, he would also become eligible for her to dream about. Maybe someday they could even have that godly marriage that she wanted and needed and had been praying for. Maybe Etienne was the husband God intended for her.

"Jolie," he murmured after a long time.

"Yes?"

"Would you reconsider and come to New Orleans with me? Please? I keep making this wretched, long journey just to be near you. It is insanity."

Tabitha said nothing, but merely gazed into his black, black eyes, noticing the beginning shadow of a beard on his sculpted cheek and jaw. Luke came to mind. Part of her wished this was he holding her. She pushed the thought away. Luke was so antagonistic towards God, while Etienne, perhaps, would not be any more. It felt good to be held, to have someone care about her. She really did like him, and there was no doubt he was attractive and could provide for her. If he asked, she decided, she would say yes.

He went on. "Martha will be gone soon, and you will have no one here. I hate to think of you slaving away for barely enough money to live on. I could give you a mansion. Servants. Parties. Caviar and champagne. Anything you ever wished for."

Still she looked up into his face. He was offering her everything. The world. Yet he hadn't said what she waited to hear.

"I guess," she finally prompted, "you will have to tell me more clearly what it is you want."

Etienne broke eye contact while he tried to think of a way to phrase his request. His hesitancy was all the answer Tabitha needed, and she abruptly pulled away from him and turned to walk home.

"Tabitha?" he questioned, following. "I do not understand! I made virtually the same offer once before, and you did not become nearly so angry."

"I believe 'virtually' is the key word." She never slowed down, and wouldn't face him. "Your previous offer was half in jest, and included the option of my living on your charity. I am insulted that you would believe I could ever do such a thing. And I am very upset with myself for ever giving that impression that I might consider it, though I have no idea how I did!"

When they reached the top of the bluff, and home was west and the train station and hotel were south, she still didn't pause. "I believe, *monsieur,* that this is *adieu.*" Intentionally, she used the French word for a permanent good-bye, rather than the temporary *au revoir.* "No need to walk me home. I can manage quite well on my own."

"Did he ask you ta marry 'im?" Martha asked before Tabitha had even had a chance to close the front door.

"Nothing quite so legitimate as that." "I don't believe we'll be seeing any more of Monsieur Rousseau."

"I'm sorry."

And to herself Tabitha admitted, *So am I.*

❦

The train made its rhythmic clacking, lulling passengers to sleep, steadily progressing towards Rock Island. Etienne, however, was awake, sitting on the settee in his Pullman, with his legs propped up on an expensive cherry wood table, and his cravat loosened. He could just picture Tabitha stalking away from him into the fading evening light, indignation in her every move. He gave his lopsided smile to his brandy snifter and took a drink. He had offered her everything. All the things that people desired, fought over, even killed for, and she had refused without even hesitating. Perhaps she was as good and as pure as she seemed.

Finally, after a lifetime of looking in the wrong places, he knew precisely what he wanted. He wanted Tabitha. "I'll be back, *cherie,*" he whispered. When she had had time to forgive the harshness of his test, he would return for her.

❦

In the predawn darkness Tabitha lay awake. Darkness and silence provided a lack of distractions that helped her to think clearly. The insult still stung. And despite the hurt, she knew she would miss Etienne, and that the loss was permanent this time. She knew enough about him now never to be lulled again into the temptation of dreaming about him and hoping for anything permanent or godly. She could forgive him; she already had. But she would never again trust him.

She had learned something from the episode, though. She learned that God had answered her prayers, while it had seemed for so long that He hadn't been listening. Because He *had* made her strong enough to resist temptation. She had been tried—tempted by all the world could offer. Everything money could buy, as well as the companionship of a very attractive, attentive man, and she had not succumbed. Had not even been seriously tempted to.

A test of faith had been met and passed, and she felt stronger.

Come to think of it, she had passed, sort of, a test with Luke, too. She had stood firm for God, knowing he did not want to hear it. It had driven him away, but she would not do it differently. Perhaps she was strong enough, with the help of God, to get through the upcoming day.

"Tabby!" Martha had come home unexpectedly. "I finished 'elping Mrs. Grimes with the breakfast cleanup. Then she said I could be going, because she knew I had a lot to do, and that I needn't come in any more. Said she could get along until she found other help."

She made her way to the back room and saw Tabitha, nearly ready for church, dressed in the yellow dress, with her hair in the net. "What are you doing?" she asked.

"Isn't Mr. Luke fetching you after church?"

"Fetching us. Yes."

"Why are you wearing that?"

Tabitha shrugged and looked away.

"You usually wear your skirt and blouse to church, and do something more with your 'air." Then understanding dawned. "Ah! You're sad about Mr. Etienne. So ya don't 'ave the 'eart to make yourself pretty. Right?"

"Not right."

Martha scowled, trying to figure out her friend. "Then ya must be dressing poorly on purpose. And I'm wondering why. Could it be because o' Mr. Luke?"

Tabitha's blush gave her away.

"But why?" Martha sat near her on the edge of the bed. "I would think ya'd want to look your best for 'im!"

Tabitha said nothing.

"Now don't be giving me that mind-your-own-business look. I 'ave been minding my own business. Too long, I'd say. Mr. Etienne is a very nice man, but I don't think 'e's what's best for you. What's best for ya is Mr. Luke."

Tabitha's mouth opened to make a shocked protest, but Martha wouldn't let her speak. "I can see the way 'e looks at ya, and it's plain on 'is face that 'e's in love with ya. An I know my own feelin's well enough ta recognize the same in you. You, Tabitha Bradford, are in love, an' it's clear to me, if not to you, that it's Mr. Luke, not Mr. Etienne, 'oo 'olds your 'eart. So get ya off the bed and change your clothes, an' then I'll 'elp with your 'air. Ya should be settin' out ta make 'im see 'e loves ya, not settin' out ta bore 'im 'alf ta death."

"No!" Tabitha argued. "I will not set out to attract the man. I will not attach myself to a man who strives with God, so why should I put the idea in his head?"

Martha made a noise that was half laugh and half sigh. "Strives with God is right. Tabitha, your 'ead knows more than your 'eart will admit. Mr. Luke believes in God, and in Jesus an' all that. 'E only is 'striving.' Ya told me yourself that 'e resents 'is wife's death. That's not a matter of unbelief! 'E only needs to work it out in 'is own mind 'ow a lovin' God could do that."

"God didn't 'do that'!"

"It's 'im you need to tell, not me."

Tabitha swallowed hard and grew still. Martha was right. But it couldn't be she who spoke to him, who tried to help him make sense of a world that sometimes seemed to be harsh and make no sense. She was too close. What he said, what he thought, and what he finally decided were ultimately too important to her.

An ember of hope let her allow Martha to assist her with her hair and dress, and an hour later they were seated in church, both attired in their finest. But Tabitha was not listening to the sermon. She was thinking of Luke and praying for him. Scriptures came to mind in a flood, strengthening her prayers.

"Whosoever believeth in him should not perish, but have eternal life." *Oh, dear heavenly Father, yes! Don't let him perish!* "The Lord is not slack concerning his promise," came the Lord's reply, "not willing that any should perish." And the Lord was aware when a sparrow fell. How much more did he care about a man? "The Lord shall preserve thee from all evil: he shall preserve thy soul." And if the Lord had begun a good work in Luke, He would be faithful to complete it.

Assured in her heart that God would not let Luke be taken from His hand, Tabitha was, at last, content to wait on Him and rest in the assurance that God was for her. And for Luke.

From the top of the church steps, Tabitha spotted Luke before he saw them. He was easy to identify in the crowd of people leaving the church, or standing around visiting, because Amanda was sitting in the wagon in her new pink shirt. For once, the sight of him did not give her the flippety-flops. It gave her a warm glow.

He was a remarkable man, in whom God had indeed started a good work. She would love to be able to run down the steps to him, or better yet, have him there with her, leaving the church. Perhaps someday. But God had not promised her that she would be his. Perhaps He had something else in mind, someone else. That was all right, because she believed that whatever He declared would be in her best interest. Meanwhile, she would wait and trust, and not push, either towards Luke or against him.

Her gaze moved to Amanda. Even though the girl wore trousers, she looked quite pretty and feminine. Her hair was braided and held a ribbon. The work shirt had a ruffle inserted around the yoke, and, Tabitha was glad to see, it fit well. She noted that Luke had placed a board across the back of the wagon for extra seating room. Mostly, though, she noticed Luke. He was so strong and confident. Handsome, too, though in a rougher way than Etienne or Martha's Jeremy.

Amanda saw them and pointed them out to her father. Luke's eyes met Tabitha's and softened. He straightened from where he had been leaning against the side of the wagon and walked toward them. In spite of herself, Tabitha's heart beat faster.

Luke tipped his hat to Martha, then asked if they were ready. Tabitha nodded, and he placed his hand on her lower back to guide her across the street to his wagon.

An overall-clad man in a ratty derby came up beside them. "Hey, Hayes," he chuckled, "Didja make that writin' desk?" His self-satisfied laugh only lasted until Luke's fist connected with his jaw with a loud thud, sending him sprawling in the dirt.

A communal gasp, then silence fell over the parishioners. Gloved, fluttering hands covered open mouths, and men shuffled closer for a better view of what they hoped would be a good fight. Tabitha was astonished and embarrassed, horrified to see this new side of Luke. Bits of shocked conversation penetrated her cloudy thoughts.

"Can you imagine?"

"In front of the church!"

Luke reached a hand to help the dazed man to his

feet. "You all right, Palmer?"

The man jerked his head in an abrupt nod and walked away even more abruptly, rubbing his jaw.

"What was that all about, Luke?" Tabitha asked.

He gave a wry smile. "I was hoping you wouldn't ask."

"Not ask?! You just hit a man! With a large audience, and no apparent provocation! Why would I not ask?"

The "audience" was dispersing, some disappointed, leaving the three alone to continue towards the wagon. Tabitha was a bit disappointed, too. How could Luke be so violent, and unexpectedly so? Martha wore a smug "I told you so" expression.

"There was plenty of provocation."

"Oh really? You must be the only one who saw any."

"It's good for you that I am the only one who saw it." There was an angry spark in his look, and it somehow made her feel as if she was the one in the wrong. "He was questioning your virtue."

"Oh." She could think of nothing else to say to this explanation. Then a frown furrowed her forehead. "A writing desk?"

A grin broke through his clouded expression. "Never mind. It's a long story."

Waiting in the wagon, Amanda was about bursting with curiosity. She jumped down. "Papa! Why did you hit Mr. Palmer?"

"He said something rude about Tabitha."

"He's an ol' mean man! I wish you woulda hit him once for me, too!"

"Must be a Hayes trait," Luke said, "wanting to defend you."

Tabitha turned to face him. "Couldn't you have used a less forceful means of defending my honor? Not that I don't appreciate it."

He chuckled. "I used less force last time. A little less."

Last time! Merciful heavens! Was she that much talked about? "Just how many times," she asked, steeling herself for the answer, "have you been called upon to defend me?"

"Today makes twice."

"Same man?" She surely hoped so.

"Yeah. Only last time he was with MacDonald."

She was disgusted that two men should be talking about her that way, but relieved that it was only two. She wasn't, it would appear, the town's most notorious painted lady.

While this conversation went on, Martha and Amanda formed a quick conspiracy and climbed up onto the back bench, forcing Tabitha to sit in front with Luke.

He drove the horse south to Belvidere Street, then headed west.

"How far away is your farm?" Tabitha asked.

"About five miles."

They drove for a time in silence. It didn't take long to get out of town, and Tabitha looked around eagerly. She hadn't yet seen any of America that wasn't a town or city. There were a lot of trees on either side of the road, and thick undergrowth. Squirrels chattered in the trees. At one point, the trees thinned to a grassy clearing, but she could see more trees ahead. The grass was dotted with purple chicory flowers, and a deer watched them pass. It was so untamed compared to what she had known in England! There were horses in pastures, the same as in England, but everything here was larger and wilder.

"Do you ever have trouble with animals?" she asked, excited at the prospect of being in what she considered wilderness. "Bears or wolves?"

Luke hid a smile at her naïveté and childish enjoyment. She was breathtakingly lovely, and her face held a touch of both excitement and fear. He didn't want to spoil the adventure for her, or for him, by telling her that there hadn't been any serious wildlife trouble for years. "There was a wolf trying to get my chickens last winter, but they're thinning. Too many people."

Too many people! Tabitha looked around and saw only the little town shrinking behind them and one farm away towards the south. She remembered the teaming multitudes of London, and even the countryside of England, which was dotted with farms and villages everywhere. It was difficult to believe that what was around her was too many.

"Must be almost four thousand folks in Waukegan now. Did you know that Waukegan wasn't always what the town was called?"

"Yes, I'd heard that it used to be called Little Fort. I don't know which I prefer. Little Fort sounds more charming. Waukegan is unique."

"Guess it wasn't so little anymore."

"But Waukegan is so odd sounding. Where did they come up with the name?"

"Indian word. Algonquin. It's not such an unusual name for the area. 'Wau' means 'land.' Lots of place-names use it. Waukesha, Milwaukee."

"This is lovely!" Martha said as they pulled into the Hayes farmyard. "Just like a picture book!"

Sinbad, the dog, bounded to meet them, and Tabitha had to laugh. He was large and very hairy, with weeds and grass stuck in his fur and an expression of mindless joy.

"I'm afraid it isn't what you're used to." Luke directed his reply to Tabitha, apologizing. His gaze, she noted, was not on the dog, but on the farm buildings.

Why was it men judged their value by what they owned? She looked around at the tidy two-story house and the snug barn and outbuildings. He had put a lot of work into his home and farm, and if he hadn't known that Samuel had been rich, he would have been proud of it.

"No." She purposely misunderstood him. "It's not what we're used to. Our little place in town is much smaller, and not nearly so well built."

"That's not what I meant, and you know it!"

"Yes," she agreed, letting her irritation show. "You're referring to the mansion I lived in when I was married. A mansion that was drafty, had no personality, and that Samuel did nothing to acquire. You've worked hard to achieve what you have, and it's charming. Besides, the house I grew up in wasn't much bigger than this. Now stop apologizing and show me around!"

"Yes, ma'am," he replied with a grin.

He helped her from the wagon, sending an unwanted rush of tingling warmth up from where his hand held hers. Tabitha knew that meeting his eyes would not be a good idea. Her feelings would show, and she was afraid of seeing those same feelings reflected back to her. Instead, she focused her attention on the house.

Amanda climbed up into the front of the wagon and took the reins. "I'll put Dolly in the barn, Papa!"

"Thanks, Mandy."

"Could I come along?" Martha asked her. "I would love to see the barn."

Tabitha rolled her eyes, wishing she could wring one matchmaking neck. "This is very nice," she said, referring to the house, as the wagon rattled away.

Luke still didn't look convinced.

Tabitha sighed. "All right. Bradford Hall was beautiful. It had three floors, and more rooms than I could count. I had two rooms that were just for me. The walls were hung with heavy drapes or ancient, valuable tapestries. There were separate rooms and even separate stairs for the servants. And I enjoyed having servants. Someone to draw my bath, clean my clothes, serve my meals. To a point. I was also bored. The most excitement in my day was to sit in the perfectly sculpted and tended gardens and read, or do a bit of needlepoint. The house was cold and gray and lonely, and devoid of love except for Samuel.

"I prefer my little shop, even if I do have to work hard. I want my home to be full of love, whether it's a mansion or one of those sod houses you Americans use."

"Will your shop be full of love when Martha leaves and you're alone there?"

"No." She conceded his point. But it was still better than what she'd left in England. "At least it won't be full of greed and contempt. Or hedonism."

"Hedonism?" Luke raised a curious eyebrow.

"Yes. I would be a hedonist if I searched for servants and mansions and the luxuries of life for their own sake. If I only wanted life's comforts, I could have stayed in England. Or I could have gone with Etienne. He was back, you know, and he offered me all of those things. And a life of slaving to please oneself."

"I'd heard he'd been around again. Like a hungry wolf." He had known the man was around, almost from his arrival in town. So he had avoided the town, not wanting to run into Etienne, not wanting to see him, and afraid all the while that Tabitha would leave with him. He had snapped at Amanda out of his feeling of helplessness, yet was unable to keep his fear away. He hadn't slept a decent night until he heard through the Garfield grapevine that the Frenchman was gone and Tabitha was still here. Now he was trying to ferret out some information, to learn how she really did feel about The Frog.

"Yes," she answered, not letting the hurt show. "He

was here. For about a week. He even let Jeremy share his suite, to save the boy money. He's really a gentleman." In every way except the most important one.

"Gentleman? If having hands as smooth as a baby's bottom and dressing like a fop make a gentleman, then I guess he is."

"Fop?!" she cried. No matter that he had asked the unspeakable of her, she was not ready to stand by and let him be called something so vile. "He is not a fop," she protested. "He is elegant!"

"So if he's so wonderful, why didn't you go with him? Take him up on his offer of rich living?"

Tabitha clutched her purse and looked away. How could she explain something so personal? It wasn't just Etienne's immoral request, but also it was the death of a friendship, and it still hurt. "It wasn't marriage he offered, Luke, and I am determined to do what's right. So you see, I am still here. He's not, and he won't be back."

Then, desperate to talk about something else, she asked, "Could we go measure the windows, now?" Her emotions were too mixed up to control. She stood by the man she wanted and couldn't have, at least not yet. And discussing Etienne brought a fresh anger at what he had thought of her, as well as the sadness at his going. A single tear escaped from her eye, and she wiped it quickly away.

Strong emotions also swept through Luke. Depression and anger. He was depressed by the degree of emotion she felt for that worthless Frenchman. Maybe, someday, he could convince her, win her hand. But it was clear that her heart would always be with Etienne Rousseau. And anger because the man had hurt her so. The barbaric part of him would find nothing so satisfying at that moment than feeling the crunch of his fist in a very deserving face.

"Certainly," he replied and opened the door.

Tabitha was enchanted. The first floor was nearly all one large room. The kitchen end had a black cook stove, a table that could seat six, and a hand pump for water right in the house! There was a sitting room area with a horsehair sofa and a pair of matching rocking chairs. And three low tables. Most of the things, she knew, Luke had made. There was a large, braided rug on the floor, and a bookcase full of books. The only thing missing was a woman's touch. How she would love to make an afghan, doilies, and some throw pillows for this room! An open door revealed a bedroom, containing a bed much like hers. A chest of drawers, a wooden trunk, and a washstand completed the room's furnishings. Luke opened another door in the kitchen that Tabitha had assumed was a pantry. It was, instead, a stairway that led up to two more bedrooms. The first was empty. The second was obviously Amanda's.

In it was a narrow bed, a wardrobe, and the most exquisite washstand she'd ever seen. A square wooden frame held a mirror at the back. She pulled out the narrow drawer that was in the center of the front, between two smooth, tapering legs. It held a brush, comb, and the pink and white ribbons, now joined by a blue one. Tabitha leaned down to better see the drawer works, which were unbelievably smooth. He had certainly taken special care for his special little girl.

Luke leaned an arm on the washstand, watching her. When she straightened, she discovered she was very close to him.

"Do you like it?" His breath fanned her cheek.

Her eyes locked onto his. His were soft and gentle, like a gray kitten, and warm and comfortable, like a favorite blanket. She thought she could look down layers and layers of his thoughts through those eyes, and read a new aspect of him in each.

"It's beautiful," she managed to whisper. It was difficult to swallow, and her heart was thudding painfully in her chest.

Sixteen

apa!" The scream, coming from outside, effectively drove thoughts of kisses from his mind. He was down the steps before Tabitha could run to the window to look down over the yard to see what was happening. She could see nothing, and followed him outside and then into the barn.

Martha was lying in a heap on the barn floor. Luke was checking for broken bones. "She's breathing," he said, aware that Tabitha had just come in.

"What happened?"

"I think Dolly kicked her!"

Amanda waved her arms and jumped from one foot to the other. "I was giving Dolly some oats, and Miss Martha took the curry comb. I felt Dolly kick, and when I looked, Martha was falling down! Oh, Papa, is she all right?"

"I don't know."

Tabitha prayed, unknowing and uncaring that her

words were not heard by God alone. She prayed quietly but earnestly for Martha to be well, for God to heal any damage done.

Martha moaned.

"Are you all right?" Luke asked. "Can you hear me?"

She groaned something vaguely affirmative, and her hand went to the back of her head. Then she opened her eyes and tried to sit up, wincing painfully.

"Don't move." Luke easily lifted her weight and started for the house. Tabitha followed Luke and Amanda, who scampered back and forth around him. He laid Martha on the sofa, then sent Amanda off to get a cool rag.

"Are you all right?" Tabitha echoed Luke's question as she sat down by Martha on the edge of the sofa, bracing her legs on the floor to keep from sliding off its slippery surface.

"I will be. Lucky for me, I've got an 'ard 'ead."

"What happened?"

"I saw the 'orse was going to kick me, so I tried to jump out of the way. I escaped the 'orse, and tripped on me own petticoat. I must've 'it me 'ead on the way down."

Amanda came in with the rag, hearing most of the explanation. "I'm sorry, Miss Martha," she said.

"I shoulda told ya I didn't know one end of an 'orse from the other, much less 'ow to use one o' them combs. Not your fault."

"You just stay here for a while," Tabitha instructed. "You should feel better soon."

"Anyone hungry?" Luke asked. Not because he thought anyone was, but because there was nothing anyone could do for Martha, and it was awkward for the three of them to stand around the sofa.

"No." Martha had never sounded so disgusted. It would be awhile before her appetite returned.

Luke produced a picnic basket for the rest of them, but Amanda said she needed to finish with Dolly first, and ran outside.

"Cooking is not my strong suit," he admitted. "I had Evelyn put this together for us."

"Which I'm sure she was loathe to do," Tabitha commented, joining him in the kitchen. Luke smiled at her little reminder of the woman's meddling.

"You're not the only one she's tried to pair me off with."

"Oh?" Tabitha tried to sound nonchalant, while actually she was dying of curiosity.

"She invited us to supper one night several months ago. Before you got to town. There was another guest, a Miss Lillian Morton. Attractive girl. Blonde."

Tabitha tried not to be jealous.

"Apparently she hadn't known about Evelyn's devious intentions, either. She hardly spoke all night."

His face clouded then, remembering the girl.

"And?" Tabitha prompted.

"The issue of slavery came up, briefly. Miss Morton suddenly wished to go home, so I walked her. On that walk, she told me that her father was very much against slavery, but her brother owned a slave. There was a big rift in the family. A week later she was dead. Drowned herself in the lake."

"How sad!"

"I'm afraid that's not the end of it. We will go to war with our fellow Americans over this issue before we're through. The thought terrifies me."

"War? Do you really think so?"

"Yes, I do. The politicians and the intellectuals will go to war because of the Union and the Constitution that holds us together as a nation. The men on the battle-fields will be there for state's rights, or to free the slaves, or to preserve their homes and ways of life. Men will be gone, fighting and dying. Women and children will be home with no protection, struggling to run the farms and businesses."

The more Luke had thought about the statements of the stranger in the crowd outside Garfield's store, the more he realized that the man was right. He thought about it, and the coming war, a lot.

"Tabitha?" He glanced into the far section of the room, and saw that Martha was sleeping. "Would you consider doing a big favor for me?"

"Of course."

"If anything happens to me, would you take Amanda?"

Tabitha felt suddenly chilled. "Happens to you? What do you mean? Do you want to go to war?"

"No, I don't want to go to war. But even without a war,

I'm not immortal. Anything could happen. If it does, I want to be sure about Mandy."

When she said nothing, he said, "I know it's a big thing to ask. I can ask Al and Evelyn. I just thought, well, Mandy thinks so highly of you. . . ."

"Certainly, Luke. I'll take her and love her and raise her, if that's what you want. But I don't want to think about war or death right now." She changed the subject. "So. If you can't cook, what do you usually eat?"

He followed the lead of her conversation, not wanting to talk about war and death any longer than necessary either. At least he knew Mandy would be cared for.

"I can do bacon and eggs and pancakes. And I'm a wonder with beans." With a grin he produced crispy fried chicken, a jar of pickles, fresh bread, butter, and a chocolate cake from the basket.

"How do you find time to make furniture?" she asked, needing to keep conversation flowing, and on a safe subject.

"A lot of long winters," he said, smile still intact. "Mandy reads to us for hours, while I work on a table or bed or whatever we need."

Tabitha smiled, but inside she felt like crying at the cozy word picture he painted. She didn't want to leave, ever. She wanted to stay and sew those pillows and curtains and quilts, and fill those other chairs with Luke's children. And she wanted him to love her as completely as he did Rachel, because she loved him. It was, she realized, not a passing attraction. Even if he was burned or injured in such a way that ruined his looks, she would love him. And it was also not just a reaction to her own physical and emotional need for a husband. It was more than that, for she was wanting to fill the void in *his* life, instead of the other way around.

Lord God, she prayed silently, *please let it be him. My life is yours. I will go where You lead and wed whom You would have for me. But this man is truly what my heart desires. Please let his heart come back to You soon, and please give me strength to be circumspect in my behavior and in my thoughts. Please, please, let it be him.*

Her forced smile faded, and she bit her lip to keep back the sudden tears. She sat in one of the six chairs while he got out plates, silver, and cups. "Why so many chairs?" It was the first thing that came to mind.

"Rachel wanted a big family."

Rachel's house, Rachel's chairs, Rachel's wants. Rachel's husband.

"You must have had some happy times here." She tried to keep her voice light. "Everything so normal. So American."

"Sure. But there was a lot of hard work, and a lot of sweat. It wasn't always fun. I'd like to see your Etienne cut hay all day long."

He noticed the shimmer in her eyes. "Sorry. I won't mention him again." To comfort her, he reached for one of her hands.

Amanda came in, and right away Luke sent her to the well for milk.

Tabitha breathed a mental sigh of relief. He thought her tears were for a broken heart, caused by Etienne! Better that than having him know how desperately she wanted *him!*

"Pardon me." Her brain was struggling with what he had just said to Amanda. "Did you just send your daughter to get milk from a well?"

"Truly the land flowing with milk and honey," he teased. "It's in a jug suspended by a rope into the water to keep it cool."

Amanda returned with the jug, and he poured milk into three cups. As they filled their plates, Tabitha was surprised to discover that she was actually hungry. So short a conversation about something so ordinary as milk had gone a long way to make her feel normal.

Martha joined them at the table, but she wouldn't eat anything.

"Do you like our house, Tabitha?" Amanda asked, washing down her last bite of cake.

"Amanda!" Luke scolded. "To you, she is Mrs. Bradford!"

An unrepentant Mandy mumbled, "I wish she was Mrs. Hayes."

Tabitha wished she could crawl under the table, but Luke just laughed. Martha started to join in, but winced at the sudden pain and stopped.

"Seems everyone agrees but Tabitha." Luke tugged Amanda's braid, his words leaving Tabitha in a quandary. Was he saying that he agreed, too?

"Even if she doesn't want to marry you," Amanda pouted, "I wish she didn't have to work in town, so she could live here always."

The color drained from Luke's face. "You don't know what you're saying, young lady!" he began, and as far as Tabitha could tell, he was winding up for a long lecture. Wanting to spare the girl the embarrassment of it, and suddenly afraid of learning his true thoughts with others around, she grasped for words.

"I like it here very much," she said, "but I do have to work in town, so it wouldn't be possible. But thank you, Mandy, for the compliment of wanting my company. But what about Martha? Don't you want her to live here, too?"

"She can't!" Amanda looked startled to see the ignorance of an adult. "She's gonna get married an' live in Chicago!"

"Silly me!" Tabitha toyed with her cake, twirling her fork through the frosting. "How could I have forgotten that?"

"If you didn't have to work, you'd like it here. My papa can do anything! An' he reads to me, an' he made all the furniture! Well," she amended, "almost all the furniture. The sofa was Mama's."

"A wedding present," Luke explained, trying to steer the conversation onto a more socially acceptable track. "From an uncle who had little use for me and didn't want her to live in the wilderness without some touch of civilization. The rug," he went on, "was my mother's, and I must say that the two things looked particularly out of place in the ratty little shack we lived in the first year."

Tabitha rose from the table. First it was Rachel's chairs and Rachel's family. Now it was Rachel's sofa. She did not want to listen to the history of all her things all afternoon. She did not want to listen to how life had been with Rachel. Rachel, Rachel. She was learning to hate a dead woman, God help her.

"The curtains," she said abruptly. "That's what we came here for. I'd like to tend to them."

Luke watched in confusion while she measured the windows and Martha wrote down the numbers. The conversation had gone awry, but he wasn't sure how or why.

Finished measuring, Tabitha stood back to imagine what type of curtains would look best, and decided that the yellow curtains she had pictured earlier would look perfect.

"All done?" Amanda asked.

"Yes, we're finished."

"Then will you come see the babies? Two lambs and a calf," she amended. "They were born this spring. Now they're getting big!"

They all trooped out through the grass to the fenced barnyard to view the baby animals.

"This is Mercury." Amanda patted the brown calf. "Because he's so fast. And the lambs are Romulus and Remus, the twins. And that's Hamlet!" She ran to the next pen, where a fat pink pig oinked for the scraps Amanda tossed him. Hamlet was huge, and clearly not one of the spring babies.

"I told you we read a lot," Luke said, with an affectionate glance at his bouncing daughter.

Tabitha said they really should be heading home. She knew Luke would have evening chores to do, and didn't want him to get back too late.

"May I hitch up Dolly?" Amanda asked.

"I don't know if you're strong enough."

"Me 'ead feels better. I'll 'elp," Martha quickly volunteered.

Tabitha shook her head while the two of them went back to the barn. She didn't know whether Martha needed a spanking or a hug.

"I should apologize for Amanda's remarks earlier," Luke said. "She just said what she thought, and didn't know how embarrassing it would be."

"Embarrassing for whom?"

"Both of us, I suspect, but I'm not sorry she said it. I know she wants a mother. And I commend her choice. I didn't mention it earlier," he added, "but you look wonderful today. I was going to tell you before, but that's when Palmer came up and, well, it didn't seem appropriate then."

"Thank you. You look nice today, too."

"But not elegant, eh?" He winked. "Sorry. I promised not to mention him, didn't I?"

"That's quite all right." She nearly laughed. "Perhaps not elegant, but very nice. Maybe better than elegant."

Astonishment was in the gray eyes that flew to hers,

and she was not a little dismayed at her forwardness. *Oh, dear.* It would be a dreadful mistake to let him think she was encouraging him or flirting with him. The comment had come out without her weighing her words. She would have to take care to choose her words with more discretion.

"Etienne never dressed up just for me," she said, thinking quickly. "He always dressed like that. You, I assume, wore your good clothes for me. Or," she added, striving to cover what sounded to her like she was digging a deeper hole, "am I grievously mistaken, and you had another motive?"

"No other motive," he chuckled. "How about you? Did you dress for me, or do you always wear that to church?"

Tabitha counted her blessings at his phraseology, and also that she hadn't finished her new dress. "I always wear this."

"I'm crushed," he said, but he was smiling. "Lucky congregation."

"Thank you. That is one of the nicest compliments I've ever had."

"You deserve compliments. You are beautiful today. Although I hope I give no offense by saying that I prefer your hair the other way."

She blushed furiously, unable to think of anything to say. His effusive compliments were more disconcerting than those of Etienne, probably because he gave them more sparingly. She was very glad to hear the wagon's approach.

That night as they lay in the dark, waiting for sleep, Martha apologized.

"For what?"

"For me poor timin'. I could tell by your blush and Mr. Luke's scowl that I shoulda taken a bit longer with that 'orse. By 'is expression, I don't think 'e was any too pleased to see me just then."

"That's nonsense. He'd merely complimented my dress."

"What about that scowl?"

"I wouldn't know. Maybe the sun was in his eyes."

"Or maybe 'e was buildin' up ta somethin', and I tromped right in the middle of it."

"That's silly."

Was it silly? Tabitha asked herself over and over the next day while sewing the ruffly, yellow curtains. After all, he had gone to the trouble of looking his best for her. He had admitted that. And those had been no ordinary compliments.

On the other hand, why did he hate God if not because he blamed Him for taking Rachel, whom he loved? He had had plenty of opportunity to speak, yet had given no clue of serious intentions, though Amanda had given him a perfect opening.

Tabitha was glad he hadn't. If he did have serious intentions, she would have to keep him at arm's length until he worked things out with God, and she didn't know if she could do that without driving him away. And if he had no intentions, that would be a disappointment she would like to put off as long as possible.

The curtains were finished by Monday night, and she left a message for Luke with Mr. Garfield when she went to work on Tuesday.

For the moment, she was out of hired sewing. All her jobs were done, and she could take some time to work on her own new lavender dress. Even Martha's wedding dress was done, and just in time. Tomorrow her friend would be gone, headed for Chicago and her wedding.

Lots of ruffles or gathers, she thought, her mind back on the new dress. The fabric would drape well, and she should take advantage of it. Before she knew it, she had a mental image of the design she wanted. High collar. Leg-o'-mutton sleeves. A deeply gathered skirt, but no hoops. White lace at the collar and cuffs, and pearl buttons down the back. She bought the lace and buttons she would need and headed home.

On the way, she saw a handbag in a store window that would finish off the new dress perfectly. It was white, and so was the parasol she'd bought earlier and never used. She bought the purse, which would look nice with her mauve and white skirt and blouse, and would also be acceptable with both the yellow and gray dresses. Better, anyway, than the old beige bag she'd had for so long.

Her pleasure with her purchase didn't last. She knew she was substituting things for what she really wanted, impatient for the Lord to get on with things. It was a poor substitute. How long must she wait?

She walked down to the beach north of the piers and wandered. Unmindful of her skirt, she sat in the sand and gazed out over the expanse of water. It seemed to stretch endlessly until it lapped on the sand. Then came the long stretch of bluff, and beyond that, forest and prairie, more vast than she could comprehend.

There was a small boat out on the water, and the setting sun tinged its white side pink. Pink clouds dotted a bright blue sky. The world was so beautiful, and God was so good. She was ashamed that she had questioned His timing.

It was time for her to be getting home. Martha would be worried, and besides, this was their last night. Tomorrow Martha would be going to Jeremy.

At the top of the bluff, Tabitha noticed the same man she'd seen outside Mr. Garfield's store. He had been around, here and there. Often, come to think of it, for the average new face in town. Was she being followed?

Of all the ridiculous ideas she had ever had, that had to be the silliest. Why on earth should anyone follow her!

By the time she got home it was nearly dark, and there was a surprise in store for her. Yes, Martha had been worried. So were Luke and Amanda, who had stopped by for the curtains, and, on hearing that she wasn't home and Martha didn't know where she was, had been about to set out in search of her.

"My goodness! I only took a walk on the beach. I'm sorry to cause a stir."

"Well, I'm glad to see you back safely," Martha said.

"I guess I lost track of time. I was just thinking and enjoying God's creation. Look what I bought myself." She held up the new purse, which already contained her things, and set the package of lace and buttons on the table.

Martha opened the package and showed the pretty lace to Amanda while Tabitha set down her handbag and fetched the yellow curtains to show Luke. She was holding them up the window to let him get an idea of how they would look, when she saw the sky.

Thick, dark clouds were rolling in from the west, and the wind had picked up. Trees were flapping back and forth like flags.

She stopped talking to watch, and Luke looked out to see what had captured her attention. Lightning, followed by a loud thunderclap, got the attention of Martha and Amanda.

"Are we going to ride home in this, Papa?" Terror was evident on Amanda's face.

Gray eyes questioned Tabitha, but it was Martha, ever practical, and not one to let such an opportunity pass by, who answered.

"Certainly not! You'll be soaked through and catch your death of cold. That's if you're not lost or struck by lightning first. There's an old building out back that I believe used to be a stable. It will suit as a shelter for Dolly."

Luke went out through the back door into the growing storm to tend to the horse, and Martha said to Amanda, "Well, miss. 'Ow would you like a cooking lesson? When ya grow up, ya'd like to be able to feed your 'usband something besides beans, wouldn't ya?"

The overworked conspirators went to the kitchen to prepare supper, and Tabitha leaned her head on the cool glass to watch the storm. She could see it approaching like a black wall. Martha's plan to have Luke join Tabitha in the front room was foiled when he came in the back door. Tabitha could hear him in the kitchen, talking to them.

The first raindrops splattered on the glass, and Amanda's voice rose in exasperation. "I want to surprise you, Papa!" In other words, go away.

Not foiled after all.

Luke said nothing, but came and stood near Tabitha, watching the storm with her. It was almost totally dark now, but they could see shadows of wind-tossed trees, and an unbelievable amount of water falling from the sky. Except for when lightning lit up the scene, they could not even see across the street.

"Do you realize that those two are always conspiring to get us alone together?" Tabitha turned to face Luke. Then, realizing that her movement placed her too close to him, she crossed over to a chair and sat down.

He followed, placed one stockinged foot on the other chair, and leaned on his knee, looking down at her with eyes that crinkled at the corners in amusement. "Do you find it offensive?"

"Do you find it amusing?" she countered.

"Mildly amusing."

"Martha only wants everyone in the world to share in her glorious experience. She means no harm. As to Amanda, I have no idea what her motives are."

"Her motive is that a pretty, grown-up lady has taken an interest in her. She likes you, and you seem to be the best, not to mention only, candidate for the stepmother she wants so badly."

The small flame in the lamp that flickered valiantly in the gloom suddenly absorbed Tabitha's attention. She had to look anywhere but at him. If she did that, he would see how his words affected her. He would see how much she loved him, and that she didn't like him joking about it.

Things had to change. She could not go on indefinitely hiding her feelings. She had not promised God that she wouldn't try to help Luke work out his rebellious attitude. In fact, it had been her idea, not God's, that someone else do it. The thought gave her a slight smile. And here she'd been asking God to hurry. Perhaps, all this time, He had been waiting on her!

"If I'm not getting too personal," she probed, not knowing how to broach the subject, but determined to do so, "how did your wife die?"

The laughter that had been lurking behind Luke's eyes vanished. He sat down, but his body was ramrod straight and tense. Then he relaxed, visibly, as if it had been a conscious effort. Again he got up and went to the window to stare out, palms resting flat against the glass.

Tabitha waited, hoping he would find words, hoping he would talk to her about it, debating whether she should tell him she was sorry for bringing the subject up and find something else to talk about. It was quiet in the room, except for the clang of pots and pans from the kitchen.

Her question had caused him great pain, and she couldn't stand it any longer. She went to him and softly touched his arm in mute apology. "Luke? I'm sorry."

He faced her, and she could see the weak light from the lamp shimmering on unshed tears. Her words sounded so inadequate, even to her. "I didn't mean to . . ." Her voice trailed off. That was inadequate, too. Surely he knew she had not intended this. Yet she sincerely regretted ever having brought it up. There had to be some way to communicate to him how bad she felt about it.

"I know you still love her, but I guess I wasn't thinking of that." She stopped talking. Maybe it would be better if she didn't say anything. Maybe her efforts to comfort him, as well as soothe her own conscience, were only making it worse for him. It would be better to leave him alone with his thoughts, to let him mourn in private. She started to sit down again. Inside, she hurt, too. Each time she saw evidence of his love for his long dead wife, it hurt.

"Stay." His voice cracked.

"What?"

"I'd rather have you stay nearby."

Silently, she went back to stand by his side. Not knowing what to say or do, she just stood there, hoping it was enough. Perhaps he just didn't want to be alone with his ghosts.

Eventually he sighed and dropped his arms from the windowpane. "I've never talked to anyone about it."

Oh, God, what do I do now? Wordlessly she stared up at him. Now that he was really going to open his heart and tell her about his wife and her death, she didn't want to hear it. She did not want to hear him speak of his undying love for someone else, and she felt unable to be any comfort to him.

Seventeen

*L*ightning flashed, momentarily flooding the room in blue light. Almost immediately, thunder roared, shaking the glass in the windows. Amanda screamed, then giggled at herself. Luke seemed oblivious to all of it and Tabitha stood by his side waiting, looking up at the anguish in his face, wishing she hadn't asked.

"You don't need to tell me, Luke."

"No, I think I do need to." Then he was silent for a long time. When he had composed himself, he began to speak. "It was my fault. Rachel was . . . timid. She never wanted to try anything on her own. She depended on me for everything.

"I'd known her since she was twelve. Even then she was that way, but then I liked it. I was eighteen, and Rachel made me feel important, needed. Not that I wasn't loved at home. I had wonderful parents. But they had each other, and three older sons to help with the farm-work. All of them were larger and more capable than I was. Sometimes I got stuck helping our mother with the wash or with heavy work. But as my little sister grew, I was needed less for that, too. I worked, sure, but I always felt like they could get along fine without me.

"So I loved it when Rachel needed me. I stuck up for her when other kids teased her. Sometimes I helped her with her chores. When she was sixteen, we got married. But her dependency that was so charming at sixteen grew less so as the years went by. Eventually I decided that she needed to grow up and stand on her own two feet. I encouraged her to do things on her own.

"One day, she was twenty-four by then, she came out to the field and said she needed something from town. I was skeptical, but proud of her attempt to be independent, so I gave her a kiss and watched her march off to the barn and then, a few minutes later, head out to town in the wagon."

Luke sighed. "I never should have let her go. Not only let her, but encouraged her. She would have waited till the next day, when I had time to take her in. She was only trying to please me. And a few days later, she was dead."

Tabitha frowned, not understanding how Rachel's death was in any way his fault, but not wanting to interrupt his telling.

After a pause, he continued. "Gangrene. Everything

went fine, except she cut herself on the harness. Just a little cut. She laughed about it."

He gave a rueful chuckle, and Tabitha heard in it his love and admiration for his wife despite her "timidity." Only now it was okay. His past was what made him the Luke she knew and loved, and she also knew, with sudden clarity, that her feelings for Etienne hadn't changed how she felt for Luke. So Luke could still love Rachel, and it didn't mean he wouldn't be able to love her, too.

"It got infected. I should have gotten a doctor for her, but we didn't have much money, and I had no idea how serious it was. By the time I realized, he couldn't do anything for her except amputate. She died anyway."

"Oh, my God!" Tabitha whispered.

"Yes, your God." Luke pulled his hand away and glared at her with pain and bitterness in his eyes. "This loving God you worship allowed that! If He's so loving and all-powerful, why didn't He stop it?" His voice cracked.

Tabitha had never encountered such misery and bitterness. What could she say?

"I killed her. I caused it. She never would've gone to town if it weren't for my trying to change her." He clenched his teeth together so that the muscles along his jaw stood out, and he was clenching and unclenching his fist in undirected fury until he slammed it into the wall, shaking the windows and denting the plaster.

"Luke, no!" Her own tears dribbled down her cheeks

and onto his shirt when she crushed him in a fierce hug. "Don't do this to yourself! It wasn't your fault!"

He said nothing, but the expression on his face said he only thought she was saying what he wanted to hear.

"Luke! You were right; you had to make her grow up. You both would have been happier. There was no way in the world you could possibly have foreseen that she would cut herself. Besides, people get cuts every day without such serious consequences."

"I was so hard on her!" He gave a bitter laugh. "I wanted her to become the strong woman I thought she could be. Tabitha, I loved her so much, and I forced her. Subtly, but I forced her. And I killed her."

"No, you didn't. There are times when we do what we think is right at the time, and then we find out it wasn't such a good idea. You were trying to do what was right; you were trying to help her. It was a tragedy, Luke, but you can't go on blaming yourself! It was horrible and unfortunate, but it wasn't your fault.

"Just like David," she continued. "Yes, he died because he followed me. But you were right about that, and I'm right about this. It wasn't my fault that he did. It's the same, Luke. You had no way of knowing."

Martha stepped in to call them to eat, took in the scene, and decided it would be better if she found an excuse to delay supper. "Mandy," she said, quietly, turning back to keep the child from following her to the front room and seeing her father so. "Wot would you think of making some dessert, too, before we call them in?"

Luke would have been grateful to Martha for the extra minutes, but he wasn't even aware that she had been in the room.

He returned Tabitha's hug with equal desperation, absorbing the love and forgiveness that flowed from her so easily. He had carried around his guilt and bitterness for years, and it felt good to talk about it. It was a great relief, and he was very glad that she hadn't rejected him, as he'd feared she would, after he admitted what had happened and his own part in it.

Gradually, Tabitha became aware of his arms around her, and hers around him, and it was an enjoyable discovery. Wonderful, in fact. Wonderful and dangerous. She took a step back, and he loosened his hold, leaving his hands around her waist. "Are you all right?" she asked.

"Yes." He released her completely and ran a shaking hand through his hair. "In fact, I feel better than I have for a long time."

"I'm glad."

"Thanks, Tabitha. For listening, and for not hating me because of what I had to tell you."

She wiped the last traces of tears from her face with the back of her hand. Quite unladylike, but now was not the time to go searching for a handkerchief. Uncertainly, she reached to wipe his face, too, and let her hand linger on his cheek. "How could I ever hate you?" she said with a tremulous voice. He stared at her, and she felt like she was getting lost in a warm fog. She wanted to get lost. She wanted to get so lost that she could never find her way out again.

She wanted to tell him that he was wonderful—the most truly decent man she had ever met. Except maybe for Samuel, but then Samuel had been so good that it had gotten tiresome at times. She wanted to say that Rachel had been a lucky, lucky lady.

Instead, she nodded towards the kitchen. "Do you think they've misplaced themselves in there?"

Just then Martha's beaming face appeared through the door. "Are you ready to eat?"

Luke glanced at Tabitha, and she was glad to see that most of the evidence of his crying was gone. She hoped hers was, too. "Yes," he said, and at the same time she said, "Certainly." They exchanged the smile of a shared joke, and he added, "I'm starved!"

Amanda took his hand and led him back to the table. "See, Papa! We fried some brats and cooked some sauerkraut, and I made the corn bread all by myself! Well, Miss Martha told me how. That's what took so long. And guess what's for dessert? Chocolate pudding! And it's still warm!"

Amanda, Martha, and Luke ate with gusto, laughing and talking. Tabitha ate a few small bites and forced her mouth to smile now and then. Her feeling for Luke had grown tremendously in the past hour. It was too strong for her to deal with on her own. She needed to find time as soon as possible to talk it over with God.

The table wasn't overly large, and she could feel Martha's knee bump hers from time to time. That didn't bother her. But when Luke bumped her from the other side, she swallowed a lump of unchewed food, and gripped her knife and fork tightly to hide the trembling in her hands. Did anyone notice?

Amanda was blissfully unaware; her face glowing with happiness at her accomplishment and her father's praise. Martha chattered like a magpie, but Tabitha knew she was watching her like a hawk, and she felt exposed. She hardly dared look at Luke. Slowly she let her eyes drift in his direction. He was complimenting Amanda on the corn bread again, not looking her way, so she felt she was safe, and could allow herself to watch him, unseen. His skin was paler than usual. He had such strong features—nose, jawline, and cheekbones. She loved the lines around his eyes.

He was, she realized, returning her gaze. She became aware of it by the fact that she was thinking what beautiful eyes he had. Strangely enough, it was not embarrassing to get caught, and she continued looking. Light from the lamp reflected little flickers in his eyes as he searched her face, questioning.

It was one of those moments that seemed longer than it actually was. Tabitha felt her soul had been read like a book, but in reality, the shared look had been so brief that Martha, who was giving Amanda a second helping of pudding, didn't even notice.

Tabitha tore her eyes away. She felt like pudding, too.

"Listen!" Luke said. Tabitha jumped, thinking he was talking to her.

They all sat quietly, listening.

"I don't hear anything, Papa."

"Exactly," he agreed, more thankful than any of the others would ever know. Tabitha, beautiful Tabitha, was, unknowingly, quite a temptress. The small house suddenly felt about the size of a closet. "Storm's over," he said abruptly. "What say we thank these lovely ladies for supper and their hospitality, and go home?"

"But Papa!" Amanda protested. "I thought we were gonna stay all night!"

"Don't be a goose, Angel. The storm's over, and we've ridden home in the dark before, many times. Besides, we need to tend the stock."

"Oh." Amanda didn't hide her disappointment well.

Tabitha felt a strange mixture of disappointment and relief.

"What about the mud?" Martha asked. "Won't you get stuck?"

Amanda brightened at the thought.

"No," Luke said, casting her hope to the wind. "It's just the horse, not a wagon. Dolly can walk in the grass at the edge of the road."

Martha said her good-byes. She would not be seeing the pair again.

Luke fetched Dolly from the old stable, and the two disappeared into the night.

Wednesday morning found Tabitha and Martha at the train station exchanging hugs and tears and promises to write and maybe even visit. Tabitha waved until she could no longer see the train, then went to work.

"Tabitha," Al Garfield said when she had no more than stepped in, "are you in some kind of trouble?"

"Trouble? What do you mean?" He seemed very serious. Whatever the problem was, he was sincerely concerned about her.

"Some fella's been asking questions about you. 'Bout Luke Hayes, too, 'cause he says he's seen you together a lot. What's this all about?"

"I don't know."

Someone was spying on her. She was being followed! Fear and a multitude of questions fought for top priority in her mind. As long as she was here with Mr. Garfield, she was safe, she told herself, and took a deep breath. But who would follow her, and why? It had to be the same man she had noticed. "Is this man tall and thin?" she asked. "Mustache? Wears a black suit?"

To all her questions, Albert Garfield nodded yes.

"Who is he?"

"I wish I knew. I've seen him frequently—more often than I thought could be coincidental. It crossed my mind that he was following me, but I dismissed the idea as ridiculous. Why would someone be following me? Mr. Garfield, I'm afraid!"

"Don't be. I'll go right now and ask the sheriff to keep an eye on this chap."

He left, and she sagged against the counter. Martha was gone, and she was alone. Someone was following her and asking questions, and there was no way of knowing why. But it had to be bad. If he was the honest type, he would just ask her his questions face-to-face.

Should she go to Chicago, too? It might be her best option. She wouldn't be alone, and she could start over again. She already had friends there, and she had a bit of money now. It wouldn't be as hard as the first time.

But then there was Luke. Well, leaving Luke and a situation that was quickly getting out of her depth might be for the best, too.

Then again, it wouldn't take much detective work to find her in Chicago, and she might be endangering her friends if she went there. "What should I do?" she asked God, out loud.

As the day passed, Tabitha's fears stilled somewhat. After all, if this person had wanted to, he could have killed her several times by now. He'd had opportunity. Why, just yesterday, when she'd gone to the beach alone

. . . she shuddered at the thought.

So, he hadn't harmed her yet, though he'd had plenty of chances. And the Lord was her protector. He could either guard her miraculously or guide her into a safer situation.

Her philosophizing didn't seem quite so convincing that evening when she went home. She had used Mr. Garfield's own arguments to keep him from feeling that he either had to go with her to her house or take her with him to his. The sheriff was, after all, watching out for her. And the man hadn't hurt her. It was probably someone hired by Leah to find out what she was doing.

That seemed the most logical explanation. Leah was probably sitting in her big house, worrying that Tabitha would come back and demand money or some other valuables.

Now, however, she walked quickly, looking over her shoulder repeatedly. As soon as she was in the house, she locked the door, then checked the lock on the back door and closed all the curtains. She didn't light any lamps, because that would make her more visible and therefore more vulnerable.

When a knock sounded at the door, she almost screamed. After a few deep breaths, she picked up her iron and went to see who was there.

Eighteen

*P*ulling the curtain back only a slight crack, she peered through, and could see the dark shadow of a man by her door. When he reached to knock again, she could see his profile more clearly. Luke.

"Thank you, Jesus!" she whispered, taking a breath. She hadn't been aware until then that she was holding it. Her legs didn't want to hold her upright, but she made her way to the door and threw it open, pulling Luke in and slamming the door after him.

"Tabitha, what is going on? I was getting worried."

"Maybe you should be. I'm being followed. And I was never so glad to see anyone in my life as I was to see you on my doorstep just now." She set the iron down on the cutting table.

"Followed? Are you sure?"

"Yes, I'm sure! Did you expect me to be afraid of an

imagined shadow?" That was probably not the thing to say, she realized, suddenly thinking of Rachel. "He even questioned Mr. Garfield about me. He's very real."

"Then what are you doing here alone? And if Al knows, why aren't you at his place?"

"Because I tried to be brave. The sheriff is aware and keeping a lookout for the man. And I convinced Mr. Garfield, and myself, that it was probably some hireling of my greedy and hysterical sister-in-law. I did believe that. But now it's dark, and I'm alone, and . . . oh, Luke, I'm frightened!"

"As well you should be! You're coming home with me."

"I couldn't," she said automatically.

"Would you forget gossip and your reputation? This could be your life we're talking about!"

"No, it's not possible." She was too ingrained in what was or was not acceptable behavior to say otherwise. And she was also afraid of herself, if she spent the night in his house. She knew now precisely why Martha had fled Jeremy. "Besides," she said, dragging up the same argument she had used before, "this man, whoever he is, has had lots of opportunities to harm me. He hasn't, so I'm sure I'll be fine."

"If you don't get your things and come with me, I'll carry you."

She stood still, mute, calling his bluff. He wouldn't be so ridiculous and melodramatic.

"Women," he muttered. Then he strode to the back room and began ransacking her personal belongings to collect a nightgown, clean clothes, her hairbrush, her purse, and even, to her horror, clean underwear. "Need anything else?"

Dumbstruck, she slowly shook her head no.

He swept her up into his arms.

"What will the neighbors say?'

"I don't care."

"You don't care?"

"Hate me for this if you want, but at least you'll be alive to hate me." He deposited her on the wagon seat next to Amanda, and she was glad for the wedge between them.

Soon Amanda was asleep with her head on Tabitha's lap, and the entire journey passed in a strained silence.

Luke put up the wagon, and Amanda and Tabitha went into the house. The girl wearily trudged up the steps with Sinbad at her heels, leaving Tabitha to light a couple of lamps. The house was, if possible, even more charming by lamplight.

Luke came in and saw her standing there. Quietly he closed the door, hung his jacket on a hook of the hall tree, and walked into the kitchen.

"I still think this is ridiculous," Tabitha said, "but thank you for caring."

"Ridiculous, is it? And what was your plan? To use an iron to defend yourself against a knife or gun?"

"But the sheriff is watching out for me."

"Short of putting you in jail, how is he supposed to do that? He has rounds to make. Or were you planning on sticking to his side all night as he makes them?"

She sighed, giving up. Luke was right, or logical, anyway. She was here. She was ruined. Now she would have to go to Chicago. Would even that be far enough?

"What did you come for tonight?"

"The curtains." He laughed. "I forgot them last night. Guess I had too much on my mind—like you."

"Me?" she asked weakly.

"Yes, you. Course, I'd thought about you plenty of other nights, but last night, I told you my worst secret, and you didn't hate me. Amazing. You even . . ." He wouldn't finish, picking up a cup for distraction.

"I even what?" she prompted, curious.

"That look you gave me at supper. That was an invitation if ever I saw one. Don't look at me like that again, unless you want me to take you up on it."

Stunned, Tabitha dropped into a chair. Yes, she had been thinking about him, longing for him, in love with him. But she had never meant to issue "invitations," and she certainly had not intended for him to pick up on her thoughts.

They could hear Amanda coming down the stairs. "Coffee?" he offered.

"Yes, please." She was trying to appear normal, but how could she?

The three of them sat around the table drinking coffee, Amanda's diluted with lots of milk. "Time for bed, Angel," Luke said when she emptied her cup. "And don't sleep right in the middle of it. Tabitha will have to sleep with you."

Happy to have her grown-up friend spending the night, Amanda kissed her father and hugged Tabitha, then skipped off to bed.

"More coffee?" he offered Tabitha.

She accepted, with a nod. She wouldn't be able to sleep tonight, anyway.

"I was quite astonished." He picked up their former conversation without a hitch. "I thought you were hopelessly in love with Etienne Rousseau."

"Etienne! In love with Etienne? Why would you think that?"

He gave a rude snort. "Not so improbable, is it? He's handsome and suave and rich. How does a boring, ordinary farmer stack up to that? And when he kisses your hand, you giggle and blush like a schoolgirl. What am I supposed to think?"

Tabitha was ashamed. Yes, Etienne was attractive and exciting, and she had let it show. She was ashamed that she had given Luke, and probably Etienne, too, the impression that she was in love with him. No wonder he had assumed she would go away with him. Her heart must be that of a harlot. The humiliating thing was that it showed.

"You're right, of course. He is attractive, and I wasn't immune. He is shallow and selfish, though." She made her eyes meet his squarely and said, "His looks are only on the surface. Yours go all the way through."

The front legs of his chair dropped to the floor, and he leaned towards her, reaching to touch her. Tabitha wanted more than anything to let him—to meet him halfway, to reach out to him, too. But first she had to know. She must know what he really thought about God, and see if she could allow the sweet answer to her dreams, or if she must build a barricade between them. God forgive her if her motives were not entirely proper.

"I've been thinking," she said in a rush, "about last night."

His hand changed course, and he reached instead for his cup. "What about it?"

"About what happened. With Rachel." She gritted her teeth, waiting for the explosion she thought might come.

He stared into the black liquid in the cup. "You really believe it was accidental, don't you? And you don't think it was my fault." It wasn't a question. He knew. It felt wonderful to have someone believe in him again.

"Of course it wasn't your fault."

"Okay," he said, putting down the mug with a thump. "Tell me what you think. I can tell you're dying to."

"I thought about this a lot last night. About God allowing it."

"God knew it would happen. I've been thinking, too. You're right about my not knowing it would be disastrous if she went to town. But God knew. If I didn't stop her, why didn't He? Or if He let her go, why didn't He keep her from getting hurt? Or protect her from getting gangrene?"

"You can't blame God for allowing it, any more than you can blame Him for any of the pain in the world."

"But if He's all powerful, if He loves us, then why didn't He stop it?"

"He could have. He is all powerful, and He does love us. When we hurt, He hurts for us. The Word says that He saves our tears. We are infinitely precious to Him. Yes, He could have stopped it any number of ways."

He was listening, and she went on.

"God was capable of changing something. He could have kept Rachel from hurting herself, or He could have protected her, as He did Paul when the apostle was bitten by the serpent and the poison didn't harm him. Maybe God was warning her, in that still, small voice, and she didn't listen."

"Then why didn't He make *me* listen? Why not shout? Why not shake me? Why not write it in the clouds?"

"He could. And at times, He has communicated with men in ways not easily missed. A burning bush isn't exactly subtle. But usually He speaks quietly, in our hearts. We can listen or not."

Luke looked stricken, as if she were accusing him.

"I'm not saying you weren't listening. I don't know. Maybe it was just her time."

"So you're saying that God just lets happen what will happen? He just sits back and watches us kill ourselves? I thought you were the type who would believe in miracles."

"Oh, I do! The Lord works miracles! But normally, He uses natural circumstances. Like your showing up tonight when I was so frightened. I do believe in miracles, but I don't believe in second-guessing God. He always does what is for the best in the greater scheme of things. When Job went through his troubles, he had no way of knowing that he would be an example of perseverance for the rest of time. So how are you to know what is or is not for the ultimate good?"

When he didn't reply, she asked, "Was Rachel a Christian?"

"Yes." He rolled his eyes. "Church all the time, and telling Mandy Bible stories."

"Then don't you think she's happier in heaven than she would have been here? There's nothing to be afraid of there."

"I suppose you're right." He picked up the cups and put them by the dishpan. Silently Tabitha prayed that she had said what he needed to hear to mend his fences with God. It was past time to try to get some sleep. She stood, feeling totally drained, intending to head for the stairs.

"You look perfect there, Tabitha."

"What?" She cast him a curious glance.

"I've pictured you in my kitchen before. Many times. I thought you would look perfect here. I was right." He came toward her. "I've been impressed by you since the first time I saw you, limping along on that broken heel. That alone would have been more than Rachel could have coped with. But you came to a foreign country by yourself, were stranded in a strange place, and you not only survived, but built a business from nothing. You're a courageous woman."

Tabitha was pleased that he found something in her worth respecting, but she was also angry and frustrated. Would he always be comparing her with Rachel, for good or for ill? Would the woman always stand between them?

"I would rather not be compared to Rachel. And if my only attraction is that I am unlike her, then I don't want to hear any more of whatever it is you have to say."

"I'm sorry. I didn't mean to compare you. I only intended to say that that was what originally caught my attention." He had moved closer to her, so close that she had to tilt her head up to see his face. "After that . . . well. I'm not blind."

Neither was the one who watched them from without, one eye peering just past the edge of the still-curtainless window.

"I've seen you work hard; I've seen you when you didn't have much." A work-roughened finger traced her jaw, then curved under her chin to tip it up so his lips could reach hers. But he didn't kiss her yet. "I've never heard you complain. I've never heard you show any disrespect for your late husband or your father, though you had reason, maybe, to resent both. I've seen the way you care about the problems of others, like Martha. Or me, with Amanda. And I've seen your eyes—the way you look at me. Like you are now." Then he kissed her softly, just a brief contact of lips. "I see your hair, and your nose." He kissed the tip of it.

"What I'm trying to say, Tabitha, is that I love you." He lowered his lips to hers, watching her for any indication that she did not want him to kiss her. What he saw was her eyelids flutter shut, and he felt her pulse, under the finger that held her chin, quicken.

She went into his embrace willingly, meeting his kiss, then with a gasp she snapped open her eyes and pulled away. She could not let this happen!

She thought he was a Christian who had merely been dealing with some difficult questions. But she wasn't sure. And still he had said nothing about marriage. In her mind she heard one of her father's favorite sayings: *Fool me once, shame on you. Fool me twice, shame on me.* She shouldn't be here, in his arms, dreaming about a forever. Not after she had seen how deceptive men could be, and how susceptible she was.

What now? What could she possibly say to him? What she wanted to say was that she loved him. She wanted to stay here with him, share his home and his life, help raise Amanda, have more children. More than anything, she wanted to kiss him again.

That desire, and all others, were driven from her mind in the next instant, as the kitchen door burst open and Etienne crashed into the room. Before either she or Luke had time to react, he had grabbed Tabitha and held a long, sharp knife to her neck.

"Don't try to be a hero, *monsieur*. I would hate to have to hurt our Tabitha."

It couldn't be Etienne! Her mind screamed denial. What was happening?

"What are you doing here, Rousseau?" Luke asked.

"Keeping you from destroying my plan."

"What plan?" Luke prompted him to elaborate.

He seemed willing enough to comply. Sounded proud of himself, even.

"I grew up in the worst parts of Paris. As soon as I learned that I only had to smile at the rich ladies, I knew I had something much better than begging or digging in the rubbish for my food. I became what they wanted. Every woman's dream. And they rewarded me well.

"Now Tabitha, she wasn't rich. But by then it didn't matter, because I had enough of my own money. She was lovely as a rose, and seemed as pure. I guess I was fooled. I thought she was a real moral lady." He tightened his hold, and the knife pressed against her skin. "You wouldn't give me a thing beyond a smile, though I offered you the world! And now here you are, melting in his arms! You're just like all the others, Tabitha, just like all the tramps and trollops up and down every coast in the world. Harlot!" he screamed, livid with rage.

"Don't you speak to her that way!" Luke took two steps towards them.

A black, enraged gaze locked onto his, and the words were punctuated for emphasis. "Not another step." To prove his intent, he carved a small cut in Tabitha's skin, and a tiny trickle of blood ran down into the fabric of her yellow dress.

Luke's face looked like wax. He stepped back.

"Now, my lovely little strumpet, where is your purse?"

"My purse?"

"Yes, your purse! Don't play dumb with me!"

"Over there." She nodded toward the door, where her handbag sat on the floor behind the hall tree.

"That's not it!"

"I bought a new one."

"What did you do that for? Where's the other?"

"In town. At home."

He thought for a minute. "Okay. You and I are going to get it. But first I'll have to tie up this plebeian. Sit down!" he bellowed to Luke.

"What do you want with my purse?" Tabitha asked, trying to distract him. "There's nothing in it."

"Almost true. It's worthless except for the diamonds in the lining."

"Diamonds!?"

He smiled wickedly. "I stole them from a rich fat lady in New York. And you were the perfect hiding place, Tabitha. Who would ever suspect a proper churchgoing lady like you of stashing diamonds for a jewel thief?"

A jewel thief. "The most beautiful diamond in America" he had called her—only now she realized he'd been referring to a real diamond! What a colossal ego she had. He had probably been on the *Freedom* in the first place because he was running from the law, and it was the first boat leaving London.

He moved her in front of Luke, so he could watch her while he tied Luke to the chair. "Make a move," he threatened her, "and I will cut him. Deep. And it would give me pleasure to do so."

Etienne was having difficulties with the rope, and Luke motioned to Tabitha to keep quiet. Then, in a sudden rush, he stood, swinging his arms back to take Etienne by surprise, knocking the rope loose and the knife from his hand. With no sign of remorse, Etienne grabbed an iron skillet and brought it crashing down on Luke's head. He crumpled to the floor in a heap as Tabitha screamed.

Once Luke was securely tied, Etienne dragged Tabitha out into the night, where a large, dark horse waited.

There was an opportunity coming. He could not mount the horse behind her while maintaining much of a threat with the knife. She shot a brief prayer for help into heaven.

"Don't try anything. Even without my steel friend, you're no match for me. And I really don't want to hurt you, Tabitha." When he said her name, it was almost a caress, and Tabitha ground her teeth together, fighting nausea, not wanting him to think of her like that. How could he heartlessly hurt Luke, perhaps even kill him, and then just walk away and speak to her in that voice?

"Where did you get the horse?" she asked. Anything to distract him. "Stolen?"

"No," he replied, his melodic accent belying the thick sarcasm. "I keep a stable here for my occasional visits."

He placed a hand on the saddle horn, and Tabitha kicked him as hard as she could in the face. Granted, in the dark and with her legs tangled in skirts and petticoats, it wasn't a stunning blow, but it was enough to make him step back, clutching his bleeding nose. She dug her heels into the sides of the horse, but it was tied, and reared back, afraid of the smell of blood and the conflicting orders of people. She slid off, on the opposite side from Etienne, and ran. He screamed a string of curses, calling her unspeakable names, but she kept running. At first she headed towards the barn. It seemed a safe place. But he would look there first. She headed into the forest.

The woods were terrifying. Branches slapped at her

face, brambles tore her skirt. She wondered about snakes and spiders and bears. They were preferable to meeting Etienne again, but she was afraid of them anyway. Coming to a huge old oak, she stepped behind it to catch her breath and sank to the ground to pray for protection. Remembered scriptures of protection came to mind. God had protected Daniel in the lions' den. He had saved Paul from the serpent's poison. He had watched over David and kept him safe from both Goliath and Saul. He could and would protect her, too. She clung to that. And she prayed as fervently for Amanda. For all she knew, Etienne had gone back into the house. And Luke! The last she had seen him, he was on the floor, and she didn't know if he was even alive.

❧❦

Amanda huddled in the stairwell, the hem of her nightgown stuffed in her mouth to muffle her cry. Sinbad whined, and her heart pounded in fear, but she managed to shush him. As soon as the angry voices outside faded with distance, she ran into the kitchen.

"Papa! Papa!"

Amanda's frightened cry seemed far off, and Luke struggled out of the black fog, knowing he had to help her. And Tabitha. "Lord Jesus," he prayed for the first time in years, "help me. They need me." With much effort and a wave of pain at the movement, he sat up, and Amanda threw herself into his lap, wrapping her arms around his neck. "I thought you were dead! He took Tabitha!"

"What?"

"The bad man who hurt you! He took her, an' Papa, I was so scared!"

He pushed her off him. "I'm okay, Angel, but I've got to go find her. You go back upstairs and hide until I come back, all right?"

She scurried to obey, terrified at the thought of being found alone in the house if the man should come back while her father was gone.

"And Amanda?"

"What, Papa?"

"Pray for us. Pray hard, Angel."

He slipped out of the house and crossed the yard. The barn was quiet and still. Luke crept inside, peering around the corner before entering. Everything seemed normal, quiet but for the nighttime sounds of the animals. It was very dark, the only light the faint moonlight at the door behind him.

Judging Luke's whereabouts by sound only, Etienne jumped out from a stall to attack him. He misjudged slightly, but now, in the barn's center, he could see his opponent silhouetted in the bluish light. He had the advantage, because there was no light behind him, and Luke had no way of knowing his exact location. He withdrew a small knife from his boot. The other he had lost in the dark when Tabitha had kicked him. Silently he cursed her again. She would pay. He lunged for Luke's legs, sending both his opponent and himself sprawling in the hay.

Luke brought his knee up to connect with Etienne's jaw, and Etienne slashed at him, narrowly missing. The blade shimmered like starlight. Luke reached for his knife hand, but in the dark, he could not find Etienne at all. He heard an evil chuckle just before Etienne jumped on him, both knees solidly in Luke's stomach, doubling him over in pain.

Etienne stood over him, hands on knees, breathing heavily, while Luke retched, rolling to his knees and elbows in the straw. "I wasn't going to hurt anyone," the Frenchman said. "I only came for Tabitha and the diamonds. But the police are on to me, so I had to follow her and wait for an opportunity to talk to her without being seen." He straightened, paced the barn floor, and continued his explanation. Luke's stomach was settling, the pain was diminishing, but his head hurt something fierce.

"Then I saw you carry her off! And I look in your window, and there she is in your arms!"

His rage was growing again, making Luke warily, slowly, move further away.

"She's mine! Do you understand me? You have no idea how long I looked for someone like her!" Again he was wielding his knife, and he started towards Luke.

Luke knew this was the end. Barring a miracle, he was about to be killed. Was he ready to meet God face-to-face?

Suddenly lantern light flooded the room. All movement stopped at the sharp, distinctive sound of a shotgun being pumped. Etienne dropped the knife, holding his hands away from him, in clear view. Luke collapsed, feeling like vomiting. His head was one huge, sharp pain.

The man with the shotgun Luke recognized as the sheriff. The tall, mustached man he didn't know, but he had never been so glad to see anyone.

He got off the floor, brushing bits of hay from his pants, still feeling ill.

"Where's the woman?" the stranger asked.

"I don't know," Luke answered.

"She ran off into the forest, I think," Etienne volunteered. The suave Frenchman was back. His ability to change like a chameleon sent a tingle of revulsion down Luke's back.

He went up to Etienne. When his face was inches from the other man's, he said "If you've hurt her, I'll strangle you with my bare hands. And I don't care if they hang me for doing it."

"She is unharmed, *monsieur*." Then, when Luke was

heading out of the barn to search for her, he called softly, "*Monsieur?*"

Luke stopped.

"You are a lucky man."

"Yes. I am."

He walked out the door. The sheriff stayed with the now handcuffed Etienne. The tall man followed Luke.

"I'll help you look for her. I need to question her."

"About what? Who are you?" Luke wasn't feeling up to being polite, and he suspected that this was the man who had followed Tabitha and frightened her so badly.

"Jake Majors. Pinkerton Detectives." He extended his hand, but Luke didn't shake. "I need to ask her about Rousseau. We need information to put him away."

"Fine. But first I need to tell my little girl that everything is okay."

❦

Tabitha huddled against the base of a great tree. It was cold. She was frightened. The scratches on her face stung. When would morning come? Did she dare go back? Where was back?

Even in the valley of the shadow of death, God was with her. She would get through the night. In the morning she could find her way. But should she go back now to help Luke and Amanda? Or should she try to find a farm or the town, to seek more help than she could give?

After a long, long, shivering time, she heard her name called out in the woods. It was so distant that it sounded more like the call of an owl than a person. The call came closer.

"Mrs. Bradford!"

So it wasn't Luke. It was a voice she didn't recognize. At first she nearly answered, but then she remembered Etienne's craftiness. It could be him. Should she run, or would her movement only draw attention to her?

Then suddenly it was Luke's voice, calling for her from a different direction.

"I'm here!" She stood and came out from behind the tree, lightheaded with relief.

When the first man got near enough to see clearly, she gasped. It was the man who had been following her!

"Jake Majors," he introduced himself. "Pinkerton Detectives. Don't worry, Mrs. Bradford. We've got Rousseau. We've been after that scoundrel for a long time."

Tears stung her eyes. *Thank You, Lord!*

She saw Luke behind the Pinkerton man and stumbled, sobbing, into his arms. He crushed her to him. Jake Majors discreetly looked away.

As they headed back to the house, Luke asked, "Why were you following Tabitha? You scared her half to death."

"We thought she might lead us to Rousseau. Didn't figure she knew about me. That is, until I started questioning folks. Figured she'd know, then, but I planned to talk to her soon. Clumsy of me."

"Why didn't you just ask her?"

"We had to establish first whether or not she was a willing accomplice."

"I think tonight was enough to answer that for you."

"Reckon so."

In the barnyard, Sheriff Carter was astride his horse. Etienne was cuffed to the saddle of his horse, his arms tied. A third horse was ready for Jake Majors. The detective mounted.

"Tabitha," Etienne said. "I almost loved you. Why could you not love me?"

She looked up at him. He was a defeated man, and she felt sorry for him. "I could have. If you had been honorable. It is my hope that God will yet change you, and make you into the man I once thought you were."

Etienne stared at his cuffed hands, unable to look at her. "Perhaps He will. I'm sorry."

The three men rode away.

When Luke and Tabitha reentered the house, the light made her blink a few times. Amanda was in her nightgown, standing in the middle of the floor, whimpering. When she saw Luke, her bare feet hurtled her across the floor to him. He carried her to a rocking chair and collapsed into it, where he held her tight, reassuring her and explaining what had happened.

"Weren't you scared, Papa?"

"Yes, I was. But I learned something important tonight."

Amanda was astonished that her father still needed to learn anything. "What did you learn?"

"I learned that God does hear our prayers, and He does care about us."

"Did God take care of you?"

"Yes, Angel, He did."

His words, overheard by Tabitha, confirmed her belief that he was indeed a Christian man. She went to the kitchen area of the room to say her thanks to God, and to wash the stinging scratches on her hands and face with cool water from the hand pump.

To the sound of the squeaking of the rocker, she made a fresh pot of coffee. Exhausted, she sat, sipping her coffee, while Luke rocked and the rocker squeaked. Which was the real Etienne? The polished gentleman with the easy smile, or the thief who could be violent without hesitation? He was a confused man, who'd had a hard life. She committed herself, right then, to pray for him daily.

The eastern sky was growing pink when Luke carried a sleeping Amanda up the stairs and put her into bed. It was a dawn Tabitha was very glad to see.

Luke came back into the kitchen and poured himself a cup of coffee, then sat with her at the table.

"I must look a sight," she said. So much had happened, between them and to them, that small talk was the only conversation she wanted to have. She did feel truly wretched looking. Her dress was torn and dirty, her face and hands were scratched, and in her mad dash through the trees she had lost her hair net. Now her hair tumbled wildly down her back, and it was full of twigs and leaves.

"You look alive. To me, that's beautiful."

"Me, too. I mean, I'm glad you're alive, too. I sat out there by that oak tree, wondering if Etienne had gone back into the house to carve you and Amanda into pieces."

"Are you glad? Really?"

"Luke! How could you ask such a thing?"

"Naturally, I know you're glad I'm alive. I guess what I'm asking is, how glad?"

"What do you mean, how glad? Didn't I run to you, blubbering like an idiot with relief to see you alive and unharmed?"

He toyed with the handle of his mug. "Earlier, I told you I love you, and I do. More than I ever knew was possible. But when I said it, you looked horrified. What is so wrong, Tabitha? I thought you cared for me. Now I don't know what to think."

"You can think you were right." She stood by his chair and took his hand. "I do love you. Very, very much."

"Then I don't understand."

"Until tonight," she explained, tracing circles on the back of his hand, "I wasn't sure how you felt about God, what you believed. And I knew I shouldn't be here, in the way of temptation. When you said you loved me, frankly, I was scared.

"I tried so hard not to love you. It was a losing battle from the start. The first time you walked into the store, you set my poor heart aflutter." She giggled. "Martha calls it the flippety-flops. Anyway, I soon began to see how much you cared for your daughter, and that started me loving you personally, instead of just being impressed with your handsome face."

Where was she getting the daring to say such things? Hesitantly, she let her hand touch his cheek.

Luke stood up and took a step to close the distance between them. She straightened to her full height, but still had to tip her head back to be able to look into those lovely, comfortable gray eyes.

"I lay awake at night, thinking about you and praying for strength not to think about you, strength to push you out of my mind and heart. Yesterday, after Martha left, I thought about following her to Chicago. Flee temptation, you know?"

The first sunbeam reached into the room through the curtainless kitchen window, catching Luke in the eye. He blinked and pulled her with him further into the room, away from the window. "Someday I might get my mind off you long enough to remember the curtains." They both smiled, thinking of the reason for the delay in getting them.

"How about today, Tabitha? Still feel the same about fleeing temptation?"

"Today I have to go. I've been here all night. I'm ruined." A flood of pink rushed to her cheeks, and she lowered her gaze.

"Are you sure you love me?"

"Absolutely."

"Good. Because there's something I need to ask you." She held her breath.

"Will you go to Chicago with Amanda and me? to Martha's wedding?"

"What?" She was bewildered. Here she'd gone and done it again, assuming honorable intentions! What a fool she was.

The twinkle in Luke's eyes stopped her train of thought, letting her know he was somehow teasing her. His hand curved around her neck, under her hair. "Of course," he said, "we would have to be married before we could travel together."

At last she was free to wrap her arms around his neck while she stretched to seek his kiss.

He complied willingly.

"Today?" he questioned, his voice low, his lips still close to hers.

Her eyes widened. "Today?"

"Someone is bound to have seen me carrying you off last night. We can turn the scandal of the year into the romance of the decade. Those gossipy old biddies will eat it up like candy, and all the men will be envious, my beautiful vixen."

Tabitha laughed. It was a perfect plan. "Yes, Luke!" she said. "Today."

Dear Reader:

We love to hear from our readers. Your response to the following questions will help us continue publishing the excellent Christian fiction that you enjoy.

1. What most influenced you to buy *Freedom's Promise?*
   - ❑ Cover/title
   - ❑ Subject matter
   - ❑ Back cover copy
   - ❑ Author
   - ❑ Recommendation by friend
   - ❑ Recommendation by bookstore sales person

2. How would you rate this book?
   - ❑ Great
   - ❑ Good
   - ❑ Fair
   - ❑ Poor

Comments:

3. What did you like best about this book?
   - ❑ Characters
   - ❑ Plot
   - ❑ Setting
   - ❑ Inspirational theme
   - ❑ Other_____

4. Will you buy more novels in the **Promises** series?
   - ❑ Yes
   - ❑ No

Why?

5. Which do you prefer?
   - ❑ Historical romance
   - ❑ Contemporary romance
   - ❑ No preference

6. How many Christian novels do you buy per year?
   - ❑ Less than 3
   - ❑ 3-6
   - ❑ 7 or more

7. What is your age?
   - ❑ Under 18
   - ❑ 18-24
   - ❑ 25-34
   - ❑ 35-44
   - ❑ 45-54
   - ❑ Over 55

Please return to
ChariotVictor Publishing
Promises Editor
4050 Lee Vance View
Colorado Springs, CO 80918

If you liked this book,
        check out these great *Promises* titles

Airwaves
by Sherrie Lord
ISBN: 1-56476-706-X

So what if Colin Michaels is traffic-stopping
gorgeous? So what if he represents every sin she knows to
flee? Emily Erickson wants only the job Colin offers at
Diamond Country KDMD. And so what if Emily goes out
with Colin a few times? God isn't happy with her anyway. It
won't matter that he's her boss. That he's definitely not a
Christian. Or maybe a thief—*someone's* stealing from the station. So what if he's a man of his own invention, a man who
can never tell what happened—*what he did*—in Oklahoma
nine years before?

When will Emily learn that an unforgiven heart can't outrun
God's love?

from Chariot Victor Publishing . . .

Mr. Francis' Wife
by Sandy Gills
ISBN 1-56476-689-6

Why did Eli die so suddenly? Their plans for the ranch were unfinished. The children were still young. What was Hannah to do? Could—should—she propose marriage to Mr. Francis, their hired man? Eli was, and would always be, the love of her life. Mr. Francis she *respected. Trusted.* True, they shared faith in God. But that alone wasn't enough to build a marriage on.

And Frank—*Mr. Francis.* He liked working the ranch well enough. He liked Hannah. But friendship went just so far. Move from his trailer to her bedroom? Did Hannah know what she was asking him to do? What would God have him do?

How will a marriage of convenience—a business proposition—grow into a loving, caring relationship?

Best Friends
by Debra White Smith
ISBN 1-56476-721-3

January
1999

Best friends—that's what Scott and Beth have been since they were teens. Why is Beth blind to his desire for more than friendship? "You'll make *somebody* a good husband," she says. How can he make her see that she's the *somebody*—especially when Michael, the latest guest at her bed-and-breakfast, is so handsome and debonair? Scott doesn't trust him or his motives for romancing Beth. Could Michael's presence have more to do with something valuable hidden in the inn than with Beth?

Lord, where are You? Scott was so sure of God's plans for him and Beth, but perhaps he didn't have a clue about perceiving God's will. . . .

Only His Kiss
by Sherrie Lord
ISBN 1-56476-707-8

June
1999

The Santa Fe Trail, 1858

"It's a girl, sir."

The wagon master's shoulders collapsed in exasperation. "I can see that," he said, eyes flashing ominously. "What I mean is, what's she doing here and where the . . . blazes did you find her? What's she doing all by herself, two weeks' ride from Independence?"

Sonja glanced from the train's commander to her captor then searched each bullwhacker's grimy face. Her heart fell. He wasn't here, the man with the brown eyes; no chance for another of his gallant rescues. *Please, Lord, make this the right train. . .*